SOUNDS IN THE DARK

Also by Michael C. Keith

Queer Airwaves: The Story of Gay and Lesbian Broadcasting (with Phylis Johnson)
Talking Radio: An Oral History of Radio in the Television Age
Waves of Rancor: Tuning in the Radical Right (with Robert Hilliard)
The Hidden Screen: Low Power Television in America (with Robert Hilliard)
Voices in the Purple Haze: Underground Radio and the Sixties
Signals in the Air: Native Broadcasting in America
Global Broadcasting Systems (with Robert Hilliard)
The Radio Station
The Broadcast Century and Beyond: A Biography of American Broadcasting (with Robert Hilliard)
Radio Programming: Consultancy and Formatics
Selling Radio Direct
Broadcast Voice Performance
Radio Production: Art and Science
Production in Format Radio

Michael C. Keith

SOUNDS IN THE DARK

All-Night Radio in American Life

Foreword by LARRY KING

IOWA STATE UNIVERSITY PRESS
A Blackwell Science Company

Michael C. Keith, Ph.D., ranks among the most prolific authors on the subject of broadcast media, in particular radio. He is Senior Lecturer of Communication at Boston College and is the author of more than fifteen books and numerous journal articles.

Cover Art by Justin Eccles and Chad Spilker.

Iowa State University Press
2121 South State Avenue, Ames, Iowa 50014

Orders: 1-800-862-6657
Office: 1-515-292-0140
Fax: 1-515-292-3348
Web site: www.isupress.com

∞ Printed on acid-free paper in the United States of America

First edition, 2001

Library of Congress Cataloging-in-Publication Data

Keith, Michael C.
Sounds in the dark : all-night radio in American life / by Michael C.
Keith; foreword by Larry King.—1st ed.
p. cm.
Includes bibliographical references and index.
ISBN 0-8138-2981-X (alk. paper)
1. Radio broadcasting—United States—History. 2. Radio
broadcasters—United States—Interviews. 3. Talk shows—United States.
I. Title.
PN1991.U6 K45 2001
384.54′0973—dc21 2001003251

The last digit is the print number: 9 8 7 6 5 4 3 2 1

Contents

The blessed candles of the night.

—William Shakespeare

Foreword

All-night radio is one of the most unique and important broadcast services we have, and I am puzzled that there has been so little written about it. It is a segment of mass media that has played a truly significant role in our society in so many interesting and compelling ways. Why is all-night radio worth reading about or studying? Well, for starters, it has the longest-form listener. The average listener puts in 20 or so minutes with daytime radio and between an hour and an hour and a half overnights. Then there's the loyalty factor, which is tremendous. Overnight listeners bond with the on-air host more than at any other time. It's worth noting, too, that all-night radio cuts a wide swath across audience demographics. All kinds of people tune in and for some pretty amazing and complex reasons, not just to be entertained. Let me tell you that in our 24-hour culture people have profound relationships with their radios at 3 in the morning. It's a truly potent form of electronic communications and certainly warrants the attention of communication scholars and researchers and anyone who is a fan of radio, which I have been since I was 5 years old.

Sure I'll admit to a particular bias for all-night radio. I had so many great moments doing it. Clinton calling at 1 in the morning when he was governor. Maybe the biggest thrill I had doing overnights was having the legendary performer Danny Kaye on the show. It's a moment you could never recapture, and I think it really demonstrates the special nature of all-night radio. Danny stayed on with me for the whole program. At about 4 in the morning a lady called in and was absolutely thrilled to talk with Danny. She never thought it would happen and admitted to having a very special connection with him. Her teenage son had died in the Korean War and had loved and admired Danny. He would pretend he was the actor and entertain his family by impersonating him. The navy returned his personal belongings after he was killed and among them was a photo of Danny, so she framed it and put it on top of the

TV along with a picture of her son in his uniform. Then came the part that had us all in tears. Every single day of her life, since receiving the tragic news of her son's death in the 1950s, she made it a point of rubbing her hand across those beloved photos. It was a moment that you couldn't buy. Choking back the tears, Danny asked what her son's favorite song was, and when she told him, he sang it for her. Time just stopped. It was incredible. After the show, Danny admitted it was experiences like this one that made being an entertainer worthwhile for him, and I think that what had just happened could only take place in the intense intimacy of early morning radio. There's no other airtime like it, and it was a great thrill and honor to be a part of it.

To my knowledge a book dealing with this extraordinary subject has never been published before, so I'm pleased that Michael Keith has finally taken on the task of making it a matter of record. All-night radio has long deserved our attention because of its special contribution to the lives of so many of us. The so-called graveyard shift has been the subject of a handful of studies probing the work habits and behavior of people up and about after midnight, but nothing has sought to assess the impact and influence of radio at a time when most of the planet is tuned to its unconscious.

Larry King

Preface

All-night radio possessed a special allure for me as an author of books on electronic media. To begin with, nothing of book length had been written about it, a fact I found especially appealing, if not irresistible. Working on groundbreaking material offers its own unique pleasures and rewards. Secondly, all-nights are a part of the broadcast schedule that contain a fascinating element of intrigue and romance. Midnight to dawn is virtually an unexplored time zone for much of the diurnal world. Thirdly, I was aware that some of the most original programming and talented on-air personalities existed on the medium's unheralded night shift. These were reasons enough for me to embark on this project.

My approach to telling the story of "all-night radio in American life" is similar to the one I took in *Voices in the Purple Haze,* when I examined the role of underground radio in the turbulent culture of the 1960s. It is a format that I feel provides the reader the fullest possible view of the subject being explored. Instead of one narrator, there are dozens. The principal voice of the book is the author's, but of equal importance are the narratives of the volume's prominent contributors (The Night People), who bring their savvy and discerning industry perspectives to the topic.

At the start, I want to make it abundantly clear that this small volume makes no attempt to be all-inclusive. Nor does it claim to be the be-all and end-all or final word on the subject. That is to say, it does not strive to cite every all-night radio station or all-night radio personality that has ever existed. To try to do this would be sheer folly and a sure way to go mad. There have been (and are) thousands of all-night stations, and it is safe to say that tens of thousands of individuals have graced the overnight airwaves since the inception of nocturnal radio in the 1920s.

In every city across the nation, men and women have filled the late night/early morning ether with their wit and talent and have made this segment of the broadcast clock one of the most extraordinary listening experiences the medium has had to offer. Therefore, this book contains but a mere sampling of the legions of radio practitioners who have made overnight radio such a very special place to tune.

Every all-night radio fan has his or her favorite station or deejay, so I apologize if the reader's has not been mentioned in this book. But it is to all those stalwart overnighters—both those cited herein and those unnamed—that this book is dedicated. A special note of appreciation is owed to the dozens of contributors to this work. Their generosity made the book possible. Likewise, the good people at ISUP, especially Judi Brown who's ceaseless encouragement inspired me to burn the midnight oil, deserve a tip of the hat for all they have done to make this tome a reality.

And now a suggestion. If you are not distracted by the sound of music while reading, you may find that Thelonius Monk's " 'Round Midnight" and Wilson Pickett's "In the Midnight Hour" are nice accompaniment to the words that follow.

The Night People: A List of Contributors in Order of Appearance

Art Bell—Host of nationally syndicated *Coast-to-Coast.*
Guy Wire—Editor for *Radio World.*
John B. Hanson—President of Nevada Broadcaster's Association.
Ira Fistell—Syndicated radio talk-show host.
Marlin Taylor—Radio programmer and consultant.
Wayne Cornils—Late broadcast association executive.
Rollye James—Host of nationally syndicated *The Rollye James Show.*
Don Barrett—Programmer and consultant.
Christopher Sterling—Author and scholar.
Gary Owens—Legendary radio performer.
Charles Willer—Longtime radio personality.
Kirk Harvey—WKAC program director.
Bill Cahill—Director of FM Operation for Clear Channel.
Greg Hardison—Longtime all-night show producer.
Rob Brown—WPBG program director.
Walter Sabo—Prominent industry consultant.
Helen Little—WUSL program director.
Donna Halper—Author, educator, and former all-night deejay.
Eric Rhoads—Publisher of *Radio Ink* and *Streaming Magazine.*
Sam Sauls—Author and scholar.
Sheldon Swartz—Broadcaster and archivist.
Elizabeth Salazar—Radio programmer and performer.
Dick Summer—Former all-night radio host.
Corey Flintoff—NPR news reporter.
Sheena Metal—Radio programmer and performer.
Ray Briem—Legendary all-night radio host.
Larry King—CNN luminary and former national all-night radio host.
Jim Bohannon—Nationally syndicated all-night radio host.

Steve Warren—Major market radio personality.
Anne Gress—Radio programmer.
Phil Knight/Pat O'Brien—Former all-night radio host.
Frank Childs—WJJZ radio personality.
Doug Stephan—Syndicated early morning radio host.
Larry Miller—Pioneer underground radio deejay.
Bill Conway—KOIT program director.
Alan Colmes—Fox TV talk-show host and all-night radio host.
Lynn Barstow—KMYZ program director.
Marvin Bensman—Scholar and broadcast historian.
Chuck Howell—Archivist and educator.
Frank Chorba—Scholar and journal editor.
Norman Corwin—Legendary radio writer.
John Gehron—Broadcast executive and programmer.
Ken Mellgren—Radio history archivist.
Van Harden—WHO program director.
Bruce Morrow—Syndicated radio-show host.
Max Myrick—WVAZ program director.
Mike Kennedy—KBEQ program director.
Ray Charron—Scholar and educator.
David Brudnoy—Radio talk-show host.
Steve LeVeille—Major market all-night radio show host.
Dick Fatherley—Former Top 40 deejay.
Doug Steckler—All-night talk-show host.
Ed Shane—Leading radio consultant and programmer.
Paul Heyer—Broadcast scholar and educator.
Josef Lenti—Radio programmer.
Greg Strassell—WBMX program director.
Charles Fitch—Former all-night deejay.
Brian Buckfink—Longtime radio professional.
Ken Kohl—Radio programmer.
Gary Berkowitz—President of Berkowitz Broadcast Consulting.
Anne Rea—WRFD Operations Manager.
Arnie Ginsburg—Legendary radio deejay.
Bob Henabery—Radio programming consultant.
Joey Reynolds—Syndicated all-night radio show host.
Lynn Christian—Radio executive and FM pioneer.
Mike J. Keith—Broadcaster and writer.
Joseph Buchman—Scholar and historian.
James Cassell—Longtime radio broadcaster.
Rich De Leo—Programmer for Forever Radio.

Allen Ogrizovich—Longtime radio professional.
Phylis Johnson—Author and scholar.
Joan Gerberding—President of the Nassau Radio Network.
Melissa—Major market all-night radio host.
Cecil Hale—Scholar and educator.
Rick Wright—Scholar and educator.
Dale Sommers—Syndicated all-night radio show host.
Alan Corbeth—Executive Vice President of Premiere Radio.
Eliot Stein—Radio programmer.
Robert Feder—*Chicago Sun-Times* radio columnist.
Jim Taszarek—President of TazMedia.
Mike Lawing—Radio programmer.
Craig Stevens—Longtime radio professional.
Michael Harrison—Publisher of *Talkers Magazine.*
Jason Insalaco—All-night talk radio producer.
Garrison Keillor—Host of *A Prairie Home Companion.*
Fred Jacobs—Radio programmer.
Nick Anthony—President of Nick Anthony and Associates.
Paul Ward—Longtime radio programmer.
Jim Tinker—Radio programmer.
Don Hallett—President of the Positioning Works.
Peter Van De Graaff—Program Director for Beethoven Satellite Network.
E. Alvin Davis—Prominent industry consultant.
Randy Lane—Radio programmer.
Joel Raab—Radio programming and marketing consultant.
John Butler—WMAL radio programmer.
Elroy Smith—Radio personality and programmer.
Ed Weigle—Overnight radio broadcaster.

SOUNDS IN THE DARK

Chapter 1

The Nature of Nights

If night has a thousand eyes, it has as many fears.

—Marlo Blais

Sitting awake at four in the morning . . . it was a thousand years till dawn and all lullabys had been canceled.

—Stephen King

There is something inherently unique, if not a bit peculiar, about the hours between midnight and sunrise. This is a time for which poets have written volumes. Indeed, it is a period that has fueled many a quill, pen, and keyboard. William Blake wrote that it is night where the "poor souls dwell," and John Milton thought night a "thievish time." They were hardly alone in their bleak estimate of the dark hours. Lord Tennyson claimed that night was the territory of "black bats and infant crying," whereas ballads of centuries long past have depicted the depth of night as the "dead hours" or "hours of the doomed." Others have had a more benevolent view of the wee hours, however. Lord Byron thought the "night was made for lovers," and John Keats perceived it as a very "tender and sweet moiety" of the clock's endless motion.

The so-called witching hours fascinate us. They are a time of legends and myths. We are told that the full moon can make people crazy, turning otherwise reasonable individuals into ranting fools and even raging, bloodthirsty monstrosities. We are beguiled and enchanted by the moon in all its orbital incarnations and attach profound and symbolic meaning to them. For most of us, the hours beyond the stroke of 12 are curious and inscrutable essentially because they are an uncharted and unfamiliar region. Most of us occupy the unconscious world after midnight. Sleep removes us from this land of things that sometimes go bump in the dark, unless our dreams or nightmares transport us there.

For those who routinely experience late night and early morning from a fully conscious and wakeful state, it is often a much less mystifying or intriguing part of the 24-hour cycle. Yet whether third-shift worker or insomniac, few would claim that being up when the rest of the planet is asleep is a totally normal thing. For myriad reasons, researchers have found that people who are awake and active overnights are more prone to experience problems and hardships than those who are safely tucked away. For example, marriages are at greater risk of failure for those working the graveyard shift. According to *USA Today,* research shows that overnight employment increases "the risk of divorce significantly compared with daytime work hours."[1] A study conducted by Harriet Presser at the University of Maryland also concluded "that men with children who worked between midnight and 8 A.M. were six times more likely to separate than those working regular hours, [and] the chances of separation in couples where women worked regular nights were three times higher than average."[2]

Adding to the downside of the all-night experience are the manifold negative implications to health and physical well-being. As reported in *New Scientist,* "The zombie zone, as night workers call it . . . is the time when most on-the-job accidents happen . . . [because third shifters] can barely stay awake to do their work."[3] Sleep specialist Dr. James B. Maas claims that the late-night workforce is "40 times more prone to accidents, more susceptible to viral infections and suffer poorer physical and mental health."[4] Maas also contends that life expectancy is decreased for those up at night. Meanwhile, studies by Dr. Claire Infante-Rivard of McGill University determined that "pregnant women who work night shifts may have a substantially higher risk of miscarriage than day workers,"[5] and research at Tel Aviv University revealed that "people who work

night shifts have been found to be at higher risk for hypertension at any time of the day than people who work normal hours."[6]

Making life after midnight an even more challenging, if not perilous, venture is the fact that the crime rate rises prodigiously after the sun sets. Assault and homicide statistics strongly suggest that the place to be after midnight is in bed. Yet despite all this there is a significant and growing segment of the population willing to spend their waking hours in what Edgar Allen Poe called "the midnight dreary." Twenty-five million shift workers, not to mention legions of insomniacs and night hawks, have redefined the meaning of overnights, and thousands of radio stations remain on the air to serve these denizens of the nocturnal world.

(As indicated in the book's preface, industry experts will share narrative duties with the author by contributing insiders' views and perspectives on the far-ranging aspects of overnight radio broadcasting. The format of the book will allow for individual comments as well as multiple participant dialogues or conversations.)

Art Bell: There's a huge population out there that needs and relies on the services of all-night radio. This is an important segment of the broadcast day, and what overnight radio offers its public is of absolute value to it. It was this feeling that motivated me to spend years of my life doing overnights.

Guy Wire: As to just how many all-night radio stations there are out there, it's difficult to calculate, since stations will often change their hours without letting anybody know. Sometimes even their listeners are left in the dark (pun intended). There are about 14,000 AM and FM stations now licensed. Daytime AM stations reduce that by maybe 2,000, but some of them do stay on the air 24/7 with flee power at night. Most all stations do remain active 24/7, except in small towns where they can automate or shut down and save money on the electric bill. Most FMs stay on 24/7, since their coverage does not change day to night. AMs in smaller markets with low power or tight directional patterns are more prone to shut off after midnight. I would guess that 80 percent of all stations stay on the air around the clock.

Someone Out There

Companionship ranks as the foremost reason people tune all-night stations. In many instances people who are up after midnight find themselves in solitary situations and the voice on the radio helps fill the void. A survey conducted by the National Association of Broadcasters over three decades ago found that over 60 percent of the late-night radio audience tuned to keep from being lonely. Writing in *Journalism Quarterly* in the 1970s, researchers Jeffrey Bierig and John Dimmick concluded that "radio, specifically, has been established for at least a decade as a medium of companionship. [It] functioned as a surrogate companion which diverted listeners from boring or routine tasks and helped individuals overcome feelings of social isolation and loneliness."[7] Bierig and Dimmick determined that this was especially true for late-night talk-show listeners.

In his recent autobiography, legendary overnight radio personality Joey Reynolds expressed it this way:

> Radio can be a constant companion, a real close friend. Maybe you can get more intimate on the phone, talking with your mother, or in an Internet chat room communicating with some fat guy posing as a lesbian. There's intimacy in that, I suppose. Other media spend zillions of dollars and hours of

research to figure out how to get the intimacy that a radio show is capable of.[8]

John B. Hanson: All-night radio provides a friend for people at that hour. When everybody else is in bed, and you're either working or just can't get to sleep, you know that you can turn on your radio and somebody will be there to keep you company.

Ira Fistell: There's something special about the voice in the night, coming out of the darkness. The contact between host and listeners is intimate. My audience is not just an audience. It's like a family. Callers get to be recognized as regulars, and the host becomes something like the paterfamilias, presiding over the various members of the tribe and linking everybody together. I can't imagine that kind of relationship developing in the daytime. It takes the darkness, particularly in the small hours, to provide the context in which that kind of relationship can evolve. This kind of closeness could never happen in television either. It's just too impersonal.

Marlin Taylor: It may be the graveyard time but millions of people are out there working or just roaming and these people are alone or feel alone and the voice on the radio is a crucial connection. It confirms to these folks that they are not the only people living in the dark hours.

Wayne Cornils: All-night radio lives with millions of lonely people. For many it becomes a trusted and faithful companion. It is something these people can count on to get them through whatever it is they're experiencing. People listen one-on-one to the radio, and this is especially true late at night.

Rollye James: Overnight radio is unique. It is a time when a significant number of people are alone lying in bed in the dark with the radio on. Maybe sleep doesn't come because they've got problems. Maybe a physical ailment. Maybe it's the emptiness of being alone that plagues them. For this group of listeners, all-night radio is a lifeline. For all-night workers, such as truckers or third-shift assemblers, there's a disenfranchisement from the daytime world. These people listen as they work for companionship.

Don Barrett: Absolutely. For certain, in our 24/7 world, late-night radio provides great companionship. This constitutes a very important service to the public.

Christopher Sterling: All-night radio is a boon to an increasingly round-the-clock workforce . . . those working into the wee hours of the evening surely appreciate some "electronic company" at their tasks (if I stayed up that late, I sure would). In a sense, the all-night service also helps make night workers more equal with their daytime colleagues. Further, most of us need and want companionship of some kind and all-night radio surely is one way of providing that when it's most needed.

Gary Owens: A good all-night host can really be a true one-on-one companion to the listener. I think loneliness is probably the common denominator for the all-night show audience.

Charles Willer: Typically you're alone at that hour and those late-night voices on the radio connect on a very personal level. There are so many jobs that require 24-hour work. Think about the life of an all-night security guard. Many times these lonely jobs turn into serious drudge. All-night radio personalities help fill the void in an otherwise dreary existence. It wasn't that long ago that most stations signed off at midnight.

Ira Fistell: Of course, talk radio is a godsend for the sightless and the sight impaired at any time of the day, but it's especially precious at night because sightless people don't sleep well through the night as a rule (day and night being the same to them as far as vision is concerned). Their sighted families and friends tend to follow a normal diurnal cycle and fall asleep at night, and that is when talk radio is there to ease the loneliness.

Kirk Harvey: I think radio in general serves as a companion but maybe at night even more so. People have problems, get lonely, want to talk about life, and radio is there when no one else is. The all-night radio personality is a comfort to so many . . . plant workers, police and fire personnel, hospital staffs, and truck drivers. The list just goes on and on.

Bill Cahill: All-night radio supplies real companionship to listeners. People who are up overnights are either night owls or third-shift workers. Either way they are looking for someone else who is also up. As a kid I'd turn on the radio in the middle of the night just to know that somebody else was awake. It is very reassuring.

Greg Hardison: Most folks up and listening at that hour are doing so as solitary beings . . . working security posts, transportation jobs, and other positions that don't lend themselves to large concentrations of people. Radio is perfect for these individuals. For them, it assumes the role of friend and confidant. Regardless of the listener's situation, the reason for tuning overnight is to glom onto a larger mass identity . . . to feel a part of the larger world.

Rob Brown: Peoria is a big third-shift town . . . world headquarters to Caterpillar and home of three large hospitals, among other "overnight" employers. At Big Oldies 93.3 we have long recognized the importance of playing to this available audience. Even though no salable Arbitron numbers come from overnights, the impact these listeners can have on morning drive (on their way home) is significant. My oldies station specifically seems to be very popular "on-line" at CAT plants because we are contacted by them frequently. The fact that we even have an overnight personality in the first place speaks volumes given how many stations across the country in cities of this size do not.

Walter Sabo: An all-night talk show with a live host is not only a source of entertainment, it is a profoundly important companion to its listener. For many, it is the only other voice they will hear for hours. Think about that. This is a valuable medium, wouldn't you say?

Helen Little: Late-night radio offers a camaraderie that is often like being a member of a club, and there are no dues required.

Donna Halper: A club is a pretty good way to describe the connection between the all-night host and his or her audience. As Gary Owens says, loneliness is the common denominator. Let me give you an example of this from my

> own experience as a late-night radio person. Mostly my listeners were students, hospital workers, taxi drivers, and a large contingent of prisoners. That's right . . . prisoners, and, of course, they couldn't call in to the show, but they could write and often did. Some of their letters resulted in friendships, and I would dedicate songs to them and their families. Many album rock stations back in the '70s had a prisoner-request show. I don't think it had much to do with a greater sense of social justice or even an interest in prison reform. I suspect that what motivated a lot of those shows was that back then drug laws were very strict and a lot of listeners had friends who had been arrested for possession of drugs or had friends who had been arrested for protesting the Vietnam War. Most of the people who wrote to me were not political prisoners or even first offenders caught with drugs. Some of my most loyal listeners were bikers from the Breed Motorcycle Club who had been involved in some kind of violent altercation with another biker club and several were doing time for manslaughter. Interestingly, there I was, Ms. Straight (having never done drugs or any other kind of stimulant), and yet the bikers and I became pen pals. I tried to answer as much mail as I could or get other people who wanted a pen pal in prison to answer, because these prison listeners really seemed lonely and wanted desperately to connect with someone in the outside world. My all-night show on WMMS in Cleveland reached some pretty needy people.

YOU'VE GOT A FRIEND

Radio programmers contend that all-night listeners are often drawn to their radios out of a need for a personal or intimate encounter, which may be lacking in their lives, especially at that hour. In some situations, a listener may be on the brink of disaster, and the all-night radio host may be called upon to provide a life-sustaining service, as this Associated Press story illustrates:

> A woman who called an all night radio show and threatened to kill herself because no one loved her was talked out of suicide by more than 50 callers who told her life was worth living. The woman, who identified herself as Irene, called Liz Lansing's talk show on station WIBX in Utica early Friday and threatened to jump from a fourth-floor hotel room in the city.

This call came in around 1:45 A.M., and Lansing preempted the 2 A.M. network news to keep Irene on the line. Utica police were monitoring the broadcast, and they went to the hotel. Irene was taken to St. Elizabeth Hospital, where she was familiar to mental health specialists, and was admitted for observation.[9]

Ira Fistell: When I was working the night shift back in Madison, Wisconsin, many years ago, a woman called me one night to ask what the best way to commit suicide was. I said I couldn't tell her and wouldn't if I knew, but then I engaged her in a conversation about why she wanted to kill herself. We talked for about 20 minutes—I figured that the longer I could keep her talking, the less likely it was that she would actually do herself in—until she hung up. I didn't know what happened to her until a few weeks later when she called up and simply said, "I just wanted you to know that I didn't do it." I never heard from her again.

Kirk Harvey: There's no telling how many overnight deejays have saved someone's life just by taking time to talk with them on the phone or how many lonely people, or people who have felt unimportant, have been made not to feel lonely or unimportant just by talking with that friendly voice on the radio.

Eric Rhoads: There is a unique kind of bonding that goes on between the late-night host and the listener. It goes way beyond most traditional forms of media, and it is unique to that particular shift.

Sam Sauls: This has a great deal to do with the fact that a different breed of listener tunes overnights. Typically, either working the late-night shift, driving the American roads, or just night owls, the overnight audience tends to relate more closely with the radio personality. It's almost as if they are making it through the night together . . . sometimes literally. For those of us who have worked as all-night deejays, we know that this airshift plays a vital role in our culture by serving this special niche of listeners.

Sheldon Swartz: Somebody talking and playing music in the night seems to be doing so directly to and for you. During the day you feel you're one among millions, but at night it's just you and that radio voice. Somehow there's an important intimacy created by the experience.

Elizabeth Salazar: Radio acts as a surrogate friend at all hours of the day. However, in the wee hours, this seems more pronounced probably because those who are awake and listening to their radios tend to be alone and therefore are able to form a more loyal bond with their air personality.

Rollye James: I know it's already been said, but it bears repeating. Late-night radio listeners are a different breed. There are less of them for sure, which is why so many stations and networks ignore nighttime programming, but while the headcount is lower, the loyalty factor is much higher. Often referred to as the "disenfranchised few," the late-night audience is somewhat removed from their daytime counterparts. Their reasons for being awake all night range from the practical (third-shift workers, over-the-road drivers, and so on) to the heartbreaking (lying awake alone and in pain with no other connection to human warmth) and everything in between. The common denominator is a body clock that beats to a different drummer, often in need of a kindred spirit to get them through another night. A host who understands this and can create that one-on-one bond becomes a godsend.

Dick Summer: There's no doubt in my mind that all-night listeners establish a greater intimacy with the host. In fact, in my case, maybe I allowed too much intimacy. I've thought about this a lot. Being on the air 5 hours a night kind of inspires a greater closeness with the listening audience. I couldn't keep secrets. If something had happened, it came spilling out of me. So maybe I was a bit too open. I was so open with the audience that it felt it could be open with me, so there was certainly something of value to be gained. No one could argue that all-night radio doesn't contribute something of real value to American life. It comforts a lot of people who really need comfort—people who have either a temporary or permanent emotional problem, people going through divorce, people in prison, people who are ailing, and people of who have chronic sleep disorders, to name a few. It makes a connection with people that television and other media can't. All-night radio contributes a lot. If it causes

> somebody not to give up the ghost and go grab a gun and start shooting people, it's done plenty. Let me take this in a slightly different, if not perverted, direction. Talk about all-night radio being intimate, when I did that shift there were women who called and told me they had orgasms while listening. Some were upset because they were afraid they were being unfaithful to their mates. Did I like doing all-night radio? How can you not like being the guy giving orgasms all night long on a 50,000-watt clear channel radio station?
>
> **Corey Flintoff:** I love all-night radio. I think that's when the intimacy of radio has its greatest power over listeners. Nighttime really concentrates the essence of radio—that intimacy between the announcer's voice and the listener. At night you may find yourself turning the radio down, but you can hear it better than ever, because all the external noise of the day is gone. It's just you and the radio.

Scholars Alan M. Rubin and Mary M. Step confirm many of these opinions in their study regarding the role of radio as a unique interpersonal medium. Their research has ascertained that the audio medium in particular "offers a mediated interpersonal communication experience for its audience. It provides listeners with a sense of personal contact and a forum to discuss and to learn societal issues. . . . [It] serves expressive, inclusive, and instructional needs of audience members." Rubin and Step observe that radio creates the "illusion of intimacy."

> Audience members often develop quasi-relationships with media personalities, similar to that with social friends. They feel they know and understand the personae. They feel comfortable with the personae, as they do with a friend, and feel the personae is natural and down to earth.[10]

Sleepless Nights

The number of insomniacs may not rival the twenty-five-million-plus third-shift worker figure, but according to some estimates we are a culture of people who either have sleeping disorders or who have experienced extended periods of sleeplessness. For this group of nocturnal dwellers, a world without overnight radio would be a far less tolerable place to inhabit.

Sheena Metal: Well, I've worked in Los Angeles, which is a city full of insomniacs. Sometimes it seems like no one can sleep here. Also, like most American cities, it's a 24-hour town where a lot of people work the graveyard shift. LA's really spread out with people sometimes driving 60 miles to work, school, or home. There's lots of downtime with nothing to do but listen to your car radio.

Ray Briem: I can attest to Los Angeles being a city that never seems to sleep. This gives all-night radio importance as a medium that is hard to rival. Being an insomniac can be a lonely experience. Radio gives these people someone to pass the time with.

John Hanson: I'm one of those people who simply can't get to sleep without the radio. Without it I'd be awake forever. That was true when I was a kid, and it holds true today.

Larry King: People who have no problem getting to sleep are always amazed at how many people stay awake late into the night. It's a good thing radio is there for these people. I can tell you that firsthand.

The sleepless zone has inspired Hollywood on a number of occasions, and the all-night radio station has served as a particularly popular backdrop for the melodramatic, comical, and bizarre story line. Who can forget Tom Hanks's reluctant conversation with an all-night radio host in *Sleepless in Seattle,* Wolfman Jack's midnight howling in *American Graffiti,* Clint Eastwood's portrayal of a stalked late-night deejay in *Play Misty for Me,* the shenanigans of an overnight disc jockey in *The Ladies Man,* Eric Bogosian's edgy talkmeister in *Talk Radio,* or the after-hours radio hosts in TV's *Midnight Caller* and *WKRP in Cincinnati*?

It is with some justification that writer Julia Brosnan calls all-night radio "the wacky twilight zone of broadcasting." Says Brosnan, "You get a funny breed of person out there after midnight—freaks and ghouls lurking about long after the rest of us [have] pulled on our bedsocks. For it isn't just car thieves who creep out of their hidey-holes in the wee small hours; it's also the people who go to make up late night radio."[11]

Jim Bohannon: Night people do seem strange to most folks. Maybe even vaguely dysfunctional, but there is a reason for this. I've had a chance to talk to my audience about this. On several occasions, I've asked listeners to talk about being night people. Now mind you, my audience is as fractured as any talk radio show, but on this topic they unite as one, pouring forth their stories of friends who won't plan parties to accommodate their schedules, bosses who won't schedule company meetings and other functions to include them. Then there are the highway work crews who tie up traffic as if anyone driving after dark couldn't possibly have any place important as a destination. By night's end these folk were ready to light torches and march! We are night people, we are strong, even if our hours seem wrong!

Dick Summer: The all-nighter is the world's bastard stepchild. We were conceived in fear, grew in indifference, and survive in contempt. We are definitely treated like second-class citizens, so some of us act that way.

Ira Fistell: Night people are a different breed, that's for sure. People who stay up late tend to be more interesting in general than early to bed types. There's something about the dark hours that appeals to a certain kind of mind. Late night is when Winston Churchill flourished, and Thomas Wolfe, and Thomas Edison, and God knows how many other exceptional people.

Elizabeth Salazar: The biggest lesson I learned in terms of my listenership at that hour of the morning was that it is heavily populated by a sub- or counterculture. These are a group of listeners unlike any other. The bottom line is that lifestyles change during the graveyard hours.

Steve Warren: All-night radio speaks to a very specialized audience of people whose work and life schedule is upside down from the rest of us, so some unique characteristics are bound to exist. Things are changing some though. As our population and technology grow, our occupational and social activities have also expanded into new parts of the day and night previously not utilized. The availability of music, news, and companionship via radio during the night hours has helped make night work and listening more like daytime, lessening the differences between the two and providing similar services around the clock.

Anne Gress: By nature of the time of day we're talking about, you have a pretty unusual bunch of characters tuned in. But, in my estimation, that's the cool thing about doing the overnight flight.

Phil Knight: I felt we had a community of our own. The people who were up at those hours and listening felt a bond with one another. We were the night, or Knight, people. We weren't better than everyone else, just a little different and maybe just a bit crazy. We had our own thing. It was a lot of fun.

Frank Childs: Speaking of the all-night audience, listeners sometimes can become a little peculiar about their perceived relationship with you, and that can lead to real problems. Listeners who become obsessive, believing they have true relationships with the host or deejay, can be frightening. They send you love letters and photos, some very candid and revealing, I might add. Then they show up in the parking lot at five in the morning wanting to go home with you to fulfill some kind of crazy fantasy they've made real in their own mind. When you try to be polite and let them down easy, saying you're flattered by their attention, they sometimes go crazy because they feel rejected. Then your life becomes a *Play Misty for Me* scenario. Your tires get slashed. Your windshield gets smashed. You change your unlisted number for a third time. The death threats come in the mail everyday, and you start carrying a baseball bat with you everywhere. Finally, the police get involved, and issue a restraining order. Things seem to be getting back to normal, and then the girl commits suicide. Granted, this is an extreme example, but these things do happen to people in this business.

MULTIFARIOUS MIDNIGHT

Donna Halper: Hey, the all-night audience is diverse. There's every kind of person imaginable out there listening to you. Something odd happens. Even back at the start of radio, when there was late-night programming being aired, the audience was comprised of a broad spectrum of people.

Doug Stephan: Who is listening at 3 A.M.? A huge cross-section of the population, and plenty of people in bars in Alaska, because they close down at 4 A.M.

Larry Miller: It's pretty much always been that way. Jump ahead to the wild and groovy '60s, if you will. At the station I worked for we got calls from shift workers, students, and people partying. You name it and we heard from them. In some circumstances, you got some very strange calls. But given where we were coming from, often as stoned as the audience, we invited this two-way weirdness. If I got a call from a party at 4 o'clock on a Wednesday morning in San Francisco during the Summer of Love, I could pretty much assume that they were fairly well fried, and I programmed accordingly. My favorite story from that era is of just such an all-night party. I was called from a very late and very stoned gathering as I was doing one of my raps between sets. As a joint was making the rounds at the party, somebody held a joint up to the radio speaker and told me to take a toke. It was as if I were right there in the room with them. That, to me, is what all-night radio is really all about. Being there.

Bill Conway: Who is listening to late-night radio? A better question might be who isn't? I've done more than a few overnight shifts in my career, and during those so-called graveyard hours, I've talked with artists, moms up with babies, writers, people winding down from dates, some drunks and druggies, a few groupies, and a lot of people who just happen to be up. You never know what type of person is liable to be tuned to you.

Alan Colmes: All-night radio is an acknowledgment that we don't live a monolithic lifestyle. That we are a nation of various patterns, life choices, and careers. We are not nine-to-five sheep marching in lockstep. The existence of all-night radio portends the diversity that is America.

Lynn Barstow: We have Tulsa's largest overnight audience here at KMYZ. As a low-end rock station, many of our listeners work nontraditional hours. Many others are young enough to have a social life that keeps them out after midnight. We have a pretty varied listening demographic.

Steve Warren: That's more the rule than the exception for overnight radio. If you want to categorize the all-night audience, this is how I would do it. There are three separate audiences tuned. First there are those who are out late or work late, often getting off their jobs around midnight. To this group, the radio is drive time entertainment and companionship. The second group, and most important to all-night radio, consists of those listeners with overnight jobs or overnight activities. The last group is comprised of early morning people who get up and out before the sun rises. These listeners catch the last hours of the all-night show as they head to work.

Art Bell: I think one of the things that is so compelling about broadcasting late nights and early morning is the variety of people out there listening to you at any given time.

Larry King: Yeah, I go along with that. It makes it a stimulating as well as challenging experience. When we started with our national overnight show, we had an enormous amount of students listening. A lot of law students. The first commencement address I gave was for the Columbia University Graduate School and I learned that all the interns tuned us. So all-night radio has a wide, diverse audience in all the demographic cells. It's hard to explain the feeling I used to get when I'd sit in my studio and see all those lights blinking from Cincinnati and Phoenix and Montreal. Hard to explain emotionally, but you felt like the whole country, or at least a good portion of it, was in the studio with you.

In the movie *Cast Away,* actor Tom Hanks reflects that no matter how long and arduous the night, the sun will rise. For millions, including those who prefer dusk over dawn, spending the wee hours without the fellowship of radio's knights of the nocturnal airwaves would be too dark a prospect to contemplate.

NOTES

1. Karen S. Peterson, "Late Night Shifts Take Toll on Marriages," *USA Today,* 3 February 2000, p. 1D.
2. "Shift Work Takes Toll on Marriage," *Scotsman,* 18 February 2000, p. 14.
3. Rose Mestel, "Escape from the Zombie Zone," *New Scientist,* 21 January 1995, p. 7.
4. Joe Armstrong, "The 10 Warnings Night Workers Should Watch For," *Irish Times,* 6 March 1998, p. 58.
5. Marilyn Dunlop, "Miscarriage Risk Higher," *Toronto Star,* 27 February 1993, p. F2.
6. Judy Siegel-Itzkovich, "The Pressures on Women and Night Workers," *Jerusalem Post,* 28 May 2000, p. 17.
7. Jeffrey Bierig and John Dimmick," The Late Night Radio Talk Show as Interpersonal Communication," *Journalism Quarterly,* (spring 1979): 92–96.
8. Joey Reynolds, *Let a Smile Be Your Umbrella* (New York: Hatherleigh Press, 2000), p. 135.
9. "Talk Show Caller Threatens Suicide," *Associated Press,* 15 August 1986.
10. Alan M. Rubin and Mary M. Step, "Impact of Motivation, Attraction, and Parasocial Interaction on Talk Radio Listening," *Journal of Broadcasting and Electronic Media* 44, no. 4 (fall 2000): 634, 639.
11. Julia Brosnan, "Crazy Goings-on in the Wee Hours," *Independent,* 30 March 1998, p. M11.

Chapter 2

The Night Has Ears

We had a large battery-powered radio in the front room that we used sparingly, and only at night.

—Jimmy Carter

Although the device for sending and receiving wireless signals existed at the turn of the twentieth century, the actual medium of radio broadcasting was not established in earnest until 1920. Prior to that time, radio transmissions were primarily propagated for maritime, military, and signal-testing purposes.

KDKA in Pittsburgh claims the distinction of being the first actual radio station because it was the only outlet offering "regularly" scheduled (daily) broadcasts as of the fall of 1920. At that time, and for a while to come, there was no established overnight radio programming to be tuned, only occasional experimental transmissions and those were relatively rare.

The 1920s saw the launch of the broadcasting industry and the beginning of a new age in mass communication. It was a decade of great vision, progress, and drama on many fronts, particularly financially, technologically, and culturally. Observes historian

Thomas C. Reeves, "Leaders were fond of labeling the 1920s the New Era, calling attention to its productivity and wealth."[1]

Radio was to become an appropriate metaphor for this exhilarating and provocative epoch, and stations began entering the airwaves in momentous profusion. Within a couple of years, over 500 radio outlets were vying for the listening audience, which itself expanded at an equally remarkable pace.

It is the aim of this chapter to attempt to ascertain when all-night (or "late-into-the-night") programming became a part of this amazing communication phenomenon and to determine its original programming form. A definitive history of overnight radio broadcasting is difficult, if not impossible, to construct, since records of early station broadcasts are few and far between. In point of fact, many stations claim they have no idea when they first began post-midnight operations. The principal culprit here is the fact that station staffs often have not been around as long as a station has been airing overnights and, in some cases, individuals affiliated with a station when it first began all-night programming may not even be alive.

In the process of posing the question to hundreds of stations regarding how long a particular outlet had been on the air after midnight, the answer most frequently provided was, "We have no idea!" It was something stations simply had forgotten, or it was information they had no idea how to obtain or locate. Testimonial evidence or artifacts regarding all-night launch dates were simply unavailable. The files and memory banks were empty in this regard, or so it seemed time and again. The frustration level of the author rose exponentially as this information was doggedly pursued.

What follows is what has been ferreted out with the considerable aid of many stalwart historians and broadcasters. No claim is made as to its breadth and depth, but at the very least it provides a sketch (however impressionistic) of overnight radio broadcasting back when the medium itself was in its infancy up to its second incarnation after the advent of television.

THE FORERUNNERS

Although over a million-and-a-half listeners tuned in the hundreds of stations in operation in 1922, only three seem to be cited with any regularity when the debate is waged over which radio outlet was the first to offer overnight programming. They are WDAF, WAAM, and WSB, and the first set of call letters seems to garner the most votes in this category. Notes radio history aficionado Bill Jaker, "I'm always a little hesitant to credit a first (something always happened before it happened), but [in the 1920s] WDAF regularly stayed on the air into the wee hours."[2]

> **Donna Halper:** WDAF in Kansas City was on the air as far back as 1922 between midnight and 2 A.M. Everyone else was signed off by then.
>
> **Marvin Bensman:** The earliest records I can locate show that WDAF was beaming signals into the very early morning hours around 1923. Maybe it was doing this a year earlier. It really appears to have been out there in front of everyone else.

Luther F. Sies's *Encyclopedia of American Radio* places WAAM and WSB in the winner's circle when it comes to first postmidnight radio broadcasts in 1922. Writes Sies, "The 'Jersey Journal' paper purchased one hour from midnight to 1 A.M. on WAAM (Newark, New Jersey) to broadcast New Year's Greetings."[3] The same year, according to Sies, a husband and wife team entertained late-night listeners at WSB.

> Kay and Ernest Rogers were the popular team that conducted the program on which the [Radiowls] club was formed. They talked, sang, and joked on the program that began at 10:45 P.M. and continued late into the morning hours, until both they and their material were exhausted. WSB contended that this was the first "late evening" variety program of its type.[4]

A year later, according to Sies, Chicago station KYW was staying on all night and offering news around the clock on the hour and half hour. It promoted itself as the "twenty-four hour station."[5]

> **Donna Halper:** It wasn't the only station in Chicago putting out a signal after midnight in 1923. At the Edgewater Hotel, WJAZ kept listeners company into the early morning hours.

On the east coast, pioneer station WBZ began flirting with the notion of late nights in 1924 by providing twice-weekly programming until midnight. Meanwhile, the same year, the *New York Times* reported that station 2XBG began airing music until 2 A.M., three days a week, from the city's Hotel Majestic.[6]

Donna Halper: 1925 was a fairly active year for late-night programming. For example, in January, Oakland, California, station KGO stayed on the air until 1 A.M. Tuesdays, Thursdays, and Saturdays.

In the south, a radio giant, WSM in Nashville, celebrated its inaugural broadcast on October 5, 1925, by staying on all night. However, after this initial venture into the wee hours, it would remain silent after midnight until many years later when it became a 50-kW powerhouse. (WSM would also garner the distinction of being the first commercial FM station in the country.)

At this time, Los Angeles radio was still content to sign off while the night was young. At KHJ the announcer on duty would regale listeners with this bit of verse before shutting down the transmitter:

God will not fail to watch thy sleep
and wake thee with his light.
And now dear friends of KHJ
I wish you all good night.

A couple years later, Los Angeles's listeners would have their first chance to tune radio deep into the night.

Marvin Bensman: KGFJ in LA was the first station to operate in that city with a 24-hour schedule. It broadcast around the clock until well into the 1930s with a 100-watt signal at 1200 kc. Despite its low power it was received all over the region because no one else was on the air at those hours.

Donna Halper: The station's call letters stood for "Keeping Good Folks Joyful" since the owner, Ben McGlashan, believed that radio was not just about making money but also about making people happy.

Ben McGlashan was not the only broadcaster intent on providing programs of a life-affirming nature for those still up in the wee hours. According to Halper, Roger Babson (founder of Babson College) put the word of God on the late-night air in Boston around this time.

Donna Halper: Babson created WBSO and decided to use his station to spread the gospel. On March 26, 1927, the station began airing a show called *Midnight Ministry* between

In the early days, when stations were few and receivers handmade, listeners logged the distant stations their sets 'brought in' and wanted verification. This Philadelphia 250-watter sent these special stamps to its listeners. (WDAS)

Figure 2.1. Stations provide verification to listeners tuning them in during the late-night hours.

> midnight and 1 A.M. It sometimes went later, too. The man in charge of these programs was Dr. Henry Hallam Sanderson, a minister and author. The show lasted until the middle of 1929.

Sies writes that not long after KGFJ launched its late-night programming, another Los Angeles station, KGF, began a round-the-clock schedule employing the same slogan—"The Twenty-Four Hour Station"—that Chicago's KWY used to promote its nonstop offerings. Thus within the medium's first decade of existence, lucky listeners in a handful of the country's largest cities actually had a choice of stations with which they could spend the night.

MUSIC IN THE NIGHT

Music was the staple of these early late-night stations and, in most cases, the principal reason they remained on the air long after other outlets had signed off. Stations were to discover that a listening public existed for all types of musical performance long after normal bedtime hours. Recalls Robert Lewis Shayon,

> WOR carried the popular big bands, Vincent Lopez and Guy Lombardo. Ordinarily these shows were called "remotes." The announcer who was assigned to "cover" them sat in a small studio late at night at 1440 Broadway where WOR was located and heard the music the band was playing for the dancers, coming by wire from the Astor Hotel or the Hotel Roosevelt. He would read the opening and closing lines of the show written for him by the "continuity" department, "signing on" or off. Occasionally, I would actually go down to the hotel and stand on the bandstand, close to Lopez or Lombardo, and sign on or close the show from there. Otherwise, we would take it easy at the studio, passing the late night shift "chewing the fat" with other members of the staff or watching the clock till it was time to go home.[7]

> **Chuck Howell:** The words "dance," "jamboree," and "orchestra" were almost always attached to programs that radio stations scheduled late evenings. Almost all of the late-night programming listed in the various radio periodicals of the time shows that music was the primary attraction.

Marvin Bensman: The earliest after-midnight feature that I've been able to document was the *Nighthawk Frolic,* aired nightly over WDAF beginning in 1923. This was a 3-hour program that ended at 1:30 A.M. central time and it featured Carleton Coon and Joe Sanders's Nighthawks Orchestra (often broadcasting from the Muelebach Hotel in Kansas City). It had Leo Fitzpatrick, known as "The Merry Old Chief," as master of ceremonies. The show drew listeners from all over the country, and "Nighthawk Club" membership cards were sent out by the station in response to fan mail. By the spring of 1924, KYW in Chicago was running a similar late-night music program, called variously *The Late Show* or *Midnight Revue.*

Donna Halper: There were some dance orchestras that liked to be on the air later in the evening. Indeed among the earliest was the Coon-Sanders Band in Kansas City. Carlton Coon and Joe Sanders had already recorded some of their songs for Columbia Records prior to their first radio appearances, but despite the common wisdom about radio airplay destroying the demand for a group's music, Coon and Sanders decided to perform live for WDAF, a station with a good signal, which was owned by the *Kansas City Star* newspaper. They gave their first performances in November of 1922, and the response was excellent. WDAF was heard all over the United States late at night, and late at night was exactly when Coon-Sanders wanted to play. Their band concerts usually took to the airwaves at 11 P.M. and lasted until near 2 A.M., something that was not commonly done yet. Coon-Sanders showed that it was a good idea, that people were awake and did want to hear "jazz" late at night over radio. As legend has it, the program director of WDAF, Leo Fitzpatrick, made an offhanded comment to the effect that "if you're listening this late at night, you must be a 'nighthawk'," and so was born a concept—the Kansas City Nighthawks. Thus a club was conceived that may have been the first fraternity of late-night radio listeners. Although Friday and Saturday nights became increasingly popular for late-night radio concerts in the mid-1920s, many were staying on a few hours after midnight during the week. For example, as I've already noted, KGO in Oakland was one. In January of 1925, it offered dance music with a local orchestra. Numerous black jazz musicians, like Duke Ellington and Cab Calloway, did late-night concerts for stations in New York and Los Angeles. Some stations had begun to do late-night remotes from clubs and hotels.

The telephone was employed early on by late-night music programs as a means to give listeners a chance to hear their favorite songs by a particular performer or group. Halper notes that one of the first stations to employ this practice was located in Boston in 1929.

Donna Halper: Beantown's WNAC began doing a midnight request and dedication show. The music was mainly love songs and romantic melodies, and the show was called *Midnight Reveries.* It proved so popular that it was expanded to every night and gradually lengthened from 1 hour to 2 hours, which kept it on until 2 A.M.

LATE-NIGHT VISITORS

Special occasions or circumstances often inspired stations to remain on after normal broadcast hours. Vaudeville performers were inclined to drop by stations after their performances to lend their talents to the airwaves.

Frank Chorba: Some big-name stars and celebrities, both of a local and national variety, would drop by these stations, especially in big cities like New York and Chicago. It would give them someplace to go to unwind after a stage performance. They'd sing a few songs or play a few tunes, and people would stay up to listen. This would mark the start of a long tradition in all-night radio.

This practice continued, albeit in a more structured and formalized way, when the networks began broadcasting in the late 1920s. In an Ohio State University report examining radio programming by the national networks between 1926 and 1956, music and variety features appear to have dominated the late-evening schedule. For example, from its inception in 1927 until the late 1930s, NBC aired programs such as *Chicago Civic Opera, Halsey Stuart Concert, Cliquot Club Eskimos* (music), *Freed Eismann Orchestra, Let's Dance* (with

Benny Goodman), *Hudson Essex Chorale, Lucky Strike Orchestra, RCA Victor Hour* (variety), *Seth Parker Hymns, Armstrong Quakers Orchestra, Atwater Kent Orchestra, Lenny Ross Trio, Cuckoo Hour* (variety), *Roxy Symphonic Concert, Jesse Crawford* (organist), *Ralph Kerbery* (singer), *Al Jolson* (singer), *Kate Smith* (singer), *Pickens Sisters* (singers), *Master Melody,* and *Minneapolis Symphony Orchestra.*

Meanwhile, during this same period, CBS's late-evening schedule included *DeForest Audios Band, Guy Lombardo Orchestra, Columbia Symphony Orchestra, Paramount Symphony Orchestra, Philco Concert Orchestra, Hank Simmons Show Boat, St. Louis Symphony,* and *Tito Guizar* (music).[8] All of these early network shows were aired after 10 P.M. and some remained on well past midnight.

Although network radio would come to dominate the program schedules of most stations, it would not be a player in the all-night arena, leaving these hours to local affiliates to fill if they were so inclined.

From Town and Country

As the 1930s began, overnight broadcasting became somewhat more commonplace, although certainly far more the exception than the rule. As already indicated, not all postmidnight broadcasts originated from the nation's populated meccas—New York, Chicago, or Los Angeles—but most did.

> **Donna Halper:** There was a station down in Texas called KSAT that according to the February 1930 issue of *Radio Digest* was doing an all-night show three nights a week (Monday, Wednesday, and Friday) from midnight to 6 A.M. The show, *Flying the Sunrise Trail,* was getting enthusiastic response from its listeners, many of whom were women.

> **Dick Summer:** These shows were out there. Not just in one place. There are night people—insomniacs and third-shift workers—in every region of the country, so it is not surprising that all-night radio existed in more remote locations from the start.

All-night radio activity, however, was certainly more prevalent in the metro areas of the country in the initial decades of the medium's life. In the 1930s, practically every major city in the country had at least one station putting out a signal after midnight.

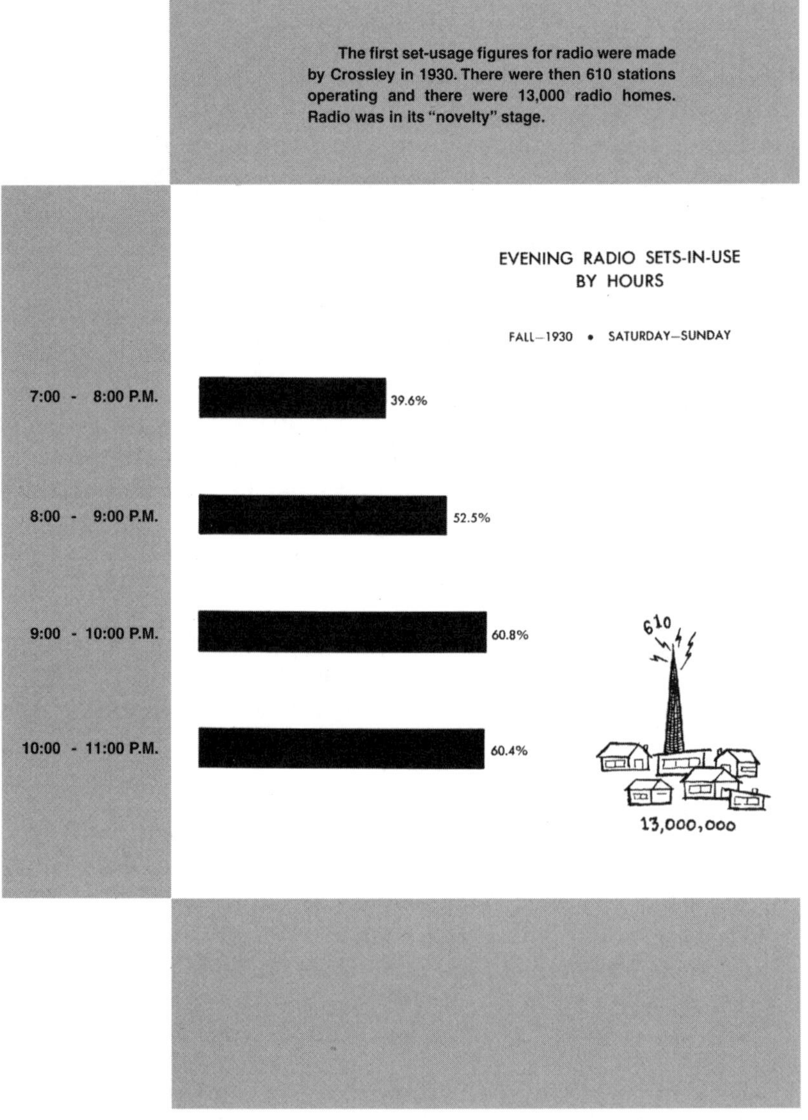

Figure 2.2. By 1930, the listening audience was tuning later and later.

Entering the fray around this time were WGN in Chicago and WNEW in New York, among others. In the latter case the station debuted its 24-hour schedule on August 6, 1935, with a feature hosted by deejay Stan Shaw called *The Milkman's Matinee.* Writes

Bill Jaker, "At first the program started up after the usual late night dance band fare had ended and ran from about 2 A.M. to 7 A.M. It later began at midnight and ran to 5:30 A.M. or 6 A.M. and remained on the station's schedule under various hosts until WNEW's demise in 1992."[9] (In his book *The Golden Web,* noted broadcast historian Erik Barnouw claims that WNEW extended its programming schedule to 24 hours in the early 1940s.)

By the middle of the decade, legendary station WLW in Cincinnati began sending an all-night signal across the country with a half-million watts. It was joined by a myriad of other radio stations around the country that perceived some value in keeping their transmitters turned on.

> **Chuck Howell:** I found some listings in *Broadcast Weekly* for stations in northern California dating back to 1935. There was something called the *Owl Program* (not Night Owl, just Owl) on KJBS San Francisco. It ran from midnight to 6 or sometimes 7 A.M. Later that year it gave up an hour on the front end for *Les Maloy's Midnite Club.* Also listed was a program on KROW called *Dance* (or *Dancing*) *Party,* which aired at midnight and ran until whenever. The station either dropped it or changed its name later that year to *Midnite Jamboree.* This program ended around 2 A.M. Another station in that area carried *The Midnite Vagabond,* described as a "DX Program." This weekly publication was also carrying listings in 1935 for a network offering called *America Dances* (on KGO, KPO, and KFI), *Morning Musicale* (on KGB), and *Dance Orchestra* (KFOX). By the way, *Broadcast Weekly* unfortunately ceased publishing in 1936.

Programming became a little more eclectic, or at least somewhat more sophisticated and varied, during the midnight hours as the decade approached its close. Perhaps taking a cue from the networks, which began to schedule a more diversified menu of late-evening features, local stations and affiliates began to mix things up and experiment a little, something that would become the hallmark of overnight radio.

> **Donna Halper:** I found a reference in Bill Jaker's book *The Airwaves of New York* wherein he mentions that WEVD (which did ethnic programming in 1938) had a guy named Gene

> King who did a show called *Midnight Matinee.* On it he promised to play requests of any song, in any language. This is something that WEVD could certainly accommodate, given all of the foreign-language shows it aired. Jaker mentions a request for a Spanish version of "Beer Barrel Polka." All-night radio had obviously come a long way.

Biographer Arthur Singer would probably agree that all-night radio was coming into its own in the 1930s, because it was taking more risks and allowing personalities, such as Arthur Godfrey, a place to flex their formidable talents and skills.

> Arthur would go on the air [at WMAL] Friday at midnight and stay on all night . . . with telephone, turntable, and a stack of records. [He] took to the air in what was the first all night call-in show in radio history, saying, "This is Arthur Godfrey. I'm going to play some records, and I'm going to be on all night. We're doing a test to see [from] how far [away] we can get listeners." Throughout the eight hours, he gave out the phone numbers and invited requests. When calls came in, he'd put the phone up to the microphone for listeners to hear the caller's comments as well as his own. . . . As morning neared he complained about the swamp and the lack of coffee. "What happened next is one of the all time believe-it-or-nots of radio," he later recalled. "Before dawn there must have been 3000 or 4000 automobiles out there with coffee, sandwiches, and cake. It was hard to believe so many people were up at that hour. . . . By the time the night was ended, I had talked on the phone to at least one person in each of the 48 states, plus a dozen from Canada, a couple from Panama, and one or two in South America.[10]

VOICES FROM THE BLACKOUT

World War II brought many more stations into the all-night arena. America became a true third-shift culture as factories worked around the clock to aid in the war effort. WJR in Detroit (a city famous for its assembly lines) was a prime example of a station stretching its schedule to provide round-the-clock programming to a growing population of third-shift workers.

Norman Corwin: It was a real turning point in this kind of radio. Until then most stations signed off, and you know, I have a hard time recalling all-night radio programs. I think there was a lot of all-night probing by listeners for long-distance transmissions. Guess I just wasn't a late-night radio person back then. Today, given to my advanced age, I often find myself listening to classical music stations at 3 A.M.

John Gehron: Norman is accurate about the majority of stations pulling the plug late evenings, but around that time, especially because of the war, more were staying on the air than ever before.

As might be expected during the war years, Washington, D.C., had more than one station putting out a signal throughout the night.

Ken Mellgren: During World War II, several stations stayed on the air 24 hours a day updating the news. Sometimes you would only hear a ticking clock until news broke in. The Pep Boys auto supply store was a frequent all-night radio sponsor in Washington and in other major cities around the country.

Van Harden: Seems to me even out here in Iowa at WHO, the war kept the signal flowing well into the night. I'm not sure when the station went postmidnight with its programming, but I suspect it predates the war.

Donna Halper: Stations that would become radio giants were flexing their overnight muscles as the medium entered the 1940s. According to a November 24, 1941, article in *Broadcasting,* WABC in New York was testing an all-night program to see what response it would get.

In the years that followed the war, the ranks of all-nighters swelled as stations looked for ways to increase their presence in communities where competition for listeners and advertising dollars increased. In Boston, WBZ went all night in 1952, and other stations in medium and large markets saw the wisdom in keeping the midnight fires burning.

NOTES

1. Thomas C. Reeves, *Twentieth-Century America* (New York: Oxford University Press, 2000), p. 83

2. Bill Jaker, "24-Hour Operation," www.old.time.radio@broadcastairwaves.com, 21 July 1998.

3. Luther F. Sies, *Encyclopedia of American Radio, 1920-1960* (Jefferson, NC: McFarland Publishing, 2000), p. 659.

4. Sies, p. 658.

5. Sies, p. 659.

6. *New York Times,* 13 July 1924.

7. Robert Lewis Shayon, *Odyssey in Prime Time* (Philadelphia: Waymark Press, 2001), p. 48.

8. Harrison B. Summers, *Radio Programs Carried on National Networks* (Columbus: Ohio State University, 1958).

9. Jaker.

10. Arthur J. Singer, *Arthur Godfrey: The Adventures of an American Broadcaster* (Jefferson, N.C.: McFarland Publishers, 2000), pp. 45–46.

Chapter 3

Designing the Dark Hours

But not without a plan.

—**Alexander Pope**

About every type of programming imaginable, and some not so imaginable, has been offered to all-night radio listeners. Although it has been traditionally pegged as the "anything goes" zone, for the most part overnight programming has been fairly reflective of radio's daytime schedule, perhaps with some subtle (and in some cases, not so subtle) variations. As already indicated, music was the mainstay of those stations pioneering the late-night hours on both the local and national levels, and this remained true well into radio's second coming following television's takeover of the living room in the 1950s.

Until the 1970s, overnight programming was the province of local programmers (after that syndicators came to dominate the late-night/early-morning airwaves), and they usually viewed the hours between midnight and 6 A.M. as an extension of their station's other dayparts. Thus if a station aired beautiful music or Top 40, it did so overnight as well, perhaps allowing the deejay a little more leeway in terms of the playlist or a greater opportunity to improvise conversation between records.

Program specialization or station formats emerged in the 1950s as the consequence of radio's abandonment by the networks. Shifting their emphasis to television, the networks left radio to its own devices and resources. The medium was then faced with the challenge of filling the huge gaps once occupied by network programs. However, this situation had little palpable impact on what stations were doing overnights, if, in fact, they were doing anything at all during those hours.

Rock and roll music took over the schedules of many stations targeting young people, while music for the adult audience was provided by those outlets airing beautiful music and middle-of-the-road sounds. Still a relatively small percentage of music stations (most located in metropolitan areas) beamed their melodies into the late-night sky. The next decade saw the introduction and rising popularity of nonmusic formats, such as news and talk, and a growing number of all-nighters left their songbooks and records behind in favor of discussion- and conversation-oriented programming.

Contemporary music's diversification (in the rock and country categories particularly) in the late 1960s and 1970s brought about new formats and variations to existing ones and inspired additional overnight radio scheduling, especially on the FM band. The all-night arena for AM radio expanded during the next couple of decades as talk programs took over the eldest listening service—the consequence of music's apocalyptic migration to FM stereo outlets. Despite the downturn in the fortunes of AM broadcasting from the early 1980s onward, the conversion to chatter actually aided in the expansion of its overnight franchise. For many, all-night radio was never more alive or abuzz than when it addressed important topical issues, and this it now did with a seeming vengeance. Fans perceived this as an era when radio truly excelled as an interpersonal and public service medium and, in doing so, felt it was once again realizing its potential. This was something many believed it had not done since television forced it to reinvent itself.

CHARTING THE NIGHT

The discussion that follows centers on the way programmers, talk-show hosts, and deejays have put together their late-hour shifts. From what follows it should become apparent that the all-night segment of the so-called broadcast "day" has been an especially unique and interesting time—some say illuminating (fully aware of the pun they have made)—to have turned on the old radio set.

Gary Owens: The first thing that should be made very clear is that the overnight shift is an important part of the programming clock. It has real intrinsic value in so many ways. Look, Arbitron has been rating it since the 1980s, so that tells you something.

Bruce Morrow: The graveyard shift, as we have called it, has developed into a very important part of the broadcast schedule, maybe not ratings-wise but for listener "glue." I, like many, have redefined my thoughts about the value of all-night programming to a station.

Max Myrick: You know, all dayparts are important. Although according to Arbitron, the number of listeners is less overnights than at other times, this is still an important piece of the clock. Overnight usage is really lifestyle usage. The all-night jock has a more intimate relationship with the listener, due to the nature of the way this individual listens. There is less button pushing, fewer distractions. The radio is more of a companion overnights. People actually listen more intently. The mood is different. Things are quiet in the world. It's a challenge to program to this audience.

Mike Kennedy: Even though the overnight audience is much smaller than the usual daytime audience, it's still very active, and let's face it, no matter how small, it is a lead-in to your most important daypart—morning drive.

Max Myrick: A good point. It has been my experience that the overnight show is an important lead-in to the morning show. This alone makes it a significant programming consideration.

Bill Conway: It's one of the reasons stations remain on all night. It's a good way to strengthen and maintain a station's "full service" image and meet its legal obligations, too.

According to overnight radio personality Blair Garner, "nearly thirty to forty percent of a single station's daytime audience share is retained overnights."[1]

Larry Miller: They're out there in bigger numbers than you might imagine. This is not a time that programmers should take lightly, though many do. It certainly poses its own unique considerations, and there are ambiguities surrounding it.

The Difference Is Night and Day

Few would argue Miller's statement. Writing in the *Toronto Star,* Gregg Quill explained overnights north of the border this way: "It's a wide open, potentially bleak landscape. No one has ever explored it, and no one seems entirely sure who is listening."[2]

Ray Charron: Yeah, there are some unique programming choices that have to be made during this segment of the broadcast schedule. That almost goes without saying.

Art Bell: There is a very sharp distinction between all-night radio and the rest of the broadcast clock. To start with, due to the time the audience is able to give more attention to what is aired. It is able to more carefully consider what is being said. The listener can sit back and think about what he or she is hearing, and this is not the case in other dayparts. It's a sound-bite society during the day, because people are just too busy to really pay attention and listen to what is being said on the radio. Depth doesn't exist. There's no time for it, but at night it gets heard and either appreciated or panned. The fact of the matter is that night people are able to digest more than their daylight counterparts. That constitutes a significant difference and a central programming consideration.

David Brudnoy: You might say the difference is night and day. The evening format takes on a different sound and feel. The issues and personalities may be the same but there is a greater opportunity to probe and explore topics after the rush of the day is over. All-night radio provides listeners with a relaxed, extended chance to consider questions because it is a less frenetic and hurried time. Unlike daytime talk, which tends to be rancorous, all-night radio is calmer and more deliberative.

Steve LeVeille: There are several different audiences I have to keep in mind when putting on my show. There are the people who are up all night and hear all or most of the show. These folks are either listening at work, listening at home, or long-distance drivers (truckers for the most part) who can pick up WBZ's signal in thirty-eight states. The next group is the people who catch the first couple of hours. These are people who work evenings and are on their way home, and people who are simply night owls and like to stay up late. Then there are the early risers who join the show around 4 A.M. Certainly there are people tuning in every night who aren't usually up at that hour and people who have some quirk of schedule that allows them to listen once a week, but the three groups referred to above are the ones who tune in every night and morning. Those are the people you have to do your show for. For them, my show is part of their day. It's something they can count on, part of their daily routine. Programming nights requires special care and attention.

Greg Hardison: Programmers perceive overnights differently (if they're paying attention—many don't), and well they should. Nighttime radio people generally aren't forced to address things like commuting problems, market fluctuations, and breaking news. Instead, they can focus on larger, more macro-type issues and viewpoints. For example, the daytime talk host might work more in the present moment—what just happened and what happens next? Whereas the overnight guy may feel more comfortable focusing on a broader and more profound tableau—how did this happen and what will it mean?

Van Harden: You know, for a broadcaster in a market large enough to be rated, the objective is the same as during the day—get as many people as possible to listen for as long as possible so that advertisers want to buy time. That's the purpose, goal, and mission. In fact, that's the criteria that decides whether a program director or host retains his job or not. I don't know that nights should be regarded as more distinctive than any other part of the program schedule. It simply needs to be as attractive to listeners as possible. Every daypart is trying to make a listener out of everyone who's awake.

Mike Kennedy: To me the only way it differs from other dayparts is the flexibility and freedom that we allow during the overnight shift. I encourage this on-air staff to get a feel for what the audience wants at that hour and run with it.

THOSE NO COUNT NIGHTS

Midnight to 6 A.M. has been viewed as the "throwaway" daypart by many station managers and programmers. This, say overnight proponents, denies the value and potential of this segment of the broadcast day. The negativity on the part of programmers for the all-night hours is typically inspired by station management's bottom-line orientation.

Rollye James: Sadly, radio stations focus on 6 A.M. to 7 P.M. weekdays for the bulk of their income. It's a comparatively easy sell, so fringe dayparts are often seen as little more than a liability. Resourceful operators turn them into cash in a variety of ways, however. Some formats, like urban and chr [contemporary hit radio] lend themselves to larger evening cumes. Others, like talk, allow for sports packaging (or the quick cash but fatal impact of infomercials). When it comes to overnights, it's almost universally unsold. Therefore, stations try to avoid spending anything on programming during that period. Networks don't want to offer good overnight shows because they're not considered profitable, and local stations don't want to originate programming for pretty much the same reason. What this means is that most stations are willing to give away the time if they stay on. The thinking is that it's a good place to run trade-off schedules and make goods. Yes, overnight is treated as a throwaway time, and that's a sad mistake, because it can be so much more.

Larry Miller: Stations used overnight to fulfill their license requirements regarding news and public affairs programming. That way they didn't have to infringe upon what they viewed as the "money" hours. For example, back in the 1970s, I recall WPLJ in New York did massive amounts of "license" stuff after hours because ABC had committed its O&Os [owned and operated] to tons of news to keep its stations in the good graces of the federales. So it became the dump zone, so to speak. Not a good reason to keep a station on the air, especially when it's a music station to start with.

Elizabeth Salazar: Many stations use this portion of their broadcast clocks to pull maintenance. That certainly says a mouthful about management's regard for the value of overnight programming. Routine tweaking and other engineering chores are often performed when listenership is thought to be low or nonexistent. Of course, if you're the all-night person, this means relinquishing your show to the oscillator and toolbox. Maintenance of this kind usually lasts for several hours. I tried to keep these interruptions a productive time by making myself available to engineers. That was better than just sitting around.

Dick Fatherley: Local stations confronted by the need to pay down debt and reduce operational costs have been forced to plug in satellite programming or dim the lights. With few exceptions, all-night programming isn't considered a profit center. It's usually a "giveaway" zone.

Eric Rhoads: Most stations automate, affiliate, or throw away the all-night shift. Those who understand the special listener network that exists and how it can become a relatable audience can build a significant following all nights. Those stations that recognize this potential and fully exploit it can end up with something genuinely worthwhile.

A Late-Night Banquet

The diversity of the all-night audience demographic was discussed in a previous chapter, and this fact is reflected in the variety of programming that is available to it. Everything from music to talk, and then some, is scheduled to meet the desires of this divergent radio-listening constituency. If anything, the all-night schedule is more eclectic and far reaching than its daytime cousin.

The labyrinthine nature of overnight radio has found its way into the literature on more than one occasion. In his most recent novel, author and radio historian John Dunning offers readers a character who works the late shift at a New Jersey radio station during World War II. What this individual does during his overnight gig is described by another station employee named Rue:

> Gus does the insomniac hour, starting at midnight. Reads poetry and prose in that great pugnacious voice, and plays the damnedest lineup of music you'll ever hear. Tchaikovsky by the Boston Symphony followed by Louis Armstrong. He's great company for nighthawks like me.[3]

Larry King: Variety was the cornerstone of my approach to nights. I had a broad outlook, no particular agenda. I was as interested in discussing sports as I was politics, movies, music, and everyday events. I liked the listener who was a little off the mark as much as the one who was on the mark. I tried to make it a lot of fun and not take the world so seriously. We got great reviews for doing this and incredible guests for that time of night. Congressman Al Gore stayed up with us until 3 in the morning. Bill Cosby dashed from his hotel in Washington in his track shoes to get to spend time with us. I was intensely curious and interested in a myriad of things and brought this to the airwaves. Clearly the audience responded.

Doug Steckler: That's certainly the key to nights. You need to keep it raw, uninhibited, and stimulating, and occasionally even smarter than its daytime stepsister.

Shel Swartz: Keep it entertaining. That's the key, pure and simple. Maybe the one thing the night audience wants more than anything is to be engaged. Providing information is a primary function, too. As they say, the news never stops. All-night news/talk radio keeps the listener in touch with the rest of the world.

Walter Sabo: All-night radio can provide vital information at a time of day when no other medium is even capable of physically delivering it. It's hard to print and distribute a newspaper in an hour. It's difficult to get a TV studio up and running in a few seconds. A live all-night show can provide exactly the same entertainment and information as the morning drive daypart. There is an interesting anomaly in Arbitron ratings that more managers should pay heed to. For stations that have all news or an information-based show on the air early mornings (5 to 6 A.M.), the shares are always the highest. It is an audience magnet. The opportunity exists for any all-night deejay or host to really talk to that audience, but few ever really do this. They do the show as if it is noon, and that's a mistake. The people tuned overnight constitute a distinctive group, and when they are identified as special, they respond in marvelous ways to both the advertiser and station.

Ira Fistell: Walter is right about the role of providing vital information when everything else is tucked away. I recall when a rare nighttime tornado struck in Madison. I was the only live personality on the air in town, and that night I instructed people what to do to stay alive—open the windows, stay away from unreinforced ceilings, go to the southwest corner of your basement and take food, water, and a flashlight with you. Not that I was a tornado expert, it was stuff I just know from my grab bag of odd knowledge. We had everyone in town listening, and the station later put out a tornado advertising brochure that must have done great things for the sales department.

Corey Flintoff: The information and entertainment that all-night stations broadcast is vital to many listeners. For example, like most stations in rural Alaska, KYUK-AM couldn't afford to stay on overnight, but the commercial fishing industry up there is what kept us on. People in the region spend most of the summer fishing for salmon in the Kuskokwim River. They have to drift their nets on the incoming tide, which means that a lot of commercial fishing periods take place during that long twilight that is an Alaskan summer night. Just like commuters, fisherman and woman need to know the time and temperature and what to expect from the weather. They also like a few tunes. We found volunteers to take the airshift, and it got to be one of our most popular shows.

In the lower forty-eight states, especially in the midwest and west, radio stations have commonly remained on the air overnight or signed on early in order to provide programming to farmers and ranchers up and at work during the predawn hours. As far back as 1925, Shenandoah, Iowa, station KMA signed on at 5:30 A.M. to serve this listening constituency.

NIGHT MOVES

In terms of pacing and mood, overnights are frequently regarded by many program directors and hosts as a time to maintain a relaxed and easygoing atmosphere. These are the hours when the screaming and loudness so familiar to other dayparts give way to a more quiet and reflective—even meditative—sound considered in keeping with this hour.

> **Larry Miller:** Definitely a more laid-back part of the radio schedule. There are fewer commercials and the jocks or hosts assume a more personal style, which fits much better at 3 o'clock in the morning.
>
> **Alan Colmes:** At night, unlike during drive time, you can delve into topics with few interruptions. In the middle of a hot issue, there is no need to break for weather or traffic updates. Time checks are less necessary too. The commercial load is usually less than that during other dayparts, so you can really get on a roll and worry less about the mechanics of fitting in all these other elements. It lets you be more yourself.
>
> **John Hanson:** When people think of overnight radio, I believe the thing that comes to mind is a mellower brand of programming. Listeners know that whether it's a music station or talk show, the deejay or host won't be screaming in their ears.
>
> **Rollye James:** Yeah, it's more like interpersonal, one-on-one communication. You don't yell into the face of the person you're talking with.
>
> **Steve LeVeille:** I haven't changed my "style" at all. The core audience for my show is people who are always up at night or at least for part of the night. They want to listen to someone who is also "up," as in "awake." They don't want to be put to sleep. So my style is the same as if I was doing morning drive or midday.
>
> **Doug Stephan:** I strive for a more inspirational tone on my show, not harsh like Rush Limbaugh or others. Wouldn't work during the early morning hours anyway.

On the subject of things inspirational, hundreds of radio stations resort to religious programming to draw listeners and sponsors to overnights. A good example is VCY America's *Music 'til Dawn,* hosted by Vic Eliason, which features "mostly conservative, ministry-oriented inspirational music."[4] Tunes are interspersed with verses from the Bible and life-affirming comments. The program is distributed by satellite to subscribers in twelve stand-alone half-hour segments.

> **Larry King:** Look, the fact of the matter is all kinds of different shows and features work overnights. It's not a monolithic programming zone. To be honest, I don't know that there is any best "single" approach to all-nights. I know that legendary late-night guy Long John Nebel succeeded with mostly cult things and this fellow [Art] Bell did very well communicating with aliens and abductees. I think what counts most is whether the program and host are entertaining and relevant.

Hitting the Right Notes

Until the late 1980s, music was by far the most widely scheduled element of all-night programming. This dominance was significantly challenged following the elimination of the Fairness Doctrine in 1987—an action that inspired a veritable explosion in the number of radio talk shows because stations no longer were required to offer time for opposing opinions and viewpoints. Yet music remains the most prevalent offering of all-night stations, and the programming of it is treated with everything from relative indifference to careful regard.

> **Frank Childs:** You have to put the time in. Music planning for that hour is very important. Choosing the right song to fit that moment is a form of art, or I should say a dying art form since many overnight programmers don't invest much time or effort in it. Maybe you have to be an all-night jock to understand the feeling you get when you make that perfect segue. When the songs are in the same key and the fade into the beginning is right there, that's a creative moment. To me that is a big part of the nighttime experience. You know the audience is with you. They get into it as much as you do. I think even more so at night.

> **Shel Swartz:** Those stations that program music overnights help make the miles pass by quickly when you're out there

driving down a long, lonesome highway. Care has to go into the playlist. It pays for the station and the listener.

Country melodies may well lead other forms of music in popularity with nighttime listeners. Hundreds of stations, both AM and FM, schedule the Nashville sound overnights. Writing in *Electronic Media* in the late 1980s, Adam Buchman conveyed the findings of an Arbitron study on this topic. The report concluded that "ratings for the so-called overnight daypart could be particularly significant to country radio because nearly one-fourth of its weekly audience listens during that time." It further determined that "23 percent of the country radio audience tunes in during the overnight daypart."[5]

Ed Shane: Overnights have always been into country music, as has Top 40. I was an occasional all-night deejay at WQXI in Atlanta during its pop music heyday in the late 1960s. My assignment was at the news desk, so when I told the PD I'd like to do an occasional disc jockey stint it was not met with particular enthusiasm. Was I that bad, I wondered? No, he told me. He just wanted to keep the news department separated from the entertainment department . . . even overnights. He was right. The station had an excellent news operation. No sense in sullying it with some disc jockey patter. Thus I became "The Music Machine." Any time the station had a hole to fill in the overnight shift, they'd plug in the Music Machine. It protected the news image, because I never used my name, and it gave me the occasional outlet beyond reporting and anchoring. Thinking about that experience from today's perspective adds odd irony. I was a live human being spinning records and doing talkups while calling myself a "machine." There was even a jingle that sang the words "The Music Machine." Today, most overnight shows are voice tracked on hard drive. They really are the music machine. The human Music Machine had one flaw. Unlike voice-tracked automation, the human can get sick. One night I got very sick, using the garbage can almost as much as I did the turntables. Joe Kelly, the voice talent who's now heard on every major rock station, was the PD at WQXI then. As the clock crept slowly toward 3 A.M. and I got sicker and sicker, I made a call I hated to make—to Joe's house in the middle of the night. The best voice in the business relieved the Music Machine that night.

Other, less mainstream, music has found its way onto the air during the wee hours. Jazz has always found it difficult to find a home in commercial radio, but many stations give it the overnight hours because it seems an appropriate form of music to be aired at that time of the broadcast schedule. Reasoned station programmers, the audience for jazz was nominal at best, and who during the daylight hours could get into the mood or gestalt conveyed by something like Thelonius Monk's " 'Round Midnight"?

In the 1980s and 1990s, new age jazz music found a significant audience, and a growing number of radio stations embraced the smooth sound as a primary format. Meanwhile, quite a few adult contemporary music stations shifted to "light" jazz at night recognizing that an audience existed for this kind of music and that it mixed well with their primary format. Found on new age jazz playlists are artists such as Janis Ian, Spyro Gyra, George Winston, Yanni, and Peabo Bryson. Among the most successful programmers of new adult contemporary (NAC) or smooth jazz is Windham Hill, which claims to stock the playlist of dozens of radio stations around the country.

> **Paul Heyer:** I'm a fan of jazz music, and when I was in high school and college I found that one of the few opportunities to hear it was by scanning the AM dial after midnight. Jazz is something you can't find in most dayparts besides overnight. This is also true for alternative rock. The all-night shift is where you're going to find it, if you find it at all on radio.

Extended Play

The moody, ethereal sound of the so-called smooth, light, and easy music programming genre especially lends itself to long, uninterrupted sweeps and nocturnal airplay.

> **Sam Sauls:** Longer music sets and extended-play cuts are a prevalent feature of all-night music programs. This is where you can do this more than at any other time of the broadcast day. Moreover, this is what the night owls want and are looking for.

> **Larry Miller:** At KMPX in San Francisco in the 1960s, I may have originated the idea of programming rock music in sets rather than airing one song at a time. Prior to that you might

> hear music played in sets on stations playing jazz or beautiful music. So we didn't exactly invent the idea. We just put it to new and more interesting use. This was first done on my overnight shift. Then it carried over into other dayparts. One source of the idea of programming music in sets actually originated late nights at WFMT in Chicago in the 1950s, as I recall. Running long music sets also frees up the all-night guy so that he can go to the bathroom, and that may very well have been the inspiration behind its creation in the first place.

> **Rob Brown:** Rotations on songs are slowed and there's more variety in the playlist from midnight to 5 A.M. More subtle adjustments are made throughout the shift. For example, we avoid saying "tonight" but use "today" or "this morning" instead. When third-shift workers are on their lunch break, it's not night to them.

While stations make adjustments for the hour, not all choose to soften or turn down the volume at night. In fact, many rock stations do just the opposite, feeling that their listeners want to party harder and stay awake and energized, rather than slip into a state of relaxed bliss.

> **Lynn Barstow:** KMYZ schedules overnights virtually the same as it does early evenings. The music is generally a little newer and a little louder by night. We also encourage our overnight jock to extend the phone-active high-energy approach of the early evening jock, at least for the first couple of hours into her midnight to 6 A.M. shift. We schedule lots of music in sets and brief talk breaks that hopefully complement the music and listener's lifestyle.

A DIFFERENT DRUMMER

No other part of the broadcast day allows for the level of experimentation as does overnights. If departure from a station's format is permitted at all, it is during this time slot when programmers believe the audience is more open to such digressions. "Programmers can take more chances at night," observes writer Ross Murray, adding that this has to do with there being less on the line. "It is taken for granted that the numbers are much smaller than in the daytime."[6]

Bill Conway: The great thing about all-nights was that you could try just about anything and have very little risk involved. If what you did worked brilliantly, then everyone benefited. If it stunk up the place, how many people did it chase away? For every caller there are probably 100 listeners who don't call. For them the extra stuff you did by experimenting and trying things was the attraction. Sure the music was the most important thing, but you could have more personality than those working the more critical dayparts. That's why some deejays would never work any other shift.

Larry Miller: This was where one could push the edge of the envelope. Parents were less likely to be up late complaining about questionable lyrics, drug songs, or dirty jokes. So you could let your hair down and go in those forbidden directions. You had more freedom overnights to develop ideas, such as playing with sound and musical effects. At KMPX in San Francisco back in the flower child era, I always had Indian music running in the background when I did breaks to create a hip-sounding atmosphere. I couldn't have done any of that during the daytime.

Steve Warren: I've always felt the overnight shift was looser and more fun. Station management seldom listened to you and rules were less strictly observed. I think management was so pleased to find someone willing to pull the shift that it tended to leave him or her alone despite the format transgressions. All-night radio personalities have always felt more at liberty to break format and play music of their own choice—music not programmed during the day.

Sheena Metal: The upside of lower listenership is that overnighters have a certain freedom to experiment on their shifts that those on the "rated" shifts don't. A lot of shows and a lot of deejays got their start on all-night radio. I guess it's viewed as a safe place to try out the new kids and ideas. Because of the "You'll never know what we'll do next" attitude found late nights, listeners seeking shows that are unpredictable and avant-garde tune in. Many people are bored by mainstream, formula radio. They're out to discover the next cool thing and sometimes they find it on overnight radio.

College radio has long been known for its alternative programming philosophy, and the night shift at these mostly noncommercial stations is emblematic of this freewheeling attitude. Gregg Quill tells about one such station in Toronto.

> At 88.1 on the FM band . . . after midnight is when some of its most provocative programming can be heard. . . . This is programming. Experimental programming. Leading edge stuff. It's fertile ground, free range. In the deep, silent hours before dawn, they [station deejays] all feel they achieve something approaching radio heaven, something daytime jocks will never have. . . . CKLN [has] a wide "alternative" mandate to deliver community based programming that is not aired elsewhere. . . . The all night slot allows more creative freedom than any other shift. . . . It gives the community a voice it wouldn't otherwise have. Radio at night has vast potential; it remains undiscovered by programmers and consultants. As daytime radio is being strip mined, the nights are where the real communication is done.[7]

Candle in the Night

Overnight programmers usually are intent on creating an atmosphere where listeners feel they can make a connection. Given the often-solitary nature of being up and about during the deep of night, the tuning public seeks a friendly voice and a place to go to mitigate the sense of disenfranchisement and isolation the midnight hour frequently fosters. In the hours before dawn, radio serves as a welcome beacon to millions, and any well-informed program director knows that and attempts to reflect this in the content of overnight shows.

> **David Brudnoy:** All-night radio should offer listeners an extended opportunity to become involved with the issues that impact their lives. They should be encouraged to join in the conversation. This on-air shift permits longer calls so that listeners can become active participants, an important quality of night radio.
>
> **Eric Rhoads:** I was an all-night jock. Though I hated the hours, it was my all-time favorite shift because I was able to interact and relate to listeners on a whole different level.

People listening and calling in became each other's family. They would phone in, and I'd put them on the air. We would talk about what was going on that night, what they were working on, what life was like living the dark shift. It's a special radio daypart, and needs to be treated as such.

Dick Summer: I never thought of my all-night radio show as a "programming service," although that's the way it was originally designed by Uncle Sam. I hated sleepless nights, but I loved all-night radio. Making love is a connection. Screwing is a "service." I loved the connection with the individuals who were sharing the night together with me. I didn't necessarily love everyone who called in, but establishing a connection was worthwhile in so many countless ways. First off, it created great radio. Secondly, especially at night, it was something you had to do if you were going to fully exploit the medium's great power and potential. I never thought of the person tuned in as a "listener." He was just another human being like me.

Tuned for the Duration

As mentioned several times elsewhere, the time spent listening by overnight audiences generally exceeds that of daytime radio. Simply put, people tuned at 3 A.M. are much less inclined to station hop. They find a program or host they like and stick with them. Loyalty is the hallmark of all-night radio users.

Rob Brown: We recognize that this daypart often has the longest-time-spent-listening opportunities as listeners are captive at workplaces for several hours in a row, and, in many places, there aren't the number of stations vying for the audience.

Helen Little: It's an opportunity to establish a longer-term relationship with listeners, because they tend to hang out with you longer all nights. This is good for many reasons, not to mention the lead-in value to the morning show.

Ray Briem: When people listen at night they listen to almost every word spoken. You have the listener's undivided attention. For the radio host, can you imagine anything better? It helps that there are fewer distractions on this shift. It's a more relaxing time, so listeners are not chased away like they often are during the day.

A Learning Experience

Many of the nation's leading radio broadcasters began their careers on the overnight airwaves. More than any other segment of the broadcast schedule, it is used as a training ground for new and aspiring radio personalities.

Anne Gress: A lot of stations use the overnight show to develop new talent. When I did overnights, that's what I was doing. God, when I think back to those shows! I was terrible! But I'm thankful to this day for the opportunity I had to work on my skills. If I were starting out today, where would I get this opportunity? It's a scary thought.

Don Barrett: When radio was fresh with live programming during the all-night hours, it was a training ground for many guys who went on to huge careers. When historic KFWB/Color Radio was launched in 1958, Ted Quillin was the all-night man. He taught me and other listeners an appreciation for the blues, and eventually he went on to success days. Bob Eubanks of *The Newlywed Game* started overnights at KRLA as did B. Mitchell Reed at KFWB.

Bill Conway: You could build a following and really develop your skills. When I was program director at WTMJ in Milwaukee in the early 1980s, we had a kid named Steve Wexler, who had interned on the afternoon show with Jonathan Green. He wanted to be a radio star, so when we suddenly had an opening all nights, we plugged him in. He immediately tried all the stuff he'd wanted to. He dubbed his listeners Wexaholics and had bumper stickers made. I knew we were growing a possible morning talent. Wex went on to mornings at another Milwaukee station. Then he went on the Portland and Seattle, where he became a program director. Now he's market manager for Journal Broadcasting's cluster in Tucson. It was amazing how fast he grew into a real talent, and it all started for him overnights.

Josef Lenti: It's where stations typically put their "lightest" jock, the person with the least experience, so that he or she can work on technique and evolve.

Greg Strassell: At Mix-98.5 in Boston, the overnight shift is for someone I might spot in a smaller market. They may have the desire, ambition, and talent to be in a top market but not the experience or polish to be in a prime daypart. This is a chance to nurture young talent, which has become a big issue in radio—where to find new talent? This makes all-night an important shift, believe me. Usually the overnight talent is more eager to do a weekly aircheck, because he or she wants to learn and grow. I welcome this kind of attitude. My goal is to provide the station with quality overnight talent, keeping it interesting and enjoyable to the overnight audience. Sara

Figure 3.1. Occasionally all-nighters left the conscious world. Courtesy Bobby Ocean, Inc.

> Rodriguez impressed me enough at a smaller station to bring her here. Sara is encouraged to do more and flex her creative muscles, because it will bring her along faster and at the same time make it pleasurable for the overnight audience that is looking for more than just jukebox radio.

The all-night shift has been used for punitive purposes as well. Low ratings of a particular daypart have resulted in the person hosting the period being exiled to the overnight slot. It is either that or goodbye in many cases. Meanwhile, the overnight person may be bumped up to an earlier slot as a reward for his or her efforts. All-nights have also been used as the cooling-off zone for personalities who have generated controversy. For example, in 2000 Dr. Laura Schlessinger's program was reassigned to all-nights in many markets where it could be heard. The uproar over her antigay statements proved the catalyst for this action.

Whether a training zone or not, all-night radio brings to its listening audience an abundant mix of programming options. Perhaps nowhere else on the commercial radio dial is one as apt to encounter the kind of uninhibited discourse and distinctive rhythms that overnight offers. As some of those in these pages have indicated, staying up to tune late-night radio can be worth any loss of sleep that may result because of the special rewards it offers.

NOTES

1. Blair Garner, www.aftermidnite.com, 29 December 2000.
2. Gregg Quill, "Free Spirits of the Airwaves," *Toronto Star,* 10 June 1989, p. E3.
3. Dunning, *Two O'Clock, Eastern Wartime* (New York: Scribner, 2000), p. 76.
4. www.vcyamerica.org, 28 December 2000.
5. Adam Buchman, *Electronic Media,* 22 February 1988, p. 18.
6. Ross Murray, "Overnight Has a Flavor All Its Own," *Gazette* (Toronto), 26 October 1991, p. E1.
7. Quill, p. E3.

Chapter 4

Distant Signals

Oh, the brave music of a distant drum.

—Edward Fitzgerald

In its earliest manifestations, overnight or late-night radio was primarily an undertaking of those stations with higher-powered signals. When radio first surfaced in the 1920s, there was very little regulation regarding the wattage a station could employ to transmit its broadcasts, yet on the whole power ratios were quite nominal. It was typical for a station to operate at somewhere between 100 and 500 watts. Later in the decade, as many more stations and the networks entered the fray, operators began to increase their output. However, by that time the government was more involved in a station's operating parameters. With the establishment of the Federal Radio Commission (FRC) in 1927, a station could no longer arbitrarily choose the strength of its "effective radiated power." If a station remained on the air at all (dozens of outlets were removed from the airwaves by the commission to reduce the problem of interference), it was told exactly the level of wattage it could use to propagate its radio frequency.

Although most early radio stations broadcast during the daylight hours and maybe into early evening, those that remained on the air were at a particular advantage because they operated on the AM band. AM signals are carried great distances at night due to a phenomenon known as the "sky wave effect." In the evening, a few hours past sunset, the ionosphere forms and radio's secondary signals, those that travel skyward, bounce off this nearly impenetrable layer of atmosphere. Thus, despite relatively low power levels, an AM station's sky wave can travel hundreds, sometimes thousands, of miles late at night.

> **Christopher Sterling:** The majority of radio stations signed off in the evening and, for those few that remained on the air, the sky was theirs.

> **Rollye James:** Jeez, until the 1950s and the advent of formula radio (Top 40), which developed in reaction to television's emergence, most radio stations did not broadcast around the clock, preferring to sign off around midnight. But with the sky wave conditions, the handful that remained on served a large part of the country. Actually, many stations got out of the way, turning off their transmitters, so that the bigger stations could be heard.

During the 1920s, the practice of "silent night" was observed by dozens of lesser-powered stations in deference to their audience's desire to hear signals from distant cities. As the decade came to a close, stations became less willing to go off the air, perhaps realizing the potential value of staying on the air hours past sundown. One such example of this occurred in Chicago in 1928. Stations in the Loop no longer felt inclined to welcome outside radio signals, or at least not on their assigned frequencies.

> Twisting the radio dial to bring in faraway stations no longer is Monday night's indoor sport for Chicago fans. The city's broadcasters have abandoned "silent night," inaugurated four years ago. At that time all local stations entered a "gentlemen's agreement" to stay off the air on Monday evenings, so the distance hounds could get what they wanted, or try to get it. Broadcasting has now been resumed every night in the week for various reasons, but principally because it was feared Chicago wave lengths would be permanently assigned on Monday nights to other stations, thus preventing even emergency broadcasting should circumstances necessitate it.[1]

The report by the Associated Press goes on to detail the contentiousness ultimately surrounding the practice of "silent night" in that midwestern city.

> Silent night had been a controversial practice. It resulted in the country's first "listener strike." Incensed because several Chicago stations continued to broadcast on Monday night, listeners banded together and decided not to tune in on them during the week. The fans won. While the family of distant hunters may not be as large as it once was, with radio taking its place in the homes with other forms of entertainment, listeners have reported almost as much luck in tuning for distance as their locals on the air Monday nights. This class, of course, includes only those with the more modern receivers. Owners of the older type sets did not have so much luck anyway on Monday night.[2]

Killer Signals

A powerful new category of radio stations was authorized by the FRC in the late 1920s. These stations were allowed to broadcast unimpeded by local stations, and their signals traveled immense distances at night.

> **Rollye James:** As radio developed early on, consideration was given to areas not served by local outlets in the form of clear-channel allocations. We're talking about AM, of course. FM was not a factor at this time, nor would it ever be in the distant broadcasting arena. Stations were divided into four categories: Class I, Class II, Class III, and Class IV. Class I facilities were designated as clear-channel allocations, both 1A nondirectional and 1B directional, and they were assigned 50,000 watts of power. Their purpose was to take full advantage of the ionosphere layer effect after dark, allowing for sky waves to bounce over greater distances. Lesser-class stations were obliged to protect these clear-channel operations, that is, get out of their way. They ruled supreme and had free reign of the nighttime airwaves. The expectation was that these stations would serve vast areas unable to get local programming after dark. Throughout the '30s, '40s, '50s,

and even in some cases the '60s, these outlets were the only source of late-night information for listeners in rural locations. Therefore, they provided a vital service.

In his book *Big Voices of the Air,* James C. Foust offers further explanation of how clear-channel operations came into existence:

As AM radio embarked upon its so-called Golden Age in the early 1930s, the industry's structure had been in many ways dictated—or at least endorsed—by government regulation.

Table 4.1. List of nation's most powerful all-night radio stations. Courtesy Rollye James.

1A U.S. clear channel facilities and formats

All are 50kW ND except WBZ and WWL which are DA-1.
(WBZ and WWL are directional in order to avoid wasted water coverage.)
There are 25 stations, 20 are news/talk, 3 are all news, 1 is sports, and 1 is country.

640	KFI	Los Angeles	N/T
650	WSM	Nashville	country
660	WFAN	New York	sports
670	WMAQ	Chicago	news
700	WLW	Cincinnati	N/T
720	WGN	Chicago	N/T
750	WSB	Atlanta	N/T
760	WJR	Detroit	N/T
770	WABC	New York	N/T
780	WBBM	Chicago	news
820	WBAP	Ft. Worth	N/T
830	WCCO	Minneapolis	N/T
840	WHAS	Louisville	N/T
870	WWL	New Orleans	N/T
880	WCBS	New York	news
890	WLS	Chicago	N/T
1020	KDKA	Pittsburgh	N/T
1030	WBZ	Boston	N/T
1040	WHO	Des Moines	N/T
1100	WTAM	Cleveland	N/T
1120	KMOX	St. Louis	N/T
1160	KSL	Salt Lake City	N/T
1180	WHAM	Rochester	N/T
1200	WOAL	San Antonio	N/T
1210	WPHT	Philadelphia	N/T

1B U.S. clear channel facilities and formats

All are directional as indicated, with 4 nondirectional exceptions: KNBR, WGY, KOA, & KNX. All are 50kW except KNZR which is 25kW/10kW. There are 33 1B stations: 21 are news/talk, 3 are news, 3 are sports, and 1 each is country, business, nostalgia, oldies, religion, and kiddie.

680	KNBR	San Francisco	ND	sports
710	WOR	New York	DA-1	N/T
	KIRO	Seattle	DA-N	N/T
810	WGY	Schenectady	ND	N/T
	KGO	San Francisco	DA-1	N/T
850	KOA	Denver	ND	N/T
1000	WMVP	Chicago	DA-2	sports
	KOMO	Seattle	DA-N	N/T
1060	KYW	Philadelphia	DA-1	news
1070	KNX	Los Angeles	ND	news
1080	WTIC	Hartford	DA-N	N/T
1090	WBAL	Baltimore	DA-N	N/T
	KAAY	Little Rock	DA-N	religion
1110	WBT	Charlotte	DA-N	N/T
	KFAB	Omaha	DA-N	N/T
1130	KWKH	Shreveport	DA-N	N/T
	WBBR	New York	DA-N	business
1140	WRVA	Richmond	DA-1	N/T
1170	WWVA	Wheeling	DA-N	N/T
	KVOO	Tulsa	DA-N	country
1190	KEX	Portland	DA-N	N/T
	WOWO	Ft. Wayne	DA-N	N/T
1500	WTOP	Washington	DA-2	news
	KSTP	Minneapolis	DA-N	N/T
1510	WLAC	Nashville	DA-N	N/T
	KGA	Spokane	DA-N	N/T
1520	WWKB	Buffalo	DA-1	sports
	KOMA	Oklahoma City	DA-N	oldies
1530	WSAI	Cincinnati	DA-N	nostalgia
	KFBK	Sacramento	DA-2	N/T
1540	KXEL	Waterloo	DA-2	N/T
1560	WQEW	New York	DA-2	kiddie
	KNZR	Bakersfield	DA-N	N/T

> Among the most significant of these structural requisites was a tripartite arrangement of individual stations in which power, frequency and hours of operation were assigned according to each station's class. Atop this allocation structure were the clear channel stations, which were assigned maximum power and given permission to broadcast on frequencies of which they had exclusive—or nearly exclusive—use. The Federal Radio Commission (FRC) reserved 40 of these frequencies in 1928 for the purpose of providing radio service to remote rural listeners, especially during night time hours. While hundreds of stations crowded the remaining 56 frequencies of the broadcast band, at night only one station was permitted to operate on each clear channel.[3]

Nearly all clear-channel stations were affiliated with a network and located in large metropolitan areas. These were among the most profitable radio outlets of their day and, in many cases, remain so today.

> **Charles Fitch:** These were the ultimate stations. In many regions of the great southwest and in other parts of the country's vast outback there were only a handful of stations. Most of these were daytimers, so the clears served these areas at night. They were our no-cost lifelines to the outside world. In trying to put all of this into historic perspective, a long-forgotten memory jumps into my head. By way of anecdote allow me to pass along a shaggy dog tale that illustrates the importance of this special category of station. Labor Day weekend in 1967, my friend and I decided to take our motorcycles for a ride through the desert to Carlsbad Caverns to see the famous bat flight. At the time there was very little around that part of the country, just the occasional El Paso gas works and a few memorial plaques relating the infamous salt wars when people got shot over salt rights. For the most part, the road was a simple two-lane blacktop with a handful of improved culverts where the old gravel road used to be. Night caught us a good many miles away from the Caverns just past El Capitan (the highest point in Texas). The only thing around was a picnic area, and so we unrolled our sleeping bags, ate dinner from a can, talked a little, and

crashed on the concrete pad under the table. Other than the desert cold, the night was calm, and we slept through till dawn. I have loved radio and DXing since the age of four, so I kept a little transistor with me whenever I went for a long ride into the wide-open spaces. The next day we did the cave and town thing and headed back out onto the desert for our return trip. As fate would have it, we ended up camping at the same picnic area as the day before. This time a goodly number of people were camping there, so we had to scurry about for a spot to lay our sleeping bags, which ended being an unsheltered area—no picnic table, that is. Now to the point of all this. Here I am half asleep and around 3 A.M. and in the deep cuddly warmth of my roll I snap on my radio deep. At a great sleepy distance I can hear the KOMA overnight guy quoting animal and feed stock prices in domestic and overseas markets. Then came the local weather report and a bulletin about New Mexico weather. Very heavy winds were forecast in the area we were camping in until sunup. This caught my attention, and I found my flashlight in my roll and turned it on. The first thing I noticed was my big chopper—that happened to be parked right next to me—swaying in the heavy winds, so I leapt to my feet and tied everything down the best I could. I honestly believe that one or two more gusts and my bike would have fallen on me. Now fully awake, I just kept tuned to that faraway broadcast signal from KOMA. In retrospect, I see where KOMA saved me a lot of grief.

Brian Buckfink: Those boomer signals intrigued and entertained me when I was growing up in North Dakota. KOMA-AM in Oklahoma City was easy to pick up at night. I once called the station (I got in trouble for making a long-distance phone call) and talked with its engineer, who said that North Dakota was one of their great listening centers at night. "FUN 1520," they called themselves. They ran a lot of livestock spots so farmers all across the west and midwest could know where auctions would be held. Another all-night sponsor was the Red River Dragway in South Dakota. I remember hearing Charlie Tuna on the station before he headed to KHJ in Los Angeles. I'd tune in the WLS (the "Big 89") in Chicago for the latest rock and roll music and

> Dick Biondi. I was a card-carrying member of his fan club. His nightly countdown was fantastic. There were many other super signals a kid could tune, such as KNX in L.A. and KSL, KNBR, KKOB, KOA. Later when I was old enough to have a car, all of these powerful stations were on the push buttons for nighttime entertainment. It was the AM sky wave phenomenon that really got me hooked on radio and led me to a career in it.

> **Ken Kohl:** My career is based on years of teenage alienation manifesting in overnight radio listening. I fell in love with radio in the middle of the night on the skip from exotic places like Salt Lake City and Buffalo.

There has been a special allure and romance associated with the late-night radio giants. To be in Danbury, Connecticut, and pick up a station in the desert southwest on an inexpensive Japanese transistor radio left a mark on many young people who dreamed of becoming the next Wolfman Jack.

> **Gary Berkowitz:** As a kid growing up, all-night radio played a major role in getting me interested in the business. Growing up in the New York area, you could scan the dial and hear great radio from as far away as Dallas and Buffalo. At the time, I'm talking the mid-1960s, talk was rare at night (I never understood why WMCA broke at 11 P.M. for Barry Gray!). I would sit in my room and dream about being the night jock on WOWO in Ft. Wayne. It was magical and inspiring.

> **Greg Hardison:** It had an impact on me, no doubt. AM radio's nighttime propagation characteristics were unique, easily crossing hundreds and thousands of miles to reach waiting receivers. Those signals made you feel like an integral part of a larger identity. I recall working an overnight test-driving gig out of San Antonio, Texas, back in the dark ages. The job required that I cover over 400 miles of west Texas roadway a night. Most of my rock-oriented listening back then was done via WLS in Chicago, KOMA in Oklahoma City, and KFI in Los Angeles. When nothing especially listenable could be found on the big three as you rolled through open country in the middle of the night, there was always something appealing about tuning mariachi music from the big signals in Mexico on XEG in Monterey or XERF in Acuna.

1,000 COUNTIES—40 STATES

It was July 18, 1922. On this day, John Glenn celebrated his first birthday in neighboring Ohio and WHAS pioneered Kentucky broadcasting as a 500-watter in Louisville.

The years flew by and WHAS helped transform a sprawling, backwoods Kentuckiana area into a rich, diversified market. WHAS has continued to pioneer with specialized departments for News, Sports, Farm, Home and Public Affairs programming.

Today, WHAS programs are airborne by a 50,000 watt, clear channel thrust and have boosters who respond from nearly 1,000 American counties in more than 40 states.

Pioneering is a good life. And in Kentuckiana, the good life for listeners and advertisers begins at eight-forty . . . WHAS 840 Radio.

WHAS

840 RADIO LOUISVILLE, KY. 50,000 WATTS, 1-A CLEAR CHANNEL

Figure 4.1. Stations promoted their powerful nighttime signals.

Jim Bohannon: To me, radio's real allure was at night when the sky waves of 50,000-watt stations had people back in the '20s and '30s glued to their crystal sets. Today, satellites do what those monster signals used to do.

THE NATION'S STATION AND BORDER BLASTERS

No other station in the history of American broadcasting was authorized to operate with more power than WLW in Cincinnati, Ohio. In June of 1932, it was given the go-ahead to generate a half-million watts between 1 A.M. and 6 A.M. According to broadcast historian Lawrence Lichty, the station "transmitted with ten times more power than any other AM station—then or now—until March 1939 when the FCC refused to continue the higher power 'experimental' license."[4]

Farm reports and hillbilly music shows drew vast audiences to the superstation during its overnight and early morning hours. Fan mail was received from every corner of the country, and WLW station management fought hard to retain their 500-kW license, claiming it provided a vital service to the country. The FCC thought otherwise and ended WLW's nighttime dominance in the early 1940s.

A decade and a half later, the country would be served by other high-powered outlets at night, but these would not broadcast from within its borders. Mexican border stations with awesome power levels cast their signals across the North American continent.

> **Rollye James:** The border blasters of the 1950s reached from the Mexican border to Canada with their quarter million watts of power. They offered a sometimes-bizarre mix of programs and dubious sponsorships that sold mail-order medical cures, among other things.

One legendary broadcaster made his mark on an across-the-border station in the 1950s. For the next couple of decades, no one would fill the nocturnal airwaves quite like Wolfman Jack. According to publisher Erik Rhoads, "Wolfman Jack was the original 'border' jock on XERF, the big gun, high-powered station from Mexico that could be heard in New York."[5]

> **Brian Buckfink:** The Wolfman howled into the midnight air from a blowtorch outlet just south of the Texas border. He was incredible. I'd never heard anything like him.

> **Larry Miller:** Man, you'd be out there driving in the cool, dark desert and all of a sudden you'd hear this howl come from your radio speaker. It was just you, the empty road, and this crazy cat, called the Wolfman, baying at the moon from hundreds of miles south across the border. He'd keep you awake.

Anne Rea: Historically, all-night radio has been a time to disseminate information over large distances (AM radio) and to provide companionship to the sleepless and overnight workers. Wolfman Jack did that in his own unique way.

Rollye James: Programming from the big-signaled AMs could consist of a wide array of things. WLAC, a clear channel at 1510 in Nashville, blanketed the south with pure rhythm and blues, supported by mail-order sales of the songs aired. WCKY in Cincinnati peddled tombstones ("Don't let your mama lay out in the cold another night without a proper marker"). Wolfman Jack worked the mail-order scheme effectively down there in Mexico.

DXing

A favorite hobby of many radio aficionados during the medium's early years (through the 1960s) was tuning in distant stations late at night and recording the transmissions in a special logbook. Dozens of DXer clubs were formed so that members could share their experiences tuning far-off radio signals.

Arnie Ginsburg: I grew up in Boston in an era when TV and FM were in their infancy. So radio was my obsession. One of my first purchases as a kid was a Hallicrafter SX-20 receiver. I spent from midnight to 6 A.M. listening to the many clear-channel AM stations east of the Mississippi that could be received in Boston. From Chicago, Dave Garroway had an all-night radio show with lots of talk and some music. Garroway had a laid-back style and one-on-one ability to communicate during the early morning hours. I was intrigued with his style and was certain he was going places. He did, of course, becoming the first host of NBC's *Today Show.* From New York, I pulled in Symphony Sid, with a jazz program broadcast directly from Birdland, one of New York's great clubs. Sid played records and featured live performances from the club. He introduced me to new jazz artists like George Shearing, Sarah Vaughn, Charlie Parker, Dave Brubeck, Stan Getz, and dozens of others. Sid had the perfect late-night voice. It had been mellowed by years of drinking fine whiskey and smoking exotic cigars. From WOR in New York, I'd also tune in Jean Shepherd, who was a storyteller who could do a 3-hour monologue at the drop of a hat. He grew up in the

Chicago area, then went into the army and finally ended up on the air, where he belonged. He could hold the listener spellbound with a 1-hour story about a Chicago Cubs game he saw when he was a kid, and he could spend another hour telling about an incident involving his army drill sergeant. No one could surpass the oratory of Jean Shepherd. He could tell a story better than anyone I'd ever heard. Still tuning my Hallicrafter after midnight, I'd catch WWVA from Wheeling, West Virginia. It was there that I discovered real country music on a program hosted by Lee Moore. I loved listening to the commercials between records. After one song there might be a spot to buy a guitar for only $9.99, and after the next song you could learn to play that guitar for only $2.99 by sending away for something. Then another record would stop and you could order 110 day-old chicks for only $4.99 or buy insurance for your future child for 10 dollars. They also sold prayer cloths that "glowed in the dark." I set several of the push buttons on my car radio to the station even though I could only get it late at night. Tuning around, I came across WLW in Cincinnati. The signal was exceptionally strong. I heard the Mills Brothers singing live on the air.

Steve Warren: This worked the other way around too. If you worked at one of these monster stations there was no telling who you'd hear from. My favorite phone call from my time on WNBC was early Christmas morning in 1976. The station had a flamethrower 50,000-watt clear-channel signal at 660 on the AM dial, and we regularly got letters and calls from all over North America. About 2 A.M. that morning I got a call from Scotland. A group of sheepherdsmen in the rural countryside could pick up the WNBC signal across the Atlantic and had been listening for several hours. They decided to call, so I'll always remember hearing from shepherds on Christmas.

Although DXing is much less a sport today than it was in the earlier years of the medium, boomer signals can still be received from the existing clear-channel AM stations still in operation. The range of these stations was reduced during the deregulation era of the 1980s, but they still put out signals that traverse amazing distances. Dave Hughes's Internet site (dcrtv.com) continues the tradition of DXing the big AM nighttime signals that reach the nation's capital. According to Hughes, these are the stations someone with a decent AM receiver could expect to hear inside the Beltway after the stroke of midnight. Among these call letters are some of the country's most prominent clear-channel outlets:

WGR, Buffalo, New York (news/talk/sports)
WCHS, Charleston, West Virginia (talk)
CMCA, St. Antonio Vegas, Cuba (Spanish)
WIP, Philadelphia, Pennsylvania (nostalgia)
WRJZ, Knoxville, Tennessee (religious)
WHEN, Syracuse, New York (sports)
WSM, Nashville, Tennessee (country)
WSCR, Chicago, Illinois (sports talk)
CFTR, Toronto, Canada (news)
WPTF, Raleigh, North Carolina (news/talk)
WLW, Cincinnati, Ohio (talk/sports)
WGN, Chicago, Illinois (talk/news)
CKAC, Montreal, Canada (French)
WSB, Atlanta, Georgia (talk)
WJR, Detroit, Michigan (talk/news/sports)
WABC, New York, New York (talk)
WBBM, Chicago, Illinois (news)
CKLW, Windsor, Canada (news/sports)
WGY, Schenectady, New York (talk/news)
WCCO, Minneapolis, Minnesota (news/talk)
WHAS, Louisville, Kentucky (talk/sports talk)
WWL, New Orleans, Louisiana (news/talk/religious)
WCBS, New York, New York (news)
WLS, Chicago, Illinois (news)
WWSW, Pittsburgh, Pennsylvania (sports talk)
KDKA, Pittsburgh, Pennsylvania (talk)
WBZ, Boston, Massachusetts (talk)
WHO, Des Moines, Iowa (talk)

KMOX, St Louis, Missouri (talk)

WOAL, San Antonio, Texas (news/talk)

Dozens of other radio signals from outside the Washington, D.C., area are also available by the flick of the dial. A testament to the popularity of all-night radio is the fact that the city also boasts dozens of local outlets on the air between midnight and 6 A.M.

NOTES

1. Associated Press, 1 January 1928.
2. Ibid.
3. James C. Foust, *Big Voices of the Air: The Battle Over Clear Channel Radio* (Ames: Iowa State University Press, 2000), p. 3.
4. Lawrence Lichty, *MBC Encyclopedia of Radio,* ed. Christopher H. Sterling (Chicago: Fitzroy Dearborn, forthcoming 2002).
5. Eric Rhoads, *Blast from the Past* (West Palm Beach, Fla.: Streamline Press, 1996), p. 404.

Chapter 5

Nights of War and Doo-Wop

There was a sound of revelry by night.

—Lord Byron

World War II established all-night radio as an integral part of the broadcast schedule. Until then, the overnight hours had been perceived as a sort of annex—a superfluous extension—of the radio programming clock.

While all-night radio would serve its country with particular distinction during the war, a rather strange twist of fate would result in it actually aiding the enemy as it prepared to launch a surprise attack on U.S. military forces based at Pearl Harbor.

> At 3 A.M., December 7, 1941, Lt. Commander Kenjiro Ono, on the Japanese aircraft carrier Akagi 250 miles northwest of Honolulu, heard Bing Crosby sing "Sweet Leilani" on an all-night radio show broadcast from the city. As Bob Hope tells it, it wasn't that Ono, a communication officer of Japan's 1st Air Fleet, was a Crosby fan—he was waiting for the weather report. The forecast was good—and so the surprise attack that was to start World War II was on.[1]

A rather inauspicious start to a period that would see overnight radio programming gain a level of stature in the industry it had yet to enjoy. Between 1941 and 1945, more Americans were up and about after midnight than ever before. Factories across the land added third shifts to generate vital materials for the war effort. Many radio stations felt it their patriotic duty to keep their signals flowing around the clock. "With the coming of World War II and the greater number of overnight workers—and with the increased information needs of wartime—many stations began to remain on the air twenty-four hours a day."[2] Stations targeted "the musical tastes of restaurant countermen, factory hands, and Rosie the Riveter, for it was World War II, and it had been concocted as a broadcast backdrop to the work of busy hands and minds, fashioning war machinery."[3] Dozens of outlets joined the handful of stations that had been operating all-nights prior to the war. Notes historian Elizabeth McLeod:

> If you examine 1942–1943 issues of "Movie-Radio Guide" you'll find a special "Swing Shift Log," offering a listing of stations on the air overnight. According to this listing, many important stations took this step. Here in the East, overnight workers could have been entertained by WNAC and WEEI Boston, WNEW and WOR New York, WKBW in Buffalo, WSYR in Syracuse, KDKA in Pittsburgh (except Mondays), WCAU in Philadelphia (also except Mondays), and WRVA in Richmond. This is by no means a complete list, but it gives the idea that a lot of stations were jumping into 24 hour broadcasting during this era as a patriotic gesture.[4]

> **Dick Summer:** Certain high-powered stations were "asked" by the government to stay on the air all night during World War II in order to provide a means of quick communication to the public in case of an emergency. When the guy who issues your license to earn a living "asks" you to do something, you suck up the costs and do it.

> **Ken Mellgren:** As I mentioned earlier, many stations kept active overnight in the nation's capital during the war. Everybody wanted to keep abreast of the latest news, and this meant at all hours.

A few stations that had kept their signals active late into the night during the war years found it financially desirable to pull the

CITY	RADIO FAMILIES U. S. CENSUS 1940	% OF RADIO FAMILIES WHO LISTEN MOST AT NIGHT TO: NBC	NETWORK B	NETWORK C	NETWORK D	OTHER STATIONS
MINNESOTA (cont'd)		%	%	%	%	%
Duluth	26,615	57	26	17	17	—
Faribault	2,893	19	80	—	—	1
Fergus Falls	2,306	80	15	—	5	—
Hibbing	4,092	85	15	—	—	—
Mankato	4,057	26	73	—	1	—
Minneapolis	137,922	52	42	1	4	1
Rochester	6,103	52	48	—	—	—
St. Cloud	5,175	25	75	—	—	—
St. Paul	77,882	62	28	4	4	2
South St. Paul	2,948	66	28	2	2	2
Virginia	3,357	75	23	—	2	—
Winona	5,782	10	67	23	23	—
MISSISSIPPI						
Biloxi	3,049	35	61	4	—	—
Clarksdale	1,949	6	87	7	—	—
Columbus	2,174	28	22	3	50	—
Greenville	3,335	5	81	—	14	—
Greenwood	2,582	19	19	62	—	—
Gulfport	2,787	4	66	30	—	—
Hattiesburg	3,396	77	23	—	—	—
Jackson	12,047	95	1	4	—	—
Laurel	3,202	88	5	5	2	—
Meridian	5,637	21	79	—	—	—
Natchez	2,351	50	41	—	3	6
Vicksburg	4,281	62	32	3	3	—
MISSOURI						
Cape Girardeau	4,560	34	20	36	—	10
Carthage	2,811	84	8	3	5	—
Clayton	3,684	67	18	5	5	5
Columbia	4,974	44	3	50	3	—
Hannibal	5,516	21	21	58	—	—
Independence	4,447	57	43	—	—	—
Jefferson City	5,304	82	3	6	9	—
Joplin	9,562	66	—	4	30	—
Kansas City	112,945	52	41	4	3	—
Kirksville	2,799	90	3	4	3	—
Kirkwood	3,130	63	28	6	3	—
Maplewood	3,572	63	28	2	7	—
Moberly	3,684	79	7	2	12	—
Poplar Bluff	2,553	28	55	—	—	17

CITY	RADIO FAMILIES U. S. CENSUS 1940	% OF RADIO FAMILIES WHO LISTEN MOST AT NIGHT TO: NBC	NETWORK B	NETWORK C	NETWORK D	OTHER STATIONS
MISSOURI (cont'd)		%	%	%	%	%
Richmond Heights	3,468	70	22	6	2	—
St. Charles	2,782	54	24	2	12	8
St. Joseph	19,002	71	17	11	1	—
St. Louis	218,457	58	31	3	6	2
Sedalia	5,349	90	4	—	6	—
Springfield	16,347	86	9	5	—	—
University City	8,895	64	26	4	4	2
Webster Groves	4,672	66	24	5	4	1
MONTANA						
Anaconda	3,066	79	21	—	—	—
Billings	6,428	99	1	—	—	—
Butte	10,737	73	27	—	—	—
Great Falls	8,475	11	88	—	—	1
Helena	4,373	84	16	—	—	—
Missoula	5,023	22	78	—	—	—
NEBRASKA						
Beatrice	2,943	64	34	2	2	—
Fremont	3,239	90	7	—	—	3
Grand Island	5,028	45	55	—	—	—
Hastings	4,043	74	24	—	2	—
Lincoln	23,327	56	30	14	14	—
Norfolk	2,774	92	8	—	—	—
North Platte	3,094	90	6	—	4	—
Omaha	58,464	72	23	2	4	—
Scotts Bluff	2,697	73	13	5	—	9
NEVADA						
Reno	6,396	47	6	47	—	—
NEW HAMPSHIRE						
Berlin	4,133	54	25	4	13	4
Claremont	3,099	70	8	—	22	—
Concord	6,427	77	8	9	6	—
Dover	3,747	76	19	4	1	—
Keene	3,564	40	41	2	17	—
Laconia	3,357	64	8	5	23	—
Manchester	19,421	68	3	26	3	—
Nashua	8,168	85	15	—	—	—

These city figures are for networks, not for individual stations.

17

Figure 5.1. A 1940 nighttime listening survey shows network dominance in several states. Courtesy Christopher Sterling.

plug once again before midnight when the global conflict ended, but the overwhelming majority let the RF (radio frequency) flow throughout the night hours.

> **Dick Summer:** When the war was over, nobody wanted to be the first guy to look cheap by going from 24/7 to 18/7, so most kept the all-night thing going. Almost none of them made any money at it, but it did give stations a chance to try out new personalities at a much lower cost than they'd have had to pay in other dayparts. Most stations paid considerably less than their daytime rates for overnight talent. I took a big pay cut to go from Indianapolis to Boston. Lots of stations broke contracts by moving the all-nighter from other dayparts. In many cases, the unwanted talent simply quit instead of working the overnight slot.

> **Bob Henabery:** Interest in the big bands continued to keep listeners tuning into the all-night shows after the war. Live music at that time was beginning to disappear though.

THE NIGHT IS GRAY

Around this time, one of all-night radio's great pioneers, Barry Gray, arrived on the scene. Gray went to work for WOR in 1945 and worked the all-night shift there until 1947. *Variety* magazine's radio editor, Robert J. Landry, had these insights about Gray in his popular 1946 book, *This Fascinating Radio Business:*

> One of the more colorful characters is WOR's Barry Gray. He specializes in facetious "insults" of those who telephone or who come into the studio to be interviewed at 4:00 A.M. Gray is of New York New Yorky, of show business smart, of jive talk glib. His chatter is about orchestra leaders, their sidemen, arrangements, talents. Or he'll discuss the latest movie or stage play or night club or comment on the style, personality, attitude, and ethics of a gossip columnist or a Broadway press agent. Now and again he drifts into a rather casual and oh-yes-I-forgot commercial on behalf of his nocturnal sponsor, the theatrical newspaper, *Variety.*[5]

Following his initial stint in the Big Apple, he headed south for the next three years to work midnight to 3 A.M. at WKAT in Miami, eventually returning to the north to ply his special skills on the

Figure 5.2. Barry Gray brought talk to all-night radio. Courtesy Library of American Broadcasting.

overnight airwaves of the nation's largest city once again. In both cities, he frequently broadcast live from popular nightspots (the Copa in Miami and Chandlers in New York). While at WOR Gray innovated the guest format, inviting celebrities to his late-night show. Gray would also use the phone to add other voices to the mix.

> Barry Gray . . . one of the longest talk show practitioners and widely considered one of the best, claims to have invented the overnight call in radio talk show in 1945. . . . According to Gray, the whole concept developed accidentally when, bored with his show at about three o'clock one morning, he answered his phone and conversed on the air with the caller, who happened to be Woody Herman. As time went on, Gray's overnight show had more talk and less music. He began inviting guests for talk in the studio and continued to take calls.[6]

> **Joey Reynolds:** Barry invented telephone talk by accident when he had trouble with a Woody Herman record and Woody called. Barry held the phone up to the mike and it was fun chatting, so the next week they hooked it up.

Crude technology at the time created challenges for Gray as he tried to include input from listeners on his show. Notes biographer Donald Bain, "Gray was the first talk personality in New York to conduct phone conversations with listeners. Because he was limited by a lack of technology, callers were not heard over the air by the audience. Gray repeated what a caller said and then answered the question or made his own comments."[7]

Over the years some of the biggest names in show business shared the microphone with Gray, including Perry Como, Frank Sinatra, Jo Stafford, Al Jolson, and Jerry Lewis, to name only a handful. Stars were not the only guests appearing on Gray's program. Major political figures, such as Eleanor Roosevelt and Robert Kennedy, also were among those who Gray would come to call "my night people." The *New York Times* described Gray's program as a "nightly kaffeeklatsch which frequently adds up to extraordinary and different radio."[8] *Variety* magazine became an enthusiastic sponsor of his show for a number of years. Gray's fame as a member of the all-night radio cabal would reach its apex over the next decade with his groundbreaking work on WMCA in New York. Often outspoken, Gray engaged in a war of words with many prominent figures of the day, most notably Walter Winchell, who condemned the overnight talker for what he felt were his "Borey Red" politics (Senator Joseph McCarthy would join the list of Gray's detractors in the 1950s for similar reasons).

While other popular overnight radio personalities around the land in the 1940s, among them Art Ford (host of WNEW's *Milkman's Matinee*), Jack Cullen (host of *The Owl Prowl*), and Joe Franklin (host of *Memory Lane*) would draw new and loyal fans to the medium's so-called forgotten zone, Gray would come to represent its first genuine luminary. His efforts to reinvent the all-night format with guests and call-in conversation gave the shift new life and credibility, helping it assume a more appealing and distinctive flavor and personality, which would help it attract larger and larger audiences.

By the late 1940s, due in great part to the war, all-night radio was a more legitimate part of the broadcast schedule. Because of the exigencies of wartime, a larger segment of the population had been exposed to late-night radio, and late-night radio had evolved into something far more than just a "music after midnight" service. This turbulent era in American history would provide impetus to what would become one of the medium's most unique listening experiences.

A Different Path

While the 1940s brought further status to the audio medium because of its laudable response to the needs of a nation caught up in a war, the decade that followed saw its fortunes seriously tested. Television had the public in thrall, and radio was in a quandary as audiences shifted their attention to the "picture" set.

> Radio's future began to look a lot less bright at the beginning of the first full post-World War II decade as "radiovision" (an ironic early moniker for television) cast its spell on the American public. The audience for "affiliate" radio was decreasing, as were its revenues (dropping by $31 million annually between 1948 and 1952), further prompting the networks to shift their attention to the TV side of the ledger. Talent raids conducted by the television networks were pillaging the audio medium of its stars and programs. William Paley's CBS network scored the biggest strike as radio luminaries such as Jack Benny, Red Skelton, George Burns and Gracie Allen, and Groucho Marx abandoned rival NBC. In 1953, half the homes in the United States had a television set, and the radio receiver was exiled to less prominent locations to make room for it.[9]

Not just a few media critics forecast grim prospects for the once triumphant medium. There were predictions that radio would be relegated to nothing more than that of a service for farmers and that it would have less than a fifth of its former audience by the end of the 1950s. These prophesies were more than a little off the mark. In fact, more stations than ever were beginning to keep their signals on throughout the night. A good example of this was Boston's powerful WBZ-AM, which expanded its programming in 1952 to serve its listening audience around the clock. In point of fact, by the end of the decade, the radio industry would be boasting larger audiences and bigger profits than during its heyday.

Several factors contributed to radio's rise from the ashes left from the firestorm that was television. A number of technological

Figure 5.3. Ray Briem, future late-night radio legend, with bandleader Jimmy Dorsey in 1949. Courtesy Ray Briem.

innovations on the audio front (the transistor and long-playing albums and 45s), the birth of a new form of popular music (rock and roll), and efforts by programmers to revive the medium's appeal by revamping its sound (format specialization) gave radio a new beginning. As the '20s had been to radio during its first incarnation, the '50s would give the medium a relevance and appeal that would have the public tuning by the millions during the first decade of its new existence—its second coming.

In fact, due in large part to the Federal Communications Commission's desire to provide local broadcast signals to rural and suburban sections of the country, the number of radio outlets actually soared (leaping from several hundred after the war to several thousand a couple decades later) at a time when the public was feverishly installing the newest symbol of the broadcast century—"sightradio"—in their homes.

Rock Around the Clock

In front of radio's discovery of rock and roll music, it was still finding an audience for nonmainstream sounds, such as jazz, late at night. Likewise, the impresarios and champions of avant-garde music on after-hours radio, the disc jockeys, were developing their own distinct styles to complement the records they spun. Writes Eric Rhoads,

> For years, a trend had been brewing that few had noticed. Deejays played 78s, 33⅓s, and 45s in the wee hours of the morning, filling non-network time on radio stations. Swing records became the rage with the original disc jockeys, Martin Block and Al Jarvis, who created "Make Believe Ballroom." Others, like Mort Lawrence's "Dawn Patrol" on WIP in Philadelphia, "Hank the Night Watchman" on KFVD, Al Fox on KGFJ and "The Nutty Club" on WBBM in Chicago were starting a new movement by playing jazz records.[10]

Stories began to abound about these hipsters of the late-night airwaves who marched to a different beat, so to speak. Rhoads recalls one incident in the early 1950s in which an all-night deejay, the legendary Al Jazzbo Collins, engaged in a spoof at a Salt Lake City station. To stir things up, he played "I'm Looking Over a Four Leaf Clover," for 3½ hours straight. Although station management was less than pleased with the stunt, the record itself went on to become a national bestseller, and it certainly helped put Collins on the map as well. He would perform his special style of all-night radio in many larger markets, New York City included.

In many ways, the all-night shift was becoming a much more colorful part of the broadcast schedule, notes historian Susan Douglas: "Hunter Hancock successfully passed as black as the hipster host of 'Huntin' with Hunter' on KGFJ and 'Midnight Matinee' on KMPC in LA, playing jazz, blues, and spirituals targeted to the audience in Watts."[11]

Meanwhile, according to consultant Bob Henabery, "Symphony Sid Torrence kept his listeners in the groove with live progressive jazz from Birdland in New York, and The Masked Spooner romanced his late night listeners with the easy side of music."[12]

Then, of course, there was the inimitable Wolfman Jack, who brought something entirely new—if not bordering on the heretical—to the radio medium, let alone the all-night shift. In the 1950s, listeners throughout the middle and western part of the country "pulled in XERF, the 250,000 watt powerhouse just over the border in Ciudad Acuna, Mexico, which featured one Big Rockin' Daddy from midnight on who played Ike Turner and his Kings of Rhythm and Louis Jordan doing 'Fatback and Corn Liquor'."[13]

All-night radio was evolving into a veritable cornucopia of programming options in the 1950s. A quick glimpse of the midnight features offered by New York radio stations on Thursday, November 13, 1952, helps illustrate this fact:[14]

12:00—WNBC—News; Symphonic music
WOR—News; Music show
WJZ—Dance music
WCBS—News; Dance music
WMCA—Barry Gray Show
WINS—News; Music
WMGM—Henry Morgan Show
WNEW—Milkman's Matinee
WOV—Ralph Cooper Show
WEVD—Symphonic music
WQXR—New York Times News; Music

Throughout most of the eastern half of the country and into portions of the west, listeners could tune WLW's mighty signal for classical music. On Washington's WTOP, Eddie Gallaher held court on *The Man in the Moondial,* while on WGN in Chicago, Franklin MacCormack presented a mixture of soft music and nostalgic poetry for his overnight listeners on a program he called *All Night Showcase.* Back on the east coast, Norm Nathan entertained late-nighters with his warm banter and jazz melodies on *Sounds in the Night* over WHDH.

HITS IN THE NIGHT

The 1950s were a watermark in all-night broadcasting because of everything that has been stated but probably even more so because of the enormous talents of two of the genre's greatest practitioners—Long John Nebel and Jean Shepherd.

By the end of the decade, stations that programmed rock and roll music led the ratings surveys in most markets, and many of these outlets put deejays on the air overnights to keep the hits coming fast and furiously. A whole new overnight market had been created by the young doo-woppers, who cruised the dark listening to the radios in their hot rods, and the kids tuned to their small transistors under the covers. (Among the countless kids to be influenced by the pop hits spun by late night deejays was Robert Zimmerman, aka Bob Dylan. In the mid-1950s, a Duluth, Minnesota radio show, called "No-Name Jive," held the future legend in thrall as it aired the early rock and roll songs that would profoundly stir his own musical impulses and aspirations.) For many years to come, some of the most prominent Top 40 deejays would launch their careers in the overnight slot. Murray the K—self-proclaimed fifth Beatle—was among them. "On April Fool's Day 1958—the same day that WMCA moved to a rock music format—'Murray the K' took over the all night shift."[15]

Philadelphia, the city that gave the world *American Bandstand*, claims the nation's first round-the-clock hit music station. "It was a very influential Top 40 radio market. One reason was that WIBG was the first 24 hour a day hit music station in America, changing from religion to Top 40 in 1956. There were others that 'block programmed' Top 40 (usually at night), but the Big 99 did it full time."[16]

A syndicated program, American Airlines' *Music Till Dawn*, provided adults an alternative to the exploding number of stations airing pop music in the nighttime. The taped program focused on easy listening instrumentals and soft ballads.

> **Marlin Taylor:** *Music Till Dawn* was popular beginning in the 1950s. It gave stations an alternative to local origination for their all-night shifts.
>
> **Lynn Christian:** The show was sponsored by American Airlines, and it picked the talent. A lot of 50-kW outlets carried it. It seems to me that it ran all during the '50s and '60s on big power AMs like WWL, WLS, WLW, KMOX, WCBS, WSB, KOA, and others. John Dorms gained fame as the *Music Till Dawn* guy for many years.

In the coming years, one of the nation's most powerful stations—WLW—would likewise broadcast an adult-oriented music program called "Moon River" (featuring many different hosts) as the audience for rock music would rise to new heights in listener popularity.

A SHEPHERD IN THE NIGHT

Arguably the greatest all-night radio personality ever, Jean Shepherd, plied his formidable talents over the airwaves of New York's WOR starting in 1956 and kept his legion of fans thoroughly enthralled for the next two decades. He was a truly remarkable presence in overnight radio—perhaps even its finest moment. He called his listeners his "Night People," and to this day—a quarter of a century after his departure from radio—they remain his devoted fans.

> **Mike J. Keith:** Was there ever anybody like Jean Shepherd on the radio? No! He was the best ever. No one can better his ability to engage the listener.
>
> **Marlin Taylor:** This is true. Shepherd did 5 hours a night with no phone calls, no records, and no quests. He just told stories, and they were amazing. Talk about ahead of his time. Station management told him to play music in his early days, and he used to say, "The show is about me. I'm more interesting than records." He was, too.

For many, Shepherd was all-night radio's greatest storyteller and quite possibly the medium's foremost raconteur, surpassing the talents of everyone from Will Rogers to Garrison Keillor. Syndicated columnist Don Kaul recalls his first encounter with Jean Shepherd:

> I was introduced to him in the mid-50s, when I happened upon his show as some friends and I were making an all night drive to New York City. We listened as he told a funny, bittersweet story about his childhood that touched our own recollections of childhood. Then, when he was done, he told another story, no less fascinating, about his time in the service. It went on for 45 minutes. Eventually we turned to each other in amazement and said, "Who is this guy?" I followed his career after that, catching the show when I could, and was never disappointed.[17]

Observes Shepherd fan and program archivist Max Schmid:

> When I was growing up as a kid in the 1960s, I listened to legendary storyteller Jean Shepherd spin wild, maniacal yarns every night for forty-five minutes on our local radio station near New York City. Shepherd told outrageous tales from his experiences working in the steel mills of Gary, Indiana, of his teenage exploits with hot rod cars, of the crazy

> boredom of his army life, and of his life as a swinger in Greenwich Village. Imagine Walt Whitman as a comedian or Garrison Keillor as a beatnik, and you might come close, but you'd miss the way Shepherd creatively hacked the medium of radio, doing things with it that would not be commonplace until the talk show era decades later.[18]

Writing about Shepherd in the *Washington Post* in the '70s, Kenneth Turan paid homage to his special talents:

> Jean Shepherd does things over those airways that no one else can even get close to. He's a tale spinner, a mood weaver, a verbal artist, disciplined yet free-form, who can set you huddled over the set, hanging on his every nuance, his every word. . . . Best of all were the stories he'd tell, weaving in and out of episodes, getting just to the good parts and then pulling back, saying "No. I've only got three listeners after midnight and I have to save the ending for them." He'd talk of fishing for crappies in polluted lakes with his buddy Junior Brunner, or maybe tell of the time he was in the army and spent a rainy afternoon shopping with his girl. . . . [Shepherd] was a humorist, not a comic.[19]

Indeed, Jean Shepherd was no ordinary storyteller, "Not only did [his] radio stories always have complete endings, but they were also often nested one inside the other, with another starting before the previous one finished. That meant that at the end of Mr. Shepherd's air time you would hear the end of each story in the reverse order that it started."[20]

Shortly after Shepherd's death in October 1999, *New York Times* writer Charles Strum cogently assessed the essential aspects of the all-night star's repertoire.

> For 21 years, from the 1950s through the 70s, Jean Shepherd held weeknight seminars on WOR-AM in New York that were part Kabuki, part commedia dell'arte, part Uncle Remus. In his flat, nasal Indiana twang, playing all the parts, and the occasional kazoo, he oozed into the darkened bedrooms of East Coast America on the battery power of cheap Japanese transistor radios. The meandering stories he told—they always came back to the point, always—were usually about him. But they also seemed to be about us—about the old man, family car trips, the Catch-22 Army and a cast of playmates from childhood and adolescence, through

> whom all the complexities of life on earth would be revealed. What was he? Social commentator? Cult leader? Or just a manic kid from a blue-collar background discovering his subversive id in the age of Eisenhower? It was Mr. Shepherd, after all, who alerted America to the scourge of "creeping meatballism," the postwar rush to a conformist society where happiness meant cars with tail fins and a refreshing, ice-cold bottle of Pepsi-Cola.[21]

Praising Shepherd, Daniel Pinkwater, host of the radio show *Chinwag Theater,* offered the following: "[He] knew how to work an audience with the modalities of class clown-cum-cheerleader call-and-response kind of comic. . . . The inventor of free-form radio, shtick radio, hip radio, he worked pranks, philosophized, concertized on jew's-harp, kazoo and nose flute, and was way, way better at radio than anybody else, then or now."[22]

Calling Shepherd "Radio's Noble Savage" in his *Harper's Magazine* article in 1966, author Edward Grossman described the opening moments of the all-nighter's show:

> Shepherd stakes his claim on the microphone. He exorcises by name the disc jockeys and the lady interviewers who have preceded him, and he tells New York ("this Sodom-by-the-Sea, this fetid hole") to stand by for something else. Some ostentatious fumbling of papers, then the recitation of an item from the *Times:* children in Sydney, Australia, have imprisoned a man in the sewer for three days, coming to watch him and to throw bread crusts. Shepherd is not amazed. It is no more than he expects of people. His "old man," he remembers with no malice, was much the same way, an incurable onlooker at catastrophes ranging from midnight refinery explosions to dirigible crashes two counties away (BRROING!).[23]

Shepherd's originality stands as a high watermark in late-night radio. To hear him as a youth was to become a fan forever, notes Bob Kaye, keeper of a website devoted to the "Twain" of the nocturnal airwaves:

> As a feckless youth growing up in Long Beach, New York, I discovered Shepherd late one night on WOR radio. My father, a musician (like myself), told me about "this crazy guy on the radio that [*sic*] tells people to put their radios by an open

> window at 2 A.M. and then plays an incredibly loud record of a train, whistles and all, for five minutes!" Well, what I heard was a bit different. This guy with a curious mixture of Indiana twang and New York tough guy in his voice, was talking about being in a troop train in the army. He was way in the back, in a car that was quite dark. I don't remember the details, but toward the end of the story, it turned out that he was in a car of coffins of returning soldiers. Needless to say, this wasn't of the Dobie Gillis or I Love Lucy genre that I was used to. In the next few nights I heard him weave stories of the foibles of growing up as a kid in Indiana, in a steel mill town. These were stories by a master.[24]

In 2000, Jean Shepherd was inducted into *Broadcasting and Cable Magazine*'s Hall of Fame. On this auspicious occasion, the publication noted that "media critic Marshall McLuhan wrote that the late Jean Shepherd 'regards radio as a new kind of novel that he writes nightly'." Continuing its praise of Shepherd's contribution to the medium of radio, it further observed:

> He attracted a large and incredibly loyal base of fans he called the "Night People." (In the mid-1970s his audience was estimated at about 260,000 each night). His shows were more than nostalgia, he talked of all the things that interested him. That was a broad canvas and he would roam from commenting on a particularly ridiculous news story of the moment to reading poems of Robert Service, all in a voice that was as expressive as an entire cast of actors.[25]

Jean Shepherd's radio artistry is credited with inspiring the work of later practitioners of the medium, such as Garrison Keillor and Ira Glass. In his book *Listening to Radio,* author Ray Barfield interviewed Shepherd fan Roger Rollin, who had this to say:

> [He was] an urban predecessor of Garrison Keillor. . . . Nothing had been heard like him before, with his reminiscences of growing up . . . his comic meditations on life, love, and the human condition . . . and his wacky schemes. I thought he was a genius. Still do.[26]

Radio's preeminent monologist possessed talents that exceeded the realm of conventional radio. "He distilled the whimsies and absurdities of middle-class life in the middle of the American century and did so in books, on television, in movies, [and] in live performance."[27]

> **Mike J. Keith:** While his twenty years of late-night WOR broadcasts are undoubtedly his greatest achievement, he was also a writer of prodigious talent whose gently humorous magazine articles and novels compare favorably, in both literary quality and insightfulness, to the works of Mark Twain, James Thurber, and fellow Hoosier George Ade. A number of his stories were adapted for television and aired by PBS. Of course, his most widely known and successful foray into the visual media was the film *A Christmas Story,* which became a holiday classic.

The death of Jean Shepherd inspired Keith (no relation to the author) to create a lasting tribute to him in the form of a poem.

I Remember Shep

I remember—doesn't everyone?—listening to Shep on WOR under the covers, on a two-inch by three-inch transistor radio, stuffed under the pillow so that no one would ever know what I was doing. Somehow the secrecy added to the effect.

I remember Shep reading his wonderful story "Wilbur Duckworth and His Magic Baton" and later playing a tape for the only girlfriend I ever had in high school, who was also in the marching band. When it was over she said, "That was cute." I don't think she got it.

I remember Shep reading George Ade's "The Fable of the Caddy Who Hurt His Head While Thinking" ("Moral: Don't try to account for anything."), and spending the next twenty years trying to understand it.

I remember Shep's laugh of infinite nuance: from derision to amusement to superiority to sarcasm to joy.

I remember listening to the radio shows again after the passage of years and realizing how much I had missed the first time around.

I remember Shep for Don Marquis and his cockroach, Robert W. Service and other literary pleasures. Had there been no Shep, would I be a writer today?

I remember Shep in Eatontown, New Jersey, and how he surpassed all expectations but one—there was no "underwater ballet." I did get it.

I remember Shep playing Stockhausen's "Gensang der Junglinge" incessantly in the background during his more scary stories—usually those involving girls.

I remember the Margate Elephant on Jean Shepherd's America, and the Great Route One Road Trip.

I remember searching for Shep records in stores' alphabetical racks, and usually only finding ones by a certain female country singer.

I remember wanting to hate A Christmas Story, because now everyone would know the greatness of Shep, and my secret would be stolen. I got over it.

I remember slob art.

I remember Shep's brilliance on The Clown, which I played one evening for some musician friends. I don't think they got it either. But the colors, man. The colors still shine.

I remember leaving the radio on one night after Shep, and hearing the Stones' "Sympathy for the Devil." Somehow it seemed fitting.

I remember Shep being the blind date. I remember being the blind date.

I remember the night Shep announced he was leaving WOR, and how he spent the whole show talking about the greener pastures beyond radio. I felt betrayed. I got over it.

I remember the "Night People."

I remember teaching myself the Jew's Harp, the Kazoo, and the art of Kopfspielen.

I also recall a decade or more wondering what a nose-flute was, and imagining how it might be played.

I remember learning of Shepherd's death by email. Would he have found this strangely, modernistically humorous? I'm not sure.

I remember the sadness of that day. Yes, his work will live forever, but there is also a stunning silence that is still hard to fathom.

I remember not ever feeling closer to a man I never met.

I remember Jean Parker Shepherd.

I remember.

A comment by Stephen L. Karph marking the passing of Radio's Noble Savage seems a fitting way to bring closure to this section. "Shepherd was pure entertainment, no politics, no conspiracies, no sidekicks. He worked alone, which for him was essential. Who would want anyone around to authenticate a good Jean Shepherd story?"[28]

NIGHTS WITH NEBEL

Rivaling, but not quite equaling, the prodigious talent and popularity of Jean Shepherd was Long John Nebel. However, Nebel was one of all-night radio's true originals in his own right. Like Shepherd, his broadcasts emanated from New York beginning in the 1950s and would attract an army of loyal fans for decades. Nebel would spend the bulk of his broadcast career at WOR and WMCA where, according to his biographer, Donald Bain, he would reign "as king of all-night radio talk."[29]

Despite some obvious similarities, the on-air styles of Nebel and Shepherd were quite different. Nebel was not the raconteur that Shepherd was. His stock-in-trade was the telephone conversation and guest interview as inspired by Barry Gray. Shepherd was not interested in talking with listeners—the microphone was his property alone. In contrast, listener dialogue served as the centerpiece of the Nebel show and no one employed it more effectively. "Telephone monitoring devices have recorded as many as forty-thousand attempts to reach him during the two-hour period between 3:00-5:00 A.M."[30]

Although Nebel could be brusque and even imperious on the phone, he was an empathetic listener and compassionate host. "For many, he has been the difference between life and death, providing the only conversation they will enjoy that day."[31] Adds Marlin Taylor, "He was the only companion for so many alone in the night."[32]

Marking the twentieth anniversary of Nebel's death in 1998, Alan Colmes called him the "grandfather of all night radio."[33]

Alan Colmes: We paid tribute to Long John on the show a few years back. He was a very special person who brought so much to all-night radio. I grew up listening to him, and he made a strong impression on me. Nebel made all-night radio important. He gave it credibility.

Whereas Jean Shepherd's radio work anticipated that of public radio's Garrison Keillor and Ira Glass, Long John Nebel was the antecedent to Art Bell, who would rise to fame and notoriety on the all-night airwaves in the 1990s with his focus on the paranormal and bizarre. Among Nebel's favorite topics in the '50s and '60s was the UFO question, something that Art Bell would later take up with a vengeance. "I sure do remember Long John's Party Line. The show originated in the '50s, mostly transmitted from WOR's radio tower in a remote area of Carteret, New Jersey. This gave added mystique to the already enigmatic atmosphere of the show."[34] Writing the foreword to Bain's biography of Nebel, performer Jackie Gleason described the late-night host as the "ringmaster of the strange" and "master of the unpredictable."[35]

Marlin Taylor: I didn't really listen to overnight radio back then, but what I do recall from the handful of times I did tune in were Nebel's unusual and unique topics. He really did foreshadow Bell.

This introduction to his program in the early 1960s gives a pretty good idea of what direction his programs often took. Strange, otherworldly music accompanied it:

Hi, neighbors. This is Long John once again. We're around from midnight to 5:00 five mornings a week, and, of course, on weekends we're around until 5:30, and that means we're on the air for some 36 hours. And during that time it's my pleasure to talk with many interesting people. We have a group with us tonight. Ed Springarm—Dr. Edward Springarm is a professor of English. Mike Gurzdansky is a linguist and a medical writer. And Kai Dee, the actor. Our guest of the morning is a gentleman by the name of Dion McGregor. Bernard Geis Associates have published a book titled *The Dream World of Dion McGregor.* And, actually, Letty Cottin must have called me about four times on this. I received a copy of the book. Letty Cottin is the gal in charge of publicity over there, and one of the top people in the publishing business as far as publicity is concerned. And, I don't know, the book was mislaid or something and she sent

> me another copy, and we've decided to do something on it. Now, I'd just like to read something from the jacket of the book. It says, "No one wrote this book. These are the tape-recorded dreams of a man who talks in his sleep." The book is published by Bernard Geis and then Decca came out with an album, *The Dream World of Dion McGregor.* And as I spoke to you, Dion, on the phone, I said I haven't had a chance—so many people, I guess they never can understand this, you'll get a record or something and somebody'll say, "Well, what'd ya think of this?" y'know, about an hour-and-a-half after you've received it. I say I haven't had a chance to play it. I have albums that a needle will never get into a groove—I just haven't had a chance. However, you are familiar with this, you've listened to it, and you said this is okay for the air.[36]

Few people before or since have brought to all-night radio the kind of ingenuity, originality, and variety that Nebel did. He represents one of post-World War II radio's creative high points and another example of the special nature of overnight programming. Along with Barry Gray and Jean Shepherd, he would come to be regarded as one of after-hours radio's true pioneers and a revered member of its cherished triumvirate.

NOTES

1. David Wallace, "War and Remembrance," *Los Angeles Times,* 1 December 1999, p. 28.
2. Bill Jaker, "All-Night Radio," www.old.time.radio.com, 21 July 1998.
3. Barry Gray, *My Night People* (New York: Simon & Schuster, 1975), p. 7.
4. Elizabeth McLeod, "Round the Clock Radio," www.old.time.radio.com, 23 July 1998.
5. Robert J. Landry, *This Fascinating Radio Business,* (Indianapolis, Ind.: Bobbs-Merrill, 1946), p. 81.
6. Wayne Munson, *All Talk: The Talk Show in Media Culture* (Philadelphia: Temple University Press, 1993), p. 36.
7. Donald Bain, *Long John Nebel* (New York: MacMillan, 1974), p. 217.
8. Nick Rado, "Barry Gray, Pioneer of Talk Radio, Dies at 80," *New York Times,* 13 December 1996, p. B10.
9. Michael C. Keith, *Talking Radio: An Oral History of Radio in the Television Age* (Armonk, N.Y.: M. E. Sharpe Publishers, 2000), p. 10.
10. Eric Rhoads, *Blast from the Past* (West Palm Beach, Fla.: Streamline, 1996), p. 259.
11. Susan Douglas, *Listening In: Radio and the American Imagination* (New York: Times Books, 1999), p. 240.

12. Personal correspondence, 8 February 2000.
13. Douglas, p. 241.
14. *New York Times,* 13 November 1952.
15. . Bill Jaker et al., "The Airwaves of New York," www.1010wins.com, 12 December 2000.
16. Classic Philadelphia Radio, www.philaradio.com, 8 December 2000.
17. Don Kaul, "Vulgarity Has Replaced Genius in Radio," *Houston Chronicle,* 26 May 2000, p. A38.
18. Max Schmid, "Jean Shepherd," *Whole Earth,* Winter 2000, p. 1.
19. Kenneth Turan, "A Cosmic Shaggy Dog," *Washington Post,* 5 January 1977, p. B1.
20. Editor, "Jean Shep's Shtick," *New York Times,* 2 April 2000, sec. 4, p. 14.
21. Charles Strum, "Remembering Jean Shepherd," *New York Times,* 26 March 2000, sec. 4, p. 7.
22. Daniel Pinkwater, "Voice in the Dark," *New York Times Magazine,* 2 January 2000, p. 21.
23. Edward Grossman, "Jean Shepherd: Radio's Noble Savage," *Harper's Magazine,* January 1966, p. 61.
14. Bob Kaye, "The Jean Shepherd Page," www.bobkaye.com, 2 February 1999.
25. "Jean Shepherd, *Broadcasting and Cable Magazine,* 13 November 2000, p. 31.
26. Ray Barfield, *Listening to Radio* (Westport, Conn.: Praeger,1996), p. 145.
27. "Jean Shepherd, Master Storyteller," *Philadelphia Inquirer,* 19 October 1999.
28. Stephen L. Karph, "Jean Shepherd, 1922-1999," *On Air,* Broadcaster's Foundation, Spring 2000, p. 6.
29. Bain, p. xii.
30. Ibid, p. 7.
31. Ibid, p. 7.
32. Personal correspondence, 8 February 2000.
33. David Hinckley, "Late Night Host Will Salute Long-Gone Nebel Tomorrow," *Daily News,* 9 April 1998, p. 128.
34. Frank Peters, Long John Nebel Chat Room, 8 September 1999.
35. Bain, p. xvi.
36. *Long John Nebel Show* transcript, 8 July 1964.

Chapter 6

Revolution and a King

A world unknown to daytime
Is forever going on
The airwaves of the nation
Between midnight and the dawn

—Bill and Taff Danoff

The 1960s saw enormous changes in American culture, and radio reflected the seismic shift that would last well into the next decade. Perhaps nowhere was the clamor and upheaval of the era more apparent (or assimilated) than during radio's overnight shift. However, changes on the technological front would have a more immediate impact on the medium as the Federal Communications Commission ruled in 1963 that AM stations could not simulcast their signals on their FM outlets in markets with a population of 100 thousand or more for more than half of their broadcast day. This was designed to give the FM medium a much-needed boost. For years it had lagged far behind the older AM band in popularity and profits, and simulcasting was perceived as an inhibiting factor in its growth.

AUTOMATED NIGHTS

It was out of this ruling that automated radio was born. Rather than staff both bands (an economic consideration), combo outlets (AM/FM licensees) purchased automation systems for their FMs. Stereophonic sound was making its mark around this time, and FM—with its larger channel width and static-free signal—seized upon it as another way of distinguishing itself from its AM counterpart. It was not long before many stations were using automation systems to cover their all-night daypart. In fact, with the introduction of automation, a growing number of stations decided to keep their FM signal active overnights.

While automation systems would reduce the need for live overnight personnel at those stations employing it, the ranks of all-nighters would continue to gradually increase throughout the 1960s. Among the names that would become familiar to late-night listeners of the period were Barry Farber, the Amazing Randi, Dick Summer, Herb Jepko, Ben Hunter, Norm Nathan, Ron Britain, Ray Briem, John McCormick, Larry Glick, Jerry Williams, Dolly Holiday, Phil Knight, Bill Mayhugh, Lee Greenwood, Jeff Kaye, and John Luther. (The preceding names represent only the tip of the iceberg, since most cities around the country had someone working the after-midnight airwaves by this time.) Already established overnighters like Wolfman Jack, Barry Gray, Long John Nebel, and Jean Shepherd would continue to expand their respective fan bases.

At the so-called big boomer stations in major metropolitan areas, new stars were being born overnights. This was especially the case at stations featuring Top 40 formats. Up until 1967, Boston's powerful WRKO had run without deejays overnight, but Jon Powers changed that when he added the human touch with the hits until dawn. Meanwhile, New York's WABC was calling itself "Music Radio 77," and throughout the 1960s (under the able direction of Rick Sklar) gave listeners a succession of popular late-night deejay shows, beginning with *Big Joe's Happiness Exchange* and followed by Bob Lewis (1962–63), Charlie Greer (1963–65), Ron Lundy (1965–69), Roby Yonge (1969), Jim Nettleton (1969), and Les Marshak (1969).

TALK AND MUSIC

The emergence of the news and talk formats in the 1960s brought more nonmusic programs to the overnight daypart. From coast to coast, but always in large markets, stations were dumping their records in favor of discourse and reportage. In the west, KYW and KABC, and in the east, WINS and WCBS were attracting audiences with their news and talk fare. The stations that adopted these formats were invariably found on the AM band. Not only were there few all-night FM stations but talk was virtually nonexistent. In all but a handful of exceptions, FM stations were music outlets, especially with the advent of automation. AM stations remained the dominant form of radio in both ratings and sheer numbers. In 1964 there were 4,009 AM and 1,270 FM stations on the air.

Despite the spread of talk on all-night radio, music remained a prime programming element. All-nights continued to be one of the only places on radio that jazz music could be found. WBZ all-night host Steve LeVeille recalls listening to it on his favorite all-night show in the 1960s, *Sounds in the Night,* hosted by Norm Nathan:

> It was supposed to be a program of popular music—singers and big bands. That was too schmaltzy for Norm's tastes. So he started playing his favorite music—jazz—around 3 A.M., figuring the boss would never be up at that hour. After a while Norm became more bold and the jazz would start around 2 A.M., or even earlier. The great music and Norm's unique sense of humor found an audience. Norm's boss started getting mail—lots of mail—from listeners thanking the station for that "great new jazz show" with the funny host that was on in the middle of the night. The boss said to Norm, "I don't know what you're doing but keep it up." And then jazz could be heard from the start of the program at 11:30 P.M. It wasn't all jazz but it was lots of jazz. Norm invited jazz musicians—from Dizzy Gillespie to Herbie Mann—into the studio for interviews when they were in town. Norm's sign-off became a sort of trademark. "Bye-bye, Old Sport," he'd say over the closing stanza of Count Basie's "Midnight Blue." Along the way it became Norm's nickname.[1]

Again, the late-night zone was often the only part of the broadcast day at radio stations when a departure from the tried-and-true playlists was tolerated.

> **Dick Summer:** Yeah, music was a big part of the all-night show. Lots of people tuned in because of the different kind

> we played. I used to get calls from people all over the country asking about our "format." The fact is, we didn't really have any. The PD would call deejay meetings about once a month, and they always boiled down to one thing: "Would you guys at least play some of the Top 40 songs I put in the studio every week." Occasionally I did. Mostly it was the wacky stuff that got the focus.

> **Ed Shane:** It was all about the music really. When I was a kid, I'd spend my allowance to collect the Howlin' Wolf blues or the gospel sounds of James Cleveland (and the Angelic Choir) or the Mighty Consolers. When I got to college, I was still faithful to the late-night sounds I'd been occasionally exposed to on Nashville's WLAC, and now I could stay up any night of the week and hear it all. What I heard was still wonderful, new, and untried music. Still the magic of all-night radio. Even though we never met, I felt a kinship with the guys at WLAC.

From the Underground

Later in the 1960s, underground radio (also called progressive, alternative, and free-form) surfaced on FM stations around the country and made special inroads into the overnight hours. The format (regarded by its practitioners and fans as the "antiformat" format) featured music not played by Top 40 stations and deejays whose presentation styles were antithetical to the shouters and screamers on pop radio stations. Underground radio's raison d'être was in step with that of the growing counterculture. It resented the mainstream gestalt of the day regarding countless social issues (war, drugs, race), but most of all it detested formula radio with its 2-minute song cuts and hyper jocks.

Underground radio had its genesis in all-nights. Regarded as one of the pioneers of commercial free-form radio, Larry Miller was the host of an all-night show on San Francisco's KMPX in 1966. The station featured foreign-language programming during the day and allowed Miller to play an eclectic mix of music during his shift.

> **Larry Miller:** I'd air artists like Screamin' Jay Hawkins and Louis Jordan, maybe some early Elvis and the Stones. I'd also intermingle an appropriate Lenny Bruce routine, a classical piece, hard rock, or maybe something from a local band.

In his memoir about his days at pioneer underground station KSAN, Scoop Nisker discussed the very diverse nature of this kind of programming approach:

> [We'd air] sublime segues and sets of sounds that took listeners on soaring, imaginative musical flights. . . . I remember deejay Ed Bear, pm freeform night on KSAN, playing a Buffalo Springfield tune that segued into a Mozart sonata, when he then mixed in and out of a Balinese gamelan piece—the counterpoints cross-culturally counter pointing with each other—and then resolved the Who set with some blues from John Lee Hooker.[2]

During the short existence (1966–72) of commercial underground radio, all-night listeners were treated to a no-holds-barred brand of programming. It was not uncommon to encounter discussions or monologues about the merits and benefits of marijuana, free love, and draft evasion. Whereas the music these stations aired during the day certainly ran counter to that found on other outlets at that hour, during overnights the musical selections often ran from the obscure to the bizarre, as did the utterances of the deejays.

By the early 1970s, the underground sound had been co-opted by big business, which purged the free-form approach to programming in favor of formula structuring. Soon these stations featured playlists and deejays reading liner-cards much like the Top 40 outlets that had inspired the underground radio movement in the first place. Reminiscing about underground radio, including one of its significant overnight performers, prior to its co-optation by the mainstream, the editor of *Spin* magazine, Bob Guccione Jr., observed in the *Los Angeles Times:*

> In 1969, FM radio was virtually underground. Innovative rock 'n' roll found a welcome there and settled into its new, and to begin with, barren homeland. In '71, FM radio was still fresh, experimental, gushingly enthusiastic, naive and fantastic. Every day, FM radio ran out of hours, not music. I'm not talking about today's classic rock, which is virtually just reheated AM radio. the silt of a great musical era. I'm talking about a spirit of musical diversity that was doomed as soon as culture's commercial value could be accurately ascertained. Because once radio stations became hot properties, they sold for ever larger prices, and their owners

> became proportionately conservative to the size of their debts. I used to listen to Alison Steele on WNEW, New York's legendary FM station. She called herself the "Night Bird." She came on at midnight, read a different poem every night and talked for the first 15 minutes of her show before she played her first song. The mystical Zac on rival WPLJ was radio's Marlin, and WNEW's Jonathan Schwartz was FM's preeminent philosopher. In L.A., it was KMET that played the same pioneering music and shaped pop culture. The early DJ's were passionate and as wide-eyed as their invisible audiences about this new music and unfolding society.[3]

At its apex, hundreds of underground stations offered unique and unconventional programming to late-night/early-morning listeners. Some believe that the underground sound was radio's finest hour—that is, during its second incarnation—claiming that creativity and freedom of expression were never as abundant, at least not in commercial radio. Recognition must be made of the fact that a number of noncommercial, public radio stations featured the free-form style of programming prior to commercial radio's discovery and application of it.

THE NIGHTS GROW RICHER STILL

The late-night airwaves would be further enhanced by talented individuals throughout the 1960s. Among those who would inspire large and loyal constituencies were Herb Jepko, Ray Briem, and Phil Knight. Each would develop a special relationship with his listener and significantly add to the reputation of overnight radio.

HERB JEPKO

At the height of his popularity, all-night host Herb Jepko had an estimated audience of ten million listeners tuned to his Mutual Broadcasting System's program.

> **Joseph Buchman:** Jepko began what would later become the Nitecap Radio Network on KSL in Salt Lake City, on February 11, 1964, and he is widely acknowledged to be the father of network talk radio. In the late 1950s and 1960s, he pursued a series of radio jobs along the California coast, Idaho, and eventually Utah. Herb was hired by KDYL in Salt

> Lake to play late-night jazz but became bored just playing music. During his late-night shift, he began talking to his listeners between records, and the show quickly gained in popularity, catching the attention of the big 50,000-watt station across town, KSL. Although the station did not remain on the air after 1 A.M., Jepko eventually convinced the station's management to do so with him at the microphone. His efforts attracted listeners, and his show became a hit almost immediately. In January 1968, KXIV in Phoenix signed on as the first Nitecap Radio Network affiliate, and network talk radio was born with Herb Jepko. Within a few years, dozens of other stations followed suit. In 1974, WBAL in Baltimore affiliated with the Nitecap Radio Network, providing the first exposure to the program for many media executives living on the east coast. On November 4, 1975, Mutual began carrying the program nationally.

(An essay written by Joseph Buchman on late-night radio legend Herb Jepko can be found in the appendices.)

> **Rollye James:** Herb's show was the butt of jokes by programmers because of the age of his audience, but to his graying listeners, he was a godsend. His experience goes far to exemplify how radio misuses overnights. Herb began on KSL. He'd buy the overnight block and resell it to direct-mail sponsors. His "gimmick" was that in order to call the show you had to be a member of the Nitecaps. It was free to join, but it gave Herb an instant mailing list in the 1960s long before computerization. Herb was as much an insurance salesman as a host. As soon as you signed up, the letters started coming. He'd also tout everything from Icy Hot (to alleviate arthritis pain in a manner that sometimes sounded more like a sexual aid—first it's cold, then it heats up, and finally it's cool and soothing, or something along those lines) to travel (who can forget the "all riding, no walking tour of Hawaii?"). In addition to KSL's clear-channel coverage, Herb added other clears—KVOO in Tulsa for a while, then KIRO in Seattle, WHAS in Louisville, and finally in the mid-'70s WBAL. I'm sorry to say I suggested that one—sorry because of what follows. When WBAL was added, the show came to the attention of Mutual Radio, which was taken with the idea of having the first overnight network offering. And so it was

Figure 6.1. Herb Jepko interviews guests on his popular all-night radio show. Courtesy Joe Buchman.

that they struck a deal with Herb—by then a millionaire from his direct-response business—that would bankrupt him. Mutual was to handle the sales and marketing, and Herb would pay for the land lines (in a presatellite era) and news. The problem that erupted then is one that plagues late-night radio even today—daytime radio is sold differently. During the day, national radio is sold on a cost-per-thousand basis to advertising agencies at attractive rates, far cheaper than they would get if they bought stations individually. The problem is that while late-night listeners are loyal, there aren't enough of them in raw head count to be financially attractive. Going after direct response business, which thrives in the overnight atmosphere, is a very different animal, one that networks were not interested in developing. Not only did it require different sales approaches, but it also netted less dollars. And so it was that overnight radio was quickly used as a lever to force stations to carry daytime inventory (either in the form of hourly newscasts and the commercials in them, or just commercials alone). Herb, who was doing well with direct response previously, was quickly reduced to paying more than he was receiving and in about two years he was doomed. Mutual rather than understanding the marketing dynamic blamed the failure on his aging audience. They brought in Long John Nebel (who in his day was indeed one of the greats) and his wife Candy, but that too was short lived (as was Long John, who succumbed to cancer not long after). At this time, the president du jour of Mutual was the former owner of WGMA in Hollywood, Florida. He used to listen to Larry King in Miami at the time, and so it was that he called him about joining the network.

Ray Briem

Another of all-night radio's revered practitioners, Ray Briem, began to make his mark in the 1960s, although he'd worked as a music deejay in the 1950s. In 1967, he was hired by KABC, which had just extended its broadcast day to 24 hours. He soon began filling the all-night shift with topics that revealed his conservative point of view. The 1960s' most outspoken and controversial radio talk-show personality, Joe Pyne, was Briem's mentor, and it was he who suggested that Briem "stop spinning records and start talking." This he did with considerable reluctance and trepidation. A proclamation ceremony placing his name on Hollywood's Walk of Fame declared:

> Briem had no idea what to talk about, but he took on the challenge anyway. He found his voice—and a huge nighttime audience—with the anti-tax movement. Briem was instrumental in bringing information to the masses, along with firebrand activist Howard Jarvis—founder of Proposition 13. When the ballot initiative won by a landslide, Briem became a legendary figure in California political history, and talk radio suddenly became recognized as a powerful communication tool. With his fine conversational skills and dedication to keeping abreast of current happenings around the world, Briem has a loyal group of listeners spanning 30 years. Guests on his programs have

Figure 6.2. In the 1970s, Ray Briem's all-night audience was as large as a city. Courtesy Ray Briem.

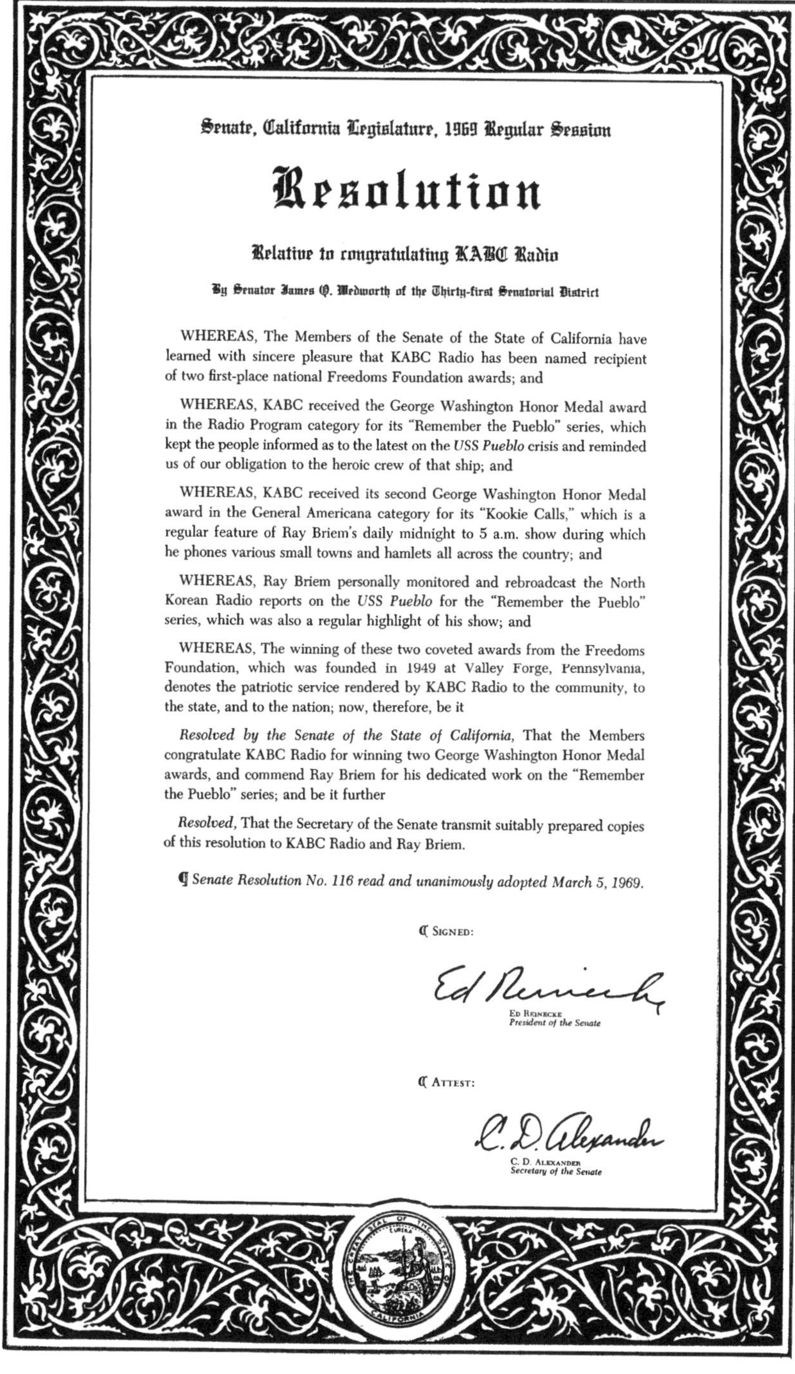

Senate, California Legislature, 1969 Regular Session

Resolution

Relative to congratulating KABC Radio

By Senator James Q. Wedworth of the Thirty-first Senatorial District

WHEREAS, The Members of the Senate of the State of California have learned with sincere pleasure that KABC Radio has been named recipient of two first-place national Freedoms Foundation awards; and

WHEREAS, KABC received the George Washington Honor Medal award in the Radio Program category for its "Remember the Pueblo" series, which kept the people informed as to the latest on the *USS Pueblo* crisis and reminded us of our obligation to the heroic crew of that ship; and

WHEREAS, KABC received its second George Washington Honor Medal award in the General Americana category for its "Kookie Calls," which is a regular feature of Ray Briem's daily midnight to 5 a.m. show during which he phones various small towns and hamlets all across the country; and

WHEREAS, Ray Briem personally monitored and rebroadcast the North Korean Radio reports on the *USS Pueblo* for the "Remember the Pueblo" series, which was also a regular highlight of his show; and

WHEREAS, The winning of these two coveted awards from the Freedoms Foundation, which was founded in 1949 at Valley Forge, Pennsylvania, denotes the patriotic service rendered by KABC Radio to the community, to the state, and to the nation; now, therefore, be it

Resolved by the Senate of the State of California, That the Members congratulate KABC Radio for winning two George Washington Honor Medal awards, and commend Ray Briem for his dedicated work on the "Remember the Pueblo" series; and be it further

Resolved, That the Secretary of the Senate transmit suitably prepared copies of this resolution to KABC Radio and Ray Briem.

¶ *Senate Resolution No. 116 read and unanimously adopted March 5, 1969.*

SIGNED:

Ed Reinecke
President of the Senate

ATTEST:

C. D. Alexander
Secretary of the Senate

Figure 6.3. All-night radio engaged in discourse that made a difference. This is one of two Freedoms Foundation awards given to KABC's Ray Briem. Courtesy Ray Briem.

> included many luminaries, from artists and writers to politicians.[4]

Briem's on-air activism resulted in his being awarded two Freedoms Foundation awards. His popularity at KABC in the 1970s led to his being broadcast nationally over ABC's Talkradio Network. "Stations in 70 cities and 36 states [could] hear Briem gabbing about all things political and newsworthy."[5] Among the high points of his career was his long association with Russia's Vladimir Pozner, who appeared on his show a number of times. Recalled Briem, "I started calling Radio Moscow in the fall of 1977. He would use our phone calls as a basis for commentaries. Nobody else was doing it."[6]

Briem retired from the all-night airwaves in the mid-1990s at the age of 65. At that time his program was "One of the longest running in the market . . . consistently [drawing] the largest ratings of any overnight talk show—attracting 15.7 percent of the available audience."[7]

PHIL KNIGHT

Phil Knight hosted one of overnight's most popular shows at WPTH-FM in Fort Wayne, Indiana, in the late 1960s and early 1970s. Calling it *Knightstime,* the host would invite callers to become involved in his creative ideas over the air. The audience therefore became an integral part of his show, which included music and a myriad of other programming elements.

> **Charles Willer:** People would call in and perform as characters, like the Shadow, for instance. Phil encouraged this. You had to be pretty creative to make it on the air. He screened callers to make sure they had something of worth to contribute. It was very hard to get through to Phil. The phone lines were always clogged. Back then, me and my buddies would stay up all night trying to get on the show. Years later, Phil told me that one night he had a peculiar call that had a suspiciously "clean" line. (This was back in the days of analog line amps on GTE.) It turns out that one of the GTE test board technicians got tired of trying to get through the "fair" way and just unplugged the actually incoming caller and patched himself in for a guaranteed chance to be on *Knightstime.*

Figure 6.4. Phil Knight was one of the midwest's most tuned overnight personalities. Courtesy Pat O'Brien.

James Cassell: You got to meet a lot of nights owls like myself, and it was pretty much a family thing. Even new callers became family. And Phil had a variety of music on from midnight until dawn. He played jazz, rock, country, soul, pretty much everything and anything. He'd even drop in bits by Cheech and Chong to spice things up. It was great. He did silly stuff that you can't get away with today, but it made his show really interesting.

Pat O'Brien: The station Phil was on had an adult contemporary music format, but the all-night show had a combination of music and talk. The music was a bit more free form after midnight than it was in other dayparts. *Knightstime* was a great deal of fun and a lot of hard work, too. The idea of the show was to involve the audience in the program. People would call in and make requests on the air. This gave listeners a chance to really ham it up. Perhaps, in some cases, they achieved their own few minutes of fame on the radio. People would dream up unique identities and situations. Everything was done in fun. Nobody was ever taken too seriously. Not everyone was playing a role. But a lot of the show's fans took the opportunity to have some fun on the program. Phil was always more than willing to play along. He had characters that ranged from well known icons of the past, like the Shadow and John Wayne, to modern-day heroes of the moment. *Knightstime* was a one-man show. Yet, the studio was a flurry of activity. Here is a typical scenario: Phil would get a record going. He would answer the phone (which was ringing 100 percent of the time) thusly, "'Knightsline,' you're on the air." The conversation would be taped on a reel-to-reel deck. Somehow Phil would manage to find and cue up the caller's request, rewind and cue the reel tape, and be ready to go by the end of the record or after a spot cluster. Frequently, Phil felt the need to "edit" the callers. This was usually done because the caller either got too boring or asked for too many songs that were not available. The reel tape would be cued up somewhere midway through the conversation. Phil would say " 'Knightsline,' you're on the air" live, then he'd punch up the tail end of the caller's chat. In extreme cases, the call would be electronically edited right then and there by dubbing it to an in-studio cart machine. This way the middle of the call could be edited out. Phil had characters of his own on the show. These included Lou—the nonexistent engineer, Garrard (Phil's cat), and most famous of all was Needa Goodbody. Needa was a character that Phil would tape ahead of time. A script of sorts was produced. Needa's first duty on the show was to read Phil's horoscope from the newspaper. Phil and Needa would have conversations during the show. Of course, Needa's lines were being punched up on a cart machine. Needa's main bit was her "Style Show." She would read (and model) descriptions of sexy outfits from Frederick's of Hollywood catalogs. Like I

Figure 6.5. Famed all-night radio personality Dick Summer at the controls of a different kind of air machine.

> said, Phil would record Needa's part ahead of time. He was able to create a pretty convincing Needa. One trick that was used to raise Needa's voice slightly and produce a unique sound quality was to wrap a layer of masking tape around the capstan of the Ampex reel-to-reel machine before dubbing "her" part to cart. This speeds up the voice, thus elevating it. Until they found out differently, virtually everyone tuned thought Needa was a real person. Even the station manager was under that impression at the time. The overnight slot gave hosts the freedom to really invent and entertain.

(Phil Knight is the alias, alter ego, and radio name of Pat O'Brien.)

From Watergate to Disco

There was no shortage of subjects to discuss on all-night radio during the early 1970s. The war in Vietnam was the topic du jour and had been for several years. It, along with issues concerning the illegal use of drugs, human rights, and ultimately the Watergate break-in—which would bring down the Nixon administration—kept the phones lines ringing long after midnight. As the 1970s began, *Life* magazine described the era as "violent, nostalgic, preposterous, maddening, amusing, sometimes immensely evocative and moving."[8] This was a good time to want to talk on all-night radio. It was a time that actor Dennis Hopper called the "age of the sleepless zombies."

If you couldn't get to sleep, so much the better for all-night "pillow personalities" like John Kingston on KWSL, Cat Simon on KHJ, Jerry Butler on WLS, Chris Bailey on WRKO, Joey Reynolds on WOR, Art Dineen on WRC, John Luther on WBEN, Steve Warren on WNBC, and Allan Allman on WNIC. All of the aforementioned and countless dozens of others in cities around the country would achieve varying measures of prominence in the nocturnal airwaves of the 1970s. In Beantown, Larry Glick would build on his growing popularity with the Midnight Marauder and his infamous Orangutan Story, and in the Big Apple, MusicRadio 77-WABC would continue to engender other nighttime luminaries, among them Jay Reynolds, Bob Cruz, Mike McKay, and Sturgis Griffin. Other New York, Chicago, and Los Angeles powerhouse outlets would likewise produce crops of radio celebrities during the postmidnight hours.

More stations extended their broadcast clocks to include overnights in the 1970s, while others brought new sounds to their listening areas.

> **Rich De Leo:** WFBG has not been 24 hours for all of its 76 years. In fact, it went round the clock in the mid-1970s when the station was in its heyday. It was one of the top pop music outlets in those days. All with overnight music. I think this was true for a lot of stations during that period. Now we run coast-to-coast AM all night. A sign of these times.

> **Allen Ogrizovich:** Rich is right. Back then KWSL was a Top 40 outlet, and I became the first overnight jock the station had because it used to sign off at midnight. I pretty much ran the show like a morning drive program with some personality. I got the typical calls everyone gets, but I do remember a guy who owned a bakery in town who called himself Baker Bob. He used to call every night and each time he'd use a different voice. He also used to make donuts for me now and then for playing his requests and helping him stay awake. I'd also get aircheck tapes of the show from listeners in Sweden. Imagine that.

Figure 6.6. Political and social issues kept people up at night and tuned to talk radio. Courtesy Bobby Ocean, Inc.

Steve Warren: We brought country music to overnights in New York at WHN and response to the format was very good. One of the things I liked most about my job was that I got to invite recording artists to the station for interviews after midnight, usually following their concerts or shows. That was fun. Later in the 1970s, I moved over to WNBC to do the 2 to 6 A.M. shift. I followed Dick Summer, the former WBZ legend, who worked the 10 P.M. to 2 A.M. slot. He usually had a studio full of friends playing trivia with the listeners, so my arrival at the studio each night was usually in the midst of a social gathering. On the other end of my shift,

> at 6 A.M., was the anticipated arrival of Don Imus. I say anticipated because Imus had some attendance problems in those days, owning and performing at his comedy club late each night and otherwise burning the candle at both ends. Many mornings I stayed past my 6 A.M. departure time to cover for Imus's late arrival. More than once I ended up doing the entire A.M. drive shift.

As the war in Vietnam came to an end and Watergate began to fade from the headlines, overnight chatter appeared to lose some of its zing. While the decade had arrived like a lion it seemed to be leaving like a lamb. On the music front, disco had captured the airwaves and many overnight radio listeners were more inclined to don leisure suits and strut their stuff than they were to engage in issues-oriented dialogue with nocturnal talkmeisters.

And Along Came the King

The individual credited with giving all-night talk radio a much-needed boost at a point when it really needed it was Larry King, dubbed "Master of the Mike" by *Time* magazine. For many he was the first realization that radio had something on after midnight. People who'd never considered tuning all-night radio did so just to hear King.

> **Frank Chorba:** Larry King brought notice of all-night radio to the world at large, and he gave it a kind of visibility and repute it had not enjoyed before, despite the efforts of many other great all-night personalities.

While others had worked all-night network (coast-to-coast) radio, it was King who really put it on the map. His show, which was aired by Mutual from midnight to 5:30 A.M., debuted on January 30, 1978. The "[network] decided to bring the local flavor of the telephone talk format to a national audience."[9] His predecessors at the network were Herb Jepko and Long John Nebel, neither of whom enjoyed what would be considered significant success due to a variety of reasons, many beyond their control. In the case of Nebel, he succumbed to cancer after a relatively short time at the overnight helm. Jepko, meanwhile, was abandoned by Mutual following a short tenure (2 years) because it was felt his audience was simply too old to entice the advertisers the network felt it had to have to reach the profit goals it had in mind.

Figure 6.7. Larry King reigned supreme during the overnights of the late 1970s through the early 1990s. Courtesy Larry King.

King was no stranger to the microphone when he joined Mutual. He had been a popular talk-show host in Miami for many years. His network show was launched with twenty-eight stations and within a few years had affiliates numbering in the hundreds. Likewise it could boast one of the largest audiences in the history of all-night radio.

Rollye James: There is no denying that he was tremendously successful, but the show didn't make any money, as was the case with those who came before him. The network just didn't know how to market the overnight show. It eventually gave up and moved him to days.

Ed Shane: KTRH in Houston was one of the first stations to carry the *Larry King Show* because its general manager at the time, Hal Kemp, was a member of the Mutual affiliates board. I was consultant to KTRH from 1978 to 1980 and then Hal

> enticed me in house as the station's program manager until the mid-1980s. So I watched the development of the King show and the huge late-night audience he attracted. It was something to behold. A real phenomenon.

King's all-night shows featured a vast array of guests, both in studio and on the phone, and topics ran from the mundane to the sublime. Politics was never far from the conversation, and over the next few years his show would become the talk of the nation's capital. Noted the *New York Times,*

> If some of the top members of the Reagan Administration have been a little red-eyed lately, it may be because they have been staying up late to appear on the all night radio talk show hosted by Larry King on the Mutual Broadcasting System. They show up at the studio at midnight and sit through three hours of questions from Mr. King and his listeners. The Administration apparently sees the show as an opportunity to deliver its message to a late-night audience of 3.5 million people without dilution or editorial interference. Among King's guests in recent weeks have been Edwin Meese 3d, counselor to the President; the White House aides Craig L. Fuller and Rich Williamson; Interior Secretary James G. Watt; R. T. McNamar, Deputy Treasury Secretary; H. Stuart Knight, head of the Secret Service; Mark Fowler, the chairman of the Federal Communications Commission; James C. Miller 3d, the chairman of the Federal Trade Commission; Anne M. Gorsuch, administrator of the Environmental Protection Agency; C. Dan McKinnon, the chairman of the Civil Aeronautics Board, and Labor Secretary Raymond J. Donovan.[10]

In 1994, after 16 years, the *Larry King Show* left overnights at Mutual. The demands on King's time, principally the result of his tremendous success at CNN, forced him to abandon all-night radio. It was not an easy decision for King.

> **Larry King:** I love radio and the all-night shift, but we did the first national all-night show. The first network all-night show. When we started the concern was "How can this work?" Would people in Phoenix be interested in what people in New York are thinking about? We spent a lot of time contemplating that, but we proved back in 1978 that this

1986 Late Night Audience Report on Larry King

Listeners: 556,000

Age: 41% 25-54 years old

Education: 57% at least 1 year of college

Salary: 26% more than $40,000 a year

Home: 90% live in large cities

Research source: Mutual Broadcasting System

Figure 6.8. Statistics on the *Larry King Show.* Courtesy Mutual Broadcasting System.

> country is very small. That people in Phoenix knew who the mayor of New York was. I think we left overnight radio a better thing for our efforts. . . . I hope so. That's what I wanted to do.

Indeed, all-night radio had reached another level by the 1980s as the result of many gifted individuals. It had become much more than the poor second cousin of daytime radio. In fact, it was making news and keeping a large segment of the nation's politerati up way past its normal bedtime. Now a daypart of substance, the industry looked upon it with newfound respect. It had only taken a half-century for it to gain this recognition.

NOTES

1. Steve LeVeille, "My Norm Nathan Page," www.radiosteve.com, 5 February 2001.
2. Scoop Nisker, *If You Don't Like the News, Go Out and Make Some of Your Own* (Berkeley, Calif.: Ten Speed Press, 1994), pp. 52-53.
3. Bob Guccione Jr., "A Commentary," *Los Angeles Times,* 14 August 1994, p. 5.

4. Samantha Hart, "Ray Briem," *Hollywood Walk of Fame* (Special Millennium Edition, 2000): 227.

5. Ray Richmond, "Ray Briem Is Still Flying High in Wee Hours at KABC," *Los Angeles Herald Examiner,* 3 July 1987, p. 34.

6. Don Barrett, *Los Angeles Radio People,* Vol. 2 Los Angeles: Don Barrett, 1997.

7. Claudia Puig, "KABC Talk Host to Call It a Night," *Los Angeles Times,* 13 December 1994, p. F7.

8. *Life,* 26 December 1969, p. 72.

9. Vincent M. Ditingo, *The Remaking of Radio* (Boston: Focal Press, 1995), p. 65.

10. Phil Gailey and Warren Weaver Jr., "Briefing," *New York Times,* 24 July 1982, sec. 1, p. 7.

Chapter 7

White Male Nights

And she don't mind the late night late night radio.

—**David Gray**

1:10-1:25 A.M. Rock 103.5-FM. In a cab on the way home. . . . The radio's on and during the entire fifteen-minute ride the station plays no women's voices.

—**Sarah Vowel**

Like many industries, radio has a history of male domination, and like many industries it also has been quite nearly the exclusive domain of Anglo-Americans. Despite this fact, women and various ethnic groups, most notably Blacks and Hispanics, have had a role in the nation's broadcasting field since its inception. This role, however, has been significantly limited due to the prevailing biases and discriminatory attitudes and actions of mainstream culture. It has only been during the last few decades that serious strides have been made to address the considerable deficits existing in the percentages of non-White and nonmale participation in radio, as well as in other areas of electronic media.

LADIES OF THE NIGHT

Female on-air radio personalities were more the exception than the rule until the 1970s. The conventional wisdom in the male-dominated industry was that women were ill suited for air work and that the audience preferred and expected to hear men. One of the medium's early female deejays, Dusty Street, explains how she came to the FM airwaves in the late 1960s by way of off-air duties:

> All the [KMPX] engineers were women—young girls, actually. I was Dusty "Super Chic" Street, and the others were Suzie Cream Cheese and Katy "The Easter Pig" Johnson. . . . We decided that the ladies should be able to get on the air because we really kept the place operating. They gave us a show that I think was called "The Chicks on Sunday" or something like that. Anyway, it was Raechel Donahue, Buzzy Donahue, and the three female engineers, and we pretty much did our own thing on Sunday.[1]

Sticking women in noncrucial shifts was a common practice and one that led to their employment in the all-night shift. Affirmative action in the 1970s provided further impetus to the hiring of women and minorities for work on microphone, but it was a slow process because substantial resistance existed to the idea of anyone but White males filling on-air slots.

> **Phylis Johnson:** I suppose the history of women on radio could be defined by the word "discrimination." However, those few female personalities on the air were "real" in the early days of radio. Women talked about what other women wanted to hear then—families, relationships, conversation, and sometimes celebrity gossip. The topics, of course, were reflective of the times. For the most part, women weren't trying to sound sexy because in many cases their target audience was other women—generally housewives. . . . By the late '50s, male programmers got it into their heads that "females prefer to listen to male voices." Twenty years later, research, primarily concerned with the effectiveness of female voice-overs in news packages, began to break down some of the myths associated with the wants and needs of listeners. In the '50s, the homemaker host was replaced by the deejay. A handful of women made the crossover. The transition meant

that they would no longer target just women. Some women did quite well. Martha Jean Steinberg's popularity grew as she gave up household chitchat to pump out rhythm and blues hits on WDIA, the first station to target African Americans. But Top 40 deejays like Dick Biondi and Wolfman Jack grew in power and popularity, especially in regards to music selection. The nature of radio was very competitive, and audiences tuned in to hear what would happen next as the male superjocks attempted to outdo each other. Women fell to the sidelines.

Donna Halper: Early on, women were restricted to "women's" shows and later on, women were simply restricted. There are few examples of women on the air late at night in radio's early years. There were a few women commentators who spoke during the evening—Dorothy Thompson on NBC Blue in the late '30s, for one—but for the most part, women were stuck to the midday or early afternoon when they were allowed on. Decades later, in the 1970s, most women still did not get equal pay with men even if we did do the same job. Album rock radio tried to portray itself as very hip and progressive, but I think the women who worked at these stations were treated like most women in the business. We were there because the FCC said we had to be. I was denied a raise when I desperately needed one, and I was really paid low wages compared to the guy I had replaced as music director. This was no surprise, I suppose, considering that a few months earlier my boss at the station had actually said that if I were "his woman" he *might* allow me to work, but he didn't know for sure. He believed women served basically three roles in life. Sex was one of them, along with doing his laundry and making his meals. I never did get the raise or equal pay.

Gary Berkowitz: To be honest, women have not played much of a role in all-night radio. Sorry to say that most of the stand-out all-night personalities have been guys. Later on, Rollye James was one woman who did stand out. There were a few others, but not many.

Elizabeth Salazar: It was the old story. Males easily dominated the airshifts in every market. This was especially true later in rock music radio. Very few women worked the format.

Joan Gerberding: Women have probably had an easier time entering the ranks of overnight performers, as opposed to morning drive, midday, and afternoon drive shifts. Why? It's simple. Most GMs or PDs don't have that strong a feeling about who's on the air overnight. You can't sell it. That's where the "trades" or "bonus" spots are run. It's the smallest audience. Arbitron overnight ratings don't count. But there's still a great deal of "old school" thinking out there for daytime hours. Like "women can't deliver the audience in morning drive" or "women's voices are not authoritative enough" or "women make better sidekicks." It's funny, since 50 percent of all radio stations in the United States are programmed to women. Fifty-three percent of all the radio station's sales departments are staffed by women. Yet, only 8 percent of all program directors are women. Does that mean that the other 92 percent know what kind of programming women want? I don't think so. The key factor in the success of any radio broadcasting company, whether a stand-alone (yes, they do still exist) or a multistation broadcasting company that covers major cities across the country, is whether or not they tap into *all* of their assets. I'm not talking financial assets here. I'm talking about the talent, the expertise, and the *heart* of its collective personnel roster. Well, actually, I'm specifically talking about the female members of its personnel roster.

Certainly there were exceptions concerning the presence of women in radio. The general manager of one of the nation's top stations in the 1930s, New York's WNEW, was a woman. Bernice Judis helped build the station's image and contributed significantly in the development of all-night radio. "She started all night radio with 'Stan the Milkman' from midnight to 6 A.M., a program of records with Stan Shaw, a staff announcer. It was soon retitled, at Walter Winchell's suggestion, 'The Milkman's Matinee,' and Art Ford was the Milkman for 12 years, from 1942 to '54."[2]

Donna Halper: WNEW was the first New York station to do 24-hour programming, an innovation by Bernice Judis, who headed the station's programming efforts and did so with tremendous creativity and vision. She's a true pioneer of the medium and all-night radio.

One of the very first women to be heard late nights was Jean King, who became know as the "Lonesome Gal" in the late 1940s and 1950s. Says historian and author John Dunning, "She took to the air with a haunting voice and a 'come hither' style, referring to her listeners as 'muffin' and 'baby'."[3]

Night Birds

The sex-kitten persona was launched by King and encouraged by the male radio establishment, which felt it would appeal to men—the largest segment of the all-night listening audience.

> **Donna Halper:** Actually during World War II, some station managers decided a sexy woman's voice would make the soldiers feel good. Interestingly, the decision was to put women in morning drive—*Beverly at Reveille* was one such show, and it was so popular that *Life* magazine did a feature on it, as did several other magazines. But this was still regarded as a gimmick and after the war, men went back to doing most of the airshifts. Of course, in the late '40s, however, the "woman with the sexy voice" gimmick resurfaced in the person of a young woman who had been an actress but decided to try her luck at radio. Her name was Jean King, who became quite popular as the "Lonesome Gal." She played romantic records, talked to the guys about love and loneliness, and got herself written up in *Time* magazine. Her program was nationally syndicated in the early 1950s.

The high priestess of this all-night radio movement was Alison Steele, known as the "Nightbird." "Through nearly three decades, she entertained late-night listeners with her sultry voice, accompanied by her dog, a French poodle named Genya, as she fielded calls. 'I'm a night person,' she once said. 'I think it has a mysterious quality. I never get lonely'."[4] Recalling publisher Bob Guccione Jr.'s earlier reminiscence about 1960s and 1970s radio, "I used to listen to Alison Steele on WNEW, New York's legendary FM station. She called herself the 'Night Bird.' She came on at midnight, read a poem every night and talked for the first 15 minutes of her show before she played her first song."[5]

Joey Reynolds: Alison had to be the sexiest voice on radio. She really got your heart pounding.

Donna Halper: Of course, *the* late-night woman with the sexy voice on FM was Alison Steele, who got her start as part of the team with Ted Steele, her then-husband in the '50s, as "Ted and the Red Head." The male program directors of FM seemed to believe that women were best suited to either late night or overnights and, of course, were told that we had to sound sexy. I personally had a very hard time doing that. I was put on overnights at WMMS in Cleveland in 1973, and while I believe I have a pleasant radio voice, I was never comfortable pretending to be somebody's nocturnal fantasy. Without trying to be sexy, I still got some truly bizarre letters from listeners. My listening audience included a prison, and I evidently developed quite a fan club at the men's reformatory. Most of the letters I got from the inmates were quite respectful, although one inmate wrote to tell me, "I listen to your show every night with my dick in my hand," which I guess he meant as a compliment.

Eventually, women were in less compromising or stereotypical roles during the overnight shift. The number of female deejays increased substantially throughout the broadcast schedule, including late nights, due in great part to those who had forged the path before them. Deejays like Yvonne Daniels (the only all-night female to be inducted into the Radio Hall of Fame), Dolly Holiday, Margaret Reichl (aka Shana), and several others had garnered impressive followings in the after-midnight radio zone.

Eric Rhoads: Daniels was a legendary all-nighter on WLS in Chicago for many years at a time when it was unusual to hear a woman on the air anywhere. I listened to her in the 1970s for several years. She was special.

John Gehron: She was a substantial talent, that's for sure. Yvonne was one of the first women to do Top 40. Her on-air sound was very personable and warm. She had a wonderfully smooth voice that went particularly well late nights. She made a real mark, because WLS had a signal that reached thirty-eight states. Her father was singer Billy Daniels.

Figure 7.1. Rollye James became a popular overnight radio host in the latter part of the century. Courtesy Rollye James.

> **Joseph Buchman:** There were others, too. For example, Candy Jones was Long John Nebel's wife and cohost when the show was picked up by Mutual after they dumped Herb Jepko in 1977. I was a local board operator for the show a few months that year. Candy served as the sole host of the Mutual show when Long John died of cancer. Larry King eventually replaced her.

Despite the seeming progress of women in radio, there remained a level of ambiguity about their role in the medium.

> **Elizabeth Salazar:** When I pulled the all-night shift in album rock radio in the early 1980s, there was no defined role for women. It seemed somewhat nebulous. At least that was my impression. I suppose it stemmed from the fact that there were still too few of us doing it, and we took what was handed to us. We had very little say in how things were done. We just followed orders. There were some exceptions, like

Figure 7.2. Yvonne Daniels would be inducted into the Radio Hall of Fame for her work.

> Alison Steele, Raechel Donahue, and Mary Turner, who probably called their own shots because of their success, but these women had already pulled their weight and paid their dues by the 1980s.

Today, the number of women all-nighters still lags far behind the number of male all-night hosts, yet a handful of women attract a disproportional share of this daypart's audience. For example, *Rhona at Night* may be heard on dozens of stations throughout the country, including:

WMRS/WHBU, Indianapolis

WZHR/WTAN, Tampa

WDEL, Philadelphia

WICC, New York
WHTH, Columbus
WBKC, Cleveland
WLKW, Providence
WETZ, Wheeling
WBCX, Roanoke-Lynchburg
WATO, Knoxville
WESA, Pittsburgh
CFYI, Toronto
WHTH, Newark
WTIX/WASO, New Orleans
WZOE, Davenport
WBGZ, St. Louis
KZNG/KSYG, Little Rock
KOKL, Tulsa
KNOR/KCRC, Oklahoma City
WMC, Memphis
KPHN, Kansas City
KZEE/KPYK, Dallas
KODI, Billings
KRLV, Las Vegas
KATD, San Francisco

Women have become an integral part of the nocturnal radio landscape despite the social and cultural forces that have worked to keep this from happening.

> **Melissa:** We're certainly a presence, but I think working the late-night or overnight shift is especially unique for female air talent. We've been socialized to think of women as more nurturing, emotional, and sympathetic, and that affects how people relate to us. Even though I often play the role of "bitch" during my show, I am constantly amazed at the advice listeners will seek from me, whether it's simple stuff like how to dress for a date or really intimate issues like how to get over an ex or how to battle addiction. I don't have a degree in psychology, but people often treat me like I do, and

I suspect my gender has a lot to do with that. Besides being able to give the male members of my audience a female perspective, I think sometimes they crave a woman's ability to analyze situations and talk about emotions. My femininity makes it a safe environment, especially during the late hours when they're letting down their guard in other areas as well. As a late-night deejay and a female, I have a unique relationship with my listeners, whether they be nighthawks, party animals, third-shift workers, or insomniacs. There is an instant feeling of camaraderie knowing that someone is awake and talking to you at such an ungodly hour. Maybe being female enhances that feeling.

COLORS OF THE NIGHT

Despite the formidable obstacles against them, minorities have worked in the radio industry from the beginning, although not in appropriate numbers and usually in token positions. At least that was the case during the first decades of the medium's existence. Black musicians were among the first to gain access to the microphone during late-night broadcasts.

Donna Halper: I can't stress enough how important music was to Black people in a segregated society in making it possible for them to get on the air, and we're talking about late-night radio. Imagine what this meant to them. Doors opened to Black musicians when they could perform on a northern station late at night. While it is undoubtedly true that the Black musicians did not receive pay equal to their White counterparts, the exposure that late-night radio provided them was invaluable in terms of record sales or future club bookings in other cities. A few of the Black performers did get a network shot, too. Noble Sissle comes to mind. He and Eubie Blake had been involved in the successful Broadway musical *Shuffle Along* in the early 1920s. It was the first Black musical to cross over to a White audience. It even got a live airing thanks to WNAC in November of 1922, since several cast members came to the station to perform songs from the touring version of the show. Sissle had a late-night show on CBS in the early 1930s. It aired at 12:30 A.M., three nights a week.

> **Cecil Hale:** The racial mix in radio changed in the middle 1930s as the result of a creative and enterprising Chicago performer. Jack L. Cooper, a true unsung media hero, became America's first full-time Black announcer. This racial change did not occur as the result of a new "enlightenment" within the communications industry. Cooper's genius was in understanding that the large Black markets in the northern cities, especially Chicago, represented substantial buying power and that the path to success was in making the cultural/social link among idealism, identity, and products. Cooper became a very wealthy person because of his unique entrepreneurial vision, but his great success was in demonstrating that race radio worked. He was a true radio pioneer. The 1940s saw the emergence of Black ownership with the purchase of Atlanta's WERD by J. B. Blayton. A Black accountant, Blayton purchased the station at a bargain-basement rate because many local stations had been economically forced out of the business by the arrival of television. His station, the first owned by an African-American, programmed music intended for Black consumption, and it was highly successful in generating a substantial audience and profits.

According to information in *Radio Ink* magazine, out of the 3,000 disc jockeys heard on more than 13,000 radio stations in the 1940s there were just 16 who were Black.

> They were Ed Baker, WJLB Detroit; Al Benson, WJJD Chicago; Bill Ranch, WEAW Evanston; Ramon Bruce, WHAT Philadelphia; Spider Burks, KXLW St. Louis; Van Douglas, WJBK Detroit; Bass Harris, KING Seattle; Eddie Honesty, WJOB Hammond; Harold Jackson, WOOK Washington, Sam Jackson, WHIN Providence; Emerson Parker, WQQW Washington; Sam Price, WPEN Philadelphia; Norfley Whiited, WDNC Durham; Woody Woodard, WLIB Brooklyn; Jack L. Cooper, WSCB Chicago; and Jack Gibson, WCFL Chicago.[6]

In 1947, the first all-Black radio format was introduced in Memphis. The station, WDIA-AM, was launched as a low-power daytime operation. It would later expand both its hours and power. The rise in Black broadcasts increased steadily over the next few years, and Black late-night deejays found audiences among third-shift workers, in particular in the industrial north. Around this time, popular Black late-night radio hosts began to surface, such as Jack L. Cooper at WCAP in Washington, D.C. (regarded as the first Black radio personality of note) and Willie Bryant, who called himself the "Mayor of Harlem" on New York station WHOM. Rufus Thomas and Martha Jean (The Queen) Steinberg were top R&B deejays in the early days at WDIA. It would be 1949 before Blacks were actually involved in station ownership. Four years later, the National Negro Network was created.

> **Rick Wright:** Black stations, or those playing mostly R&B music, offered late-night or overnight programming for the benefit of those people working the third shift in the big industrial centers. These stations took folks to work at 11 P.M., entertained them while they were on the job, and then brought them home during the morning drive time daypart. Usually the all-night shift was used to help improve the morning drive time ratings. In the case of early AM R&B or urban contemporary stations, many were daytime-only facilities that did not have nighttime broadcast operations. I'm talking about the 1950s and 1960s. There were some interesting Black all-night air personalities on full-time AMs. There was the *Gary Byrd Experience* on WWRL in New York. The show was sponsored by Bushes Jewelers. Byrd had a tremendous talent to tell stories. Yvonne Daniels and Sid McCoy had an all-night show on WCFL in Chicago. It was sponsored by Pet Milk and featured jazz and R&B. The station's 50,000-watt signal allowed this show to be heard throughout the country. Sid McCoy became the voice of *Soul Train,* the historic Don Cornelius dance music television show. In Norfolk, Virginia, Fred Correy was popular at WRAP-AM. He was the first all-night jock at the station when it went 24 hours in the 1960s. His air name was Big Daddy Nightnick Fred Correy. Eventually Correy moved on to WOL in Washington. Speaking of Washington, there was John L. Hill III at WOOK. He kept the nation's capitol cooking after midnight in the '50s and '60s. Also in town was "Mr. C.," Carl Henson at the Big 1450. He was really popular with the all-night crowd. Of course, I can't leave out "Dr. Feel Good." He was entertaining all-night listeners at WAOK in Atlanta. He

> had a real smooth "love" sound that attracted loads of listeners. Not to be overlooked, too, was Cuzzin' Linnie, who did his thing on all-nights at KLIF in Dallas during the late 1960s and early 1970s.

Today all-night Black radio is alive and very healthy. Nearly every decent-size city in the country possesses a station featuring an overnight radio host of color, and talk radio is also a successful form of Black all-night radio. According to San Francisco's KGO, its overnight personality, Ray Taliaferro, "was the first major market black talk show host." Taliaferro joined the overnight shift in the mid-1980s and has anchored it ever since. The station describes him as, "loud, edgy, and [someone who] will make you yell at your radio. His program, full of electricity, is not one to lull a person to sleep, especially since Ray himself only gets four hours of shut-eye a day. He is truly the King of Late Night Radio."[7]

Over the years, there have been syndicated late-night programs featuring Black hosts. Perhaps most notable was the 1980s *Night Talk,* hosted by Bob Law from New York station WWRL. Writes broadcast scholar William Barlow, "Law's pioneering show quickly became the most popular black radio talk program in the country."[8] Today, the number of syndicated all-night Black radio programs has increased.

In the new millennium, African-Americans occupy important positions in the broadcast industry after decades of being relegated to lesser roles. Hundreds of stations are owned by Blacks such as Dr. Cathy Liggins, who heads her own company, Radio One, following years of hard work at Washington's WOL-AM. Meanwhile, in 2001, Michael Powell was appointed to chair the FCC. He is the second Black to do so, and he replaced the commission's first Black honcho, William Kennard.

Dozens of other ethnic groups now provide all-night listening opportunities to their constituencies. For example, Spanish-language radio companies like HBC (Hispanic Broadcasting Corporation), which programs several dozen stations around the country, keep the postmidnight signals flowing. Asian and Middle Eastern programming is also offered by a number of stations around the country. All-night radio no longer is the exclusive realm of the Anglo male broadcaster. It is a place for everyone—regardless of ethnicity or gender—who is a denizen of the dark.

NOTES

1. Michael C. Keith, *Voices in the Purple Haze* (Westport, Conn.: Praeger, 1997), pp. ix-x.

2. John S. Wilson, "At 50, WNEW Is Still Sweet on Melody," *New York Times*, 12 February 1984, sec. 2, p. 29.

3. John Dunning, *On the Air: The Encyclopedia of Old-Time Radio* (New York: Oxford University Press, 1998), p. 410.

4. Obituary, "Alison Steele, Nighttime New York Disc Jockey," *Los Angeles Times*, 7 October 1995, p. A24.

5. Bob Guccione Jr., "A Commentary," *Los Angeles Times*, 14 August 1994, p. 5.

6. "Black Radio History," *Radio Ink Collector's Edition*, 10 July 1995, p. 48.

7. "Ray Taliaferro," www.kgoam810.com, 31 January 2001.

8. William Barlow, *Voice Over* (Philadelphia, Pa.: Temple University Press, 1999), pp. 254-55.

Chapter 8

Night Roads and UFOs

I threw my bag in the truck, turned the key in the ignition, and by habit rifled over the radio stations as I started to drive, all these voices suddenly speaking to me. I don't know why, but hearing them just made me feel good.

—Michael Paterniti

There's something happening here. What it is ain't exactly clear.

—Buffalo Springfield

At any given moment, day or night, there are hundreds of thousands of trucks on the interstate highways and roads of America. There are three million professional drivers—a third of these are cross-country truck drivers—and a large number clock miles after midnight. This creates a sizable potential listening audience, and this fact has not been overlooked by the radio medium.

Trucker's Radio

Perhaps no group is as tuned to all-night radio as is the nation's professional truckers. Overnight radio programming targeted at this segment of the audience has been around for quite a while.

All-nighters have long been cognizant of the fact that their programs draw listeners from the road, so to speak. Yet all-night radio for truckers evolved into its own branch or subgenre of after-midnight programming in the early 1970s, when a handful of stations decided to direct their overnight sounds to truckers.

There is some debate surrounding who was the earliest voice of trucker's radio. Both Bill Mack and Dave Nemo get the nod depending on the source consulted. Called "The most trusted voice in Trucker Radio," Nemo's show was launched on WWL-AM in New Orleans in 1972. Named the *Road Gang,* it finally gave truckers somewhere to tune. According to the *Toronto Star,* it was a bleak and lonely drive before Nemo came along. "Those were the long, dark nights before the dawn of trucking radio, when a driver sang songs to himself to stay awake, or headed blindly into winter storms, hoping his wife wouldn't worry too much if he was hours late getting home."[1]

Nemo's show struck a special note with truckers, who felt they now had someone to connect with on the long stretches of dark and lonely highway.

> "The Road Gang," heard for thousands of miles over WWL-AM's 50,000-watt clear channel (880), became an overnight sensation with interstate truckers by giving them detailed weather reports they couldn't get elsewhere; by encouraging drivers and their families to call the station's 800-number with messages; and by combining a steady diet of traditional country music with enough general trucker chatter to keep road-weary drivers awake.[2]

It was not too long after Nemo proved that all-night radio directed at this segment of the listening population could be commercially successful that others climbed on board. Over the years, truckers have found companionship in the form of late-night radio shows hosted by WLW's Dale Sommers, WRCA's Big John Trimble (voted *Open Road* magazine's second most popular trucker's deejay in 1977), Interstate Radio Network's Fred Sanders, WSM's Charlie Douglas, KVOO's Mike Rogers, and WBAP's Bill Mack, among others.

Most of these shows feature detailed forecasts and traffic reports, and almost all offer country music, seemingly the favorite with truck drivers. Plenty of road-relevant chatter is also a popular element of programming.

877-708-NEMO (6366)

Home

Talk Back

All-Nighter Club

Radio Specials

Advertisers

Find Us

All-Nighter Club

We are making some neat plans for this club....

Membership has it privileges, and that's the case when you sign up to become a member of Dave's All-Nighter Club--for free! By joining the club you'll receive specials, promotions, contests, prizes, discounts and other goodies available only to members. So join today by filling out the form and checking the box below. You'll be glad you did!

Name

Address

City

State Zip

Phone

Email Address

Occupation ☐ Trucker

☐ Other

☐ Please accept my membership to the All-Nighters Club.

Submit Reset

Figure 8.1. All-night trucker's radio personality Dave Nemo invites listeners to join his club.

> A debate about female truck-drivers was raging one morning recently on "Interstate 700," an overnight radio program for truckers on Cincinnati's WLW-AM. "When they get in tough spots, what do they do? They're always relying on somebody else," complained the Alabama Pigsticker, a male truck driver calling WLW from a pay phone at a Georgia truck stop. A few minutes later, another male trucker, who goes by the handle of Big Ugly Awful, called to defend women truckers. . . . [These] phone calls were typical of those heard early every morning on WLW.[3]

Arguably the two most popular all-night trucker's radio shows today are hosted by Bill Mack, known as "The Midnight Cowboy," and Bob Sommers, whose radio handle is "The Truckin' Bozo."

> **Sam Sauls:** Bill Mack specializes in country music. In fact, he has been the recipient of every award in the country music broadcasting field, including a Grammy Award, Country Music DJ of the Year Award, and in 1982 he received the greatest honor of all when he was placed in the Country Music Disc Jockey Hall of Fame in Nashville. Recently he was certified by BMI in its Million Air Club when "Drinking Champaign" by George Strait had been played over one million times on the radio. Incidentally, Bill wrote the song. "The Midnight Cowboy" began his radio career in the 1950s and worked at various stations throughout Texas. His happiest move (according to the WBAP webpage devoted to him) was in 1969 when he began the first radio program targeted at truckers. It was called *The U.S. 1 Trucking Show* and was broadcast by WBAP. This puts him out there before Nemo. This is some more quoting from the webpage, "In the subculture of truckers and other night time listeners, Bill Mack is more than a deejay. He is a friend. Ask any advertiser who's been on Bill's show for any length of time at all, and they'll tell you that when The Midnight Cowboy talks, the audience listens."

Bill Mack's the Midnight Cowboy Trucking Network is heard throughout the country, making his show one of the most tuned by the nation's professional drivers.

THE TRUCKIN' BOZO

Mack has formidable competition for the ears of all-night truckers in the person of Dale Sommers, better known as "The Truckin' Bozo" by his fans.

> Sommers hosts . . . what is widely regarded as America's most popular trucking show weekdays from midnight to dawn on WLW. . . . [He] specializes in comic cures for white-line fever. He improvises goofy skits with some of his regular callers, or sometimes starts his show by saying, "Look, I'm in a bad mood today, so don't bug me." Like mischievous kids, he says, drivers purposely call in with gripes, hoping he'll "blow them up" with sound effects. . . . "I try to keep my show really upbeat, and I treat 'em all like friends . . . I get involved with the issues truckers care about,

> and keep up to date on all the latest trucker legislation." . . . Sommers considers Nemo his main competition.[4]

TruckNet, a website for the trucking industry, claims that Sommers oversees "North America's largest trucking radio network—now heard in 48 states and most of Canada."

> **Dale Sommers** (aka The Truckin' Bozo): Truck radio, as it is called, is one of only two ways for radio to generate revenue in the late-night hours. The other alternative is paid religion. Regardless of the fact that roughly one-third of the American population is up and moving about at all hours of the night, it is impossible to convince American retail businesses to advertise in the late-night hours. During the late-night hours, you will find more trucks on the roads than automobiles and the reasons are obvious. Less autos mean fewer traffic jams for truckers and the less autos you have the easier it is for truck drivers to rack up some miles. You also have to consider that most businesses operate on a "just in time" basis, whereby they don't have a warehouse, so new merchandise is trucked in every day and night. This means that no matter what you use in everyday life, it was on a truck at one time or another.
>
> As far as programming is concerned, the only successful form of music on truck radio has been country, and even country music has now become so segmented that there are many variations of country radio. Most of the music I play, approximately 30 percent, is drawn from albums that we consider "great deejay records." In other words, we're talking about songs that deejays loved to play when they were current 30 or 40 years ago but for some reason they never became hits. The rest of my music format is derived from what is primarily classified as classic country from the '60s to mid-'70s. We also select a few songs from the '50s and the '80s. Our company owns close to thirteen hundred radio stations and from what I have been told, I'm the only one who gets to pick and play his own music. I pick my songs from the computer system as I go through the night.
>
> My program is syndicated and at the present time it is heard from coast to coast. For example, people in Boston can pick

up the show on WLW, WHAM, and WWVA. The last station probably comes in best because it has a directional antenna aimed at the eastern seaboard. Over the years, truck radio has been dominated by music and country comedy, but after deregulation of the industry and the subsequent bankruptcies of many well-known carriers in the mid and late '80s, I found that many drivers were wanting more information on speed laws, trucking regulations, and new and revised laws. Generally speaking, they wanted anything about the industry they could get, so I started leaning more toward discussions about problems that drivers contend with and their possible solutions. I focus on political issues that cause our economy to change and when that happens, we see a downturn in transportation stocks and trucking in general. Many truck drivers are not aware of the financial impact that the stock market has on trucking as well as the impact that trucking has on the overall economy. If the trucks stopped rolling, America would starve within days, but before that there would be riots in the streets of every major city, as soon as people discovered that once the goods on the shelves were gone there would be no more.

I attempt to mix in a little humor with music but oftentimes my eight phone lines will remain busy all night long, and they will still be ringing after we have ended the show. About 50 percent of the phone calls are from drivers themselves, which is a dramatic rise due to the advent of the cell phone and flat rate charges. Up until the "no roaming charge" billing systems went into effect, many drivers would not call on a cell phone because as they drove along, they might cross over several municipalities and consequently get a 20 to 30 dollar charge for roaming fees. Those days are over. The other 50 percent of the calls are from listeners who, for the most part, are in their homes or workplace and are usually tuning in to hear what the weather is going to be in some distant locale or they're waiting to hear us talk about a specific issue. We have learned that most people are from someplace else and quite often you find people from around the country who want to know what the weather is like back home. America is fascinated with the weather someplace else, so we provide it. There are many things that constitute truck radio, but first and foremost it is a service for those out there on the late-night road.

STRANGE NIGHTS, INDEED

The truth is out there . . . tune in.

Another form of all-night radio has enjoyed growing popularity over the past several years as well. Programs that focus on the paranormal and UFO sightings and encounters have attracted a whole new audience to late nights, not that the topic of aliens and ghostly visages is anything new. In the 1950s, Long John Nebel earned the title "Ringmaster of the Strange" for an array of topics that dealt with the odd and bizarre. Observed Malachy McCourt in his memoir, *Singing My Him Song,*

> One of the intriguing characters in all night radio had to be Long John Nebel, who'd made a name for himself by talking to people who'd been taken off on round trips by flying saucers and welcoming tales of various other odd phenomenon on his show.[5]

> **Alan Colmes:** Long John Nebel was another all-night legend who rarely dealt with the news of the day, but rather put on unusual people with bizarre theories. He explored UFOs, people who claimed to be from other planets, and other paranormal topics. He demonstrated that talk radio could be fascinating even when it wasn't topical.

Today, website chat rooms still find Long John Nebel's unusual shows worthy of discussion. Here's an example:

> Sure I remember Long John's Party Line and especially the Howard Menger interview. The show originated in the '50s and was already enigmatic. Long John's book *Way Out World* should be of interest. Menger's story, if not all then at least in part, is true. This I know [because] while investigating the case in 1956-57, we witnessed the bell shaped craft very close up prior to experiencing a complete time loss of about nine hours.[6]

The tremendously successful movies *Close Encounters of the Third Kind, Star Wars,* and *Alien* in the 1970s generated new debate about the possible existence of UFOs and extraterrestrials, and supernatural thrillers like *The Exorcist, The Omen,* and *Poltergeist* contributed greatly to dialogue about the paranormal and afterlife. In the 1980s and 1990s, these topics would come to dominate many all-night programs. In fact, the postmidnight hours at an increasing number of stations were becoming known as the domain of the strange.

Figure 8.2. Art Bell, all-night maestro of things strange. Courtesy Premiere Radio.

Elizabeth Salazar: All-night radio has become the "weird" zone over the past 20 years. It's routine to hear someone attempting to commune with fellow conspiratorists, UFO travelers, right-wing extremists, psychic friends, and paranormalists. I equate this with the same analogy that some people in public service use when seeing a full moon grace a black cat. It's when people who live or believe in counterculture lifestyles seem to come out of the woodwork or out of the cracks in the sidewalks. Sometimes it's a nightly thing, not just once a month or occasionally. I believe all-night radio has always attracted its fair share of the bizarre; it's just more open in today's world and certainly talked about more publicly than ever before. Perhaps acceptance of such diverse thinking is made easier for discussion during the all-night hours due to the fact that much of the world is asleep and a soapbox for their platform is therefore more accessible. I used to have a listener who would occasionally call the LAPD in the middle of the night to inform them that he'd planted a bomb in the building housing my radio station and another. It was such a common occurrence, the all-night jock upstairs and I knew the caller was crying wolf, but there was no convincing the police, who'd order me out of the building anyway, thereby disrupting the flow of my show and injecting it with a notoriously lethal dose of dead air. Being young and considering myself to be invincible, I began sneaking back inside to the station. More concerned for the FCC's then-stringent rules about log-keeping and entertaining my listeners, weird as they might be, I'd risk being blown up to get the show going again.

Sheena Metal: The all-night show breeds a level of weirdness not found on any other shift. My memories are cluttered with experiences that involve board ops falling asleep during the program, wacky guests having all-night pizza places deliver to the station, callers so drunk you could barely understand them. Yes, tame but weird. I remember staying up and listening to the radio all night when I was young and couldn't get to sleep. I thought that the radio station must be a magical and mystical place. In many ways it is overnights.

Steve Warren: Settings for the all-night show can inspire the weird side of the imagination too. Following a stint at WIRE, I went to WIFE in 1967. There I did overnight news from the transmitter site, thereby utilizing my First Class License. The station built a small news studio at their transmitter location in a swamp south of town. It was just me and the croaking frogs most nights. After one really bad snowfall, I was stranded in the transmitter building and had to be rescued by a bulldozer. All that certainly adds a certain ambiance to the job.

Spooky stories abound about haunted stations with scenarios that invariably unfold during the late-night hours.

Phylis Johnson: This is true. You know, things like doorbells ringing with no one there. Lights flashing and going out entirely. Ghostly cold currents of air flowing through the control room. Your mind can play funny games on you in the dead of night when you're all alone at a station.

Allen Ogrizovich: Talk about the paranormal, back in the mid-1970s I worked the all-night gig at KWSL in Sioux City, Iowa, and had to contend with strange little aliens in mice costumes. I was always catching the vermin in the trash or bypassing traps. I remember a few times giving them swimming lessons in the toilet. That's about as exotic it got for me.

Of course, what makes all-nights strange may have as much to do with the personalities of the hosts as it does with otherworldly phenomenon. This newspaper description of Toronto overnight deejay Gary Bell gives this theory some credence.

[He's] too excited to sit down between midnight and 5:30 A.M. Around the studio they call him "Space" and, in his wild eyes, framed by tiny round spectacles and fringed with wine-colored, shoulder-length hair, you can see a glimmer of the spirit of a lost planet warrior. Bell is no stranger to the lonesome, electric freeways of intergalactic air.[7]

Joey Reynolds: I don't buy into all this weirdness stuff. What do I think about the paranormal? Not much. I don't think a lot about what's not out there, but clearly a lot of people do.

Whether a believer in things that go bump in the night or not, the witching hours seem to inspire a cornucopia of unusual and sometimes irreverent behavior. A case in point is Top 40 KIEV-AM's firing of its late-night host "Kaptain Kaos" for playing a recording of Pope John Paul's album *Abba Pater.* The station argued that Kaos violated its format by playing foreign-language music and using profanity between cuts. On yet another station in the 1960s, the all-night deejay locked himself in the control room and played "They're Coming to Take Me Away" for 3 hours, until the authorities came and took him away. Meanwhile, in the late 1980s, two young deejays were ousted from a Baptist university radio station for using the devil's language on their talk show during which they described "unnatural sex acts between a dog and a cat."[8]

Larry Miller: Yes, it can and often does get a wee bit strange out there when the moon is full and the station's signal beams across the nighttime world.

Occasionally the real world of late-night radio is not far from that depicted in the novel *Fuel-Injected Dreams* by James Robert Baker. Here the author describes how his main character, a late-night deejay, opens his show:

> This is Scott Cochran, macho superstud, male feminist, and untreatable schizophrenic. You're listening to "Radio Noir." . . . I wanna get on a death trip.[9]

As the change of the millennium approached, all-night talk centered around survivalist strategies and end-of-the-world theories.

> **Lynn Christian:** As you can well imagine, the size of the all-night audience grew exponentially as the anxiety level rose in the days and weeks before the actual turn of the millennium and century. Not only were the usual paranormal shows focusing on this topic, but even many of those hosts who typically avoided such talk got in on it. It was the topic du jour.

THE BELL CURVED

As the most popular syndicated late-night host over the past decade, Art Bell has ruled the nocturnal airwaves from a modest prefabricated complex surrounded by a barbed wire fence on the barren southern Nevada desert just a few miles from the fabled Area 51. "The radio signal is beamed from the Bell family backyard—populated with dishes and antennae—via a complex bicoastal satellite system, to a network whose nighttime reach stretches from the Arctic to South America."[10] It is there that he and his callers speculate on the existence of all things strange and wondrous several hours each night. Bell became to all-night radio in the 1990s what Larry King had been to it in the 1980s. He was its reigning monarch; its foremost voice. Listeners by the millions tuned in on a regular basis and quickly became loyal fans of Bell as they had other legendary all-nighters before him, among them King, Barry Gray, Long John Nebel, Jean Shepherd, Al Jepko, Wolfman Jack, and Ray Briem.

While Bell shared many attributes in common with his preeminent late-night forerunners, he, like them, brought something uniquely and distinctively his own to the microphone. His editor, Jennifer L. Osborn, summed it up effectively in her preface to *The Art of Talk*,

> Who is Art Bell? The first time I remember listening to Art Bell was in college. I wasn't sleeping very well because of various pressures in my life, and I hit upon the idea of turning the radio on late that night for some company. I drifted away, only to be awakened later in the morning, say, 2 A.M., by the call of Art Bell's voice. Once my mind engaged with that voice, it was impossible to go back to sleep—and I didn't want to anyway at that point. I was compelled to listen; I had no choice. I was gripped by the expanse of subject material covered on the show. I was fascinated by things Art talked about that I had little or no knowledge of. Art Bell quickly became a comfortable habit at night; like a good book you just can't put down, you hope it never ends.[11]

Bell launched his radio career at KDWN, a powerful AM radio station in Las Vegas. This eventually led to the popular overnight show "West Coast AM," which would capture the attention of broadcast executive Alan Corbeth, who would suggest the idea of syndicating the program nationally as "Coast to Coast AM."

> In 1988, I met Alan Corbeth, who was visiting Las Vegas while on business. . . . I learned that he was an expert at syndicating radio programs and had been an avid listener of mine for the better part of a year after he had moved to Medford, Oregon. I met him and was delighted to discover what a nice guy he was. We both had a lot in common, radio being one thing in particular and we are also very driven; I wanted to have a bigger show and Alan wanted to see me achieve this aim.[12]

> **Alan Corbeth:** Nighttime radio was my thing. I pushed it, loved it, and had a vision for it, as did Art. So we built it together.

Eventually the program was purchased by Premiere Radio Networks, a wholly owned subsidiary of Jacor Communications—the nation's top syndicator of talk programming. By the end of the 1990s, Art Bell's *Coast to Coast* show dominated the overnight ratings, boasting a listenership approaching ten million, far surpassing the competition.

At the core of Bell's success has always been his strong desire and willingness to tread where few others do, to pursue a different path—one of his own creation. This is no ordinary talk show, writes Andrea Adelson of the *New York Times:* "Extra-dimensional beings, disasters foretold and Government conspiracies are standard fare."[13]

> **Art Bell:** I was in a fortunate position when I started out. I had complete freedom to dictate what I did, and I decided that the public was sick of the kind of radio it was getting 24 hours a day, what at that point was all political talk. It occurred to me in my life, and in the life of those who are close to me, that nobody sits at home and talks politics 3 to 4 hours a day. I was fed up and sick of the same old things on all-night radio and decided I would not do that. I had to spread my wings. Of course, station management got very uptight. Fortunately, because I was on at night and radio stations were not as sensitive to experimentation or ratings numbers, I was allowed to do things. They didn't stop me or cancel me, and the ratings showed the audience was with me. So that kind of validated the direction I was taking. I think the secret of success is not to walk in somebody else's shoes.

> Conformity was expected at the time I started doing all this. You had to be a Rush Limbaugh clone. But Limbaugh was a success to start with because he walked his own path. My advice to anybody entering talk radio today would be to avoid walking in anybody's path. Ingenuity and sincerity are important elements of success.

What has made Bell such a success with his listeners is his openness to what callers have to contribute to the program.

> Mr. Art Bell pretty much lets the listeners rule. He starts off with a basic rundown of the major news stories of the day, and poses questions about these stories in order to purposely provoke controversy. He opens up five phone lines . . . and allows listeners to call and say what they think. However, he lets callers talk about anything they wish, and they often bring up new topics for discussion. What makes "Coast to Coast" really unique are the rules that Art Bell plays by. For example, all phone calls are unscreened, and, as a result, they can get pretty weird and nasty.[14]

What Long John Nebel had begun in the 1950s, Bell expanded into a full-scale radio genre in the 1990s. Critics have called his show a radio version of *The Twilight Zone* and *The X-Files,* because of its seeming fixation on the strange and peculiar. Writes Tom Genoni:

> Living in Los Angeles, I've grown accustomed to seeing neon-signed psychic storefronts, sidewalk fortunetellers, aura readers, channelers, spiritualists, and New Age advocates of all kinds. The "fringe" is well represented here. But none of this—not even the psychic cat that occasionally shows up on Venice Beach—could have prepared me for the parade of paranormal oddities appearing regularly on the late-night radio program "The Art Bell Show." Carried live five days a week on AM stations all over the country, "The Art Bell Show" . . . is America's most-syndicated late-night radio program. . . . Bell believes there is already an "automatic skepticism" about his program's paranormal subject matter and that plenty of skeptical information is available.[15]

A critic of this type of programming, Genoni believes it contributes little of legitimate substance to the listening public.

> Not surprisingly, the real reason for the show's divergent postures—simultaneously existing solely as entertainment and presenting supposedly reliable, scientific information—has little to do with any "search for wisdom." The "Art Bell Show," and others like it, exist because of a formula, one that their producers rarely concede and one that invariably precludes any meaningful, balanced discussion of the paranormal.[16]

On two occasions, Bell has quit his show; the first time in 1998, due to domestic problems stemming from the sexual molestation of his son, and the second time in 2000 as the consequence of emotional stress derived from the experience. "Bell [left] because of ongoing torment that his family has suffered since his son was kidnapped and raped in 1997 by a substitute teacher. He also said he was leaving because of being falsely accused of being a child molester."[17]

Reported the *Washington Post,* "Somewhere deep in the nightscape of his own created world, the dark conspiracy theories became all too real for Art Bell. And so, angry, frightened, hunted, one of the country's most popular radio hosts simply walked away in Saturday's early morning hours."[18]

In April 2000, Mike Siegel took over the hosting duties at *Coast to Coast* for Bell. In a statement to the press, the management at Premiere Radio Network said it chose Siegel as Bell's successor because "he has the blend of the greatest curiosity for the issues we want to explore in the program, and because he will be able to stand the test of time of almost 25 hours a week of programming."[19]

Unfortunately, Siegel was not able to stand the test of time with listeners of *Coast to Coast* during the 10-month absence of Bell, and the ratings for the program revealed as much. After considerable soul searching about his personal life and intense negotiations with Premiere Radio, Bell agreed to return to the helm of *Coast to Coast* on February 5, 2001. In a press release, Kraig T. Kitchin, president/COO of Premiere Networks, stated "I am ecstatic to welcome Art Bell back to his program. It was a bloody negotiation—pulling someone out of retirement always is. I am wildly enthusiastic to bring the news to affiliates and listeners nationwide . . . imagine their reactions! I also want to add my thanks to Mr. Siegel."[20]

A barometer of Bell's impact on the late-night radio arena was the increasing number of shows that attempted to fashion themselves after *Coast to Coast AM.* In the 1990s, as Bell's show rose in popularity, late-night programs focusing on the paranormal surfaced around the country. In 1998, the NBG Radio Network announced its plans to venture into all-night radio syndication with a show designed to address "UFO's, History, Paranormal, Politics, Archaeology, Science, Conspiracies, Technology, Religion, The Unexplained, Current Events, and much more."[21] Eliot Stein was chosen to host the show, which never really got off the ground.

> **Eliot Stein:** We were hoping to give stations in every market that were not carrying Art Bell a show that got into other intriguing areas beside UFOs. They wouldn't bite though. Stations seemed to think that if it wasn't already on outlets in Los Angeles and New York, then it wasn't good enough for them. So after a while, we all agreed to dump it.

Art Bell, the latest reigning king of all-night radio, was not to be faced with challenges any more formidable than those arising from within his own heart and mind.

NOTES

1. Katherine Seigenthalei, "All Night Radio Keeps Truckers on the Road," *Toronto Star,* 9 April 1989, p. C6.
2. Ibid.
3. Adam Buckman, "Truckin' Across the Dial," *Electronic Media,* 27 June 1988, p. 1.
4. Seigenthalei.
5. Malachy McCourt, *Singing My Him Song* (New York: Harper Collins, 2000), p. 95.
6. Frank Peters, www.musicradio.computer.net/wwwboard/messages/34975.html, 27 January 2001.
7. Gregg Quill, "Free Spirits of the Airwaves," *Toronto Star,* 10 June 1989, p. E3.
8. United Press International, 14 April 1989.
9. Madison Bell, "Paperbacks," *New York Times,* 4 March 1986, sec. 7, p. 38.
10. Robert Koehler, "Operation Desert Talk," *Los Angeles Times,* 13 January 1996, p. F1.
11. Art Bell, *The Art of Talk* (New Orleans: Paper Chase Press, 1998), p. 7.
12. Ibid., p. 169.
13. Andrea Adelson, "Audience Left Wondering as Radio Host Disappears," *New York Times,* 26 October 1998, p. C8.
14. Keith W. Schwarz Jr., "Coast to Coast: Radio for the Late Night Studier," www.uno.edu/drif/may2/radio.htm, 31 January 2001.

15. Thomas C. Genoni Jr., "Peddling the Paranormal: Late Night Radio's Art Bell," *Skeptical Inquirer,* March 1998.

16. Ibid.

17. "Replacement Found for Radio's Art Bell," Associated Press, 12 April 2000.

18. Frank Ahrens, "Art Bell, Escaping the Voices," *Washington Post,* 4 April 2000, P. C2.

19. Judith Michaelson, "Veteran Talk Show Host Mike Siegel to Succeed Bell," *Lost Angeles Times,* 11 April 2000, P. F2.

20. Press release, Premiere Radio Networks, 5 January 2000.

21. "CompuServe Interactive Radio & Hollywood Hotline Link with NBG Radio Network," *Business Wire,* 13 August 1998.

Chapter 9

The Right of Night

If you drove through the night pushing buttons, it all turned into one long talk radio.

—**Frank Gannon**

Radio was *the* medium for conservative talk-show hosts in the 1980s and 1990s. Broadly speaking, the two things that most significantly contributed to this development were the Reagan presidency, with its right-wing politics and sweeping de/reregulation of broadcasting, and the Clinton presidency, with its left-wing politics and notorious scandals.

The crown jewel in Reagan's plan to free broadcasters, especially commercial broadcasters, of governmental constraints and strictures was the elimination of the Fairness Doctrine, created in the late 1940s to ensure that multiple viewpoints and perspectives on important issues had the opportunity to be articulated over the airwaves.

The liquidation of the Fairness Doctrine in 1987 essentially restored full freedom of speech without a requirement that other views be offered. The increased proliferation of right-wing talk shows on radio in the 1980s and 1990s was to a considerable degree the result of the abandonment of the doctrine. Whether this was an anticipated by-product of Reagan's veto is unclear.

Full freedom of speech has been modified by the courts according to the tenor of the times, and in some cases restraints on freedom of speech by the private sector have been upheld by the courts as a reflection of public opinion of the given time. Presumably, a 1937 Supreme Court opinion delivered by Chief Justice Charles Evans Hughes in a case involving a man accused of criminal conduct by conducting meetings under the auspices of the Communist Party established a modern basis for freedom of speech in general. Hughes stated:

> The greater the importance of safeguarding the community from incitements to the overthrow of our institutions by force and violence, the more imperative is the need to preserve inviolate the constitutional right of free speech, free press and assembly in order to maintain the opportunity for free political speech.[1]

Reported *Broadcasting and Cable* regarding the elimination of the Fairness Doctrine:

> The FCC . . . struck down the Fairness Doctrine, saying: "If we must choose between whether editorial decisions are to be made in the free judgment of individual broadcasters or imposed by bureaucratic fiat, the choice must be for freedom."[2]

With this action, talk-show hosts now had the opportunity to speak their minds with relative impunity, because stations did not have to offer airtime to those with opposing perspectives, something provided by the defunct canon. Talk-show hosts, nearly all conservative in their political views, took full advantage of this. Thus, right-wing radio personalities like Rush Limbaugh, Oliver North, G. Gordon Liddy, and a myriad of others were born.

During the 1980s politics came to dominate the conversation of all-night radio as it never had before, and some of overnight's biggest stars were flag-waving conservatives, such as Ray Briem, whose program at the start of the decade was the most popular overnight radio broadcast in the country. At KABC in Los Angeles, the flagship station of Briem's show, 47,600 listeners were tuned each quarter hour, Monday through Friday, between midnight and 5 A.M. These were the highest numbers delivered by any all-night show at the time. Among the markets carrying Briem's syndicated program were New York, Boston, Chicago, Detroit, Philadelphia, Houston, Atlanta, and Los Angeles. Of the dozens of stations airing the show, only one, KGB in San Diego, was an FM outlet.

Outspoken late-night hosts espousing liberal views and perspectives were certainly in the minority, but they did exist. Among the most famous, perhaps infamous, talkers of this persuasion was Alan Berg, remembered more for the tragic consequences of his rants against right-wing extremists than his on-air performances. In June 1984, Berg was machine-gunned down in the driveway of his Denver home because of his stands against anti-Semitism and racism.

> A self-proclaimed "Wild Man of the Airwaves," the controversial, belligerent Berg managed to enrage, abuse, provoke and fascinate . . . while carrying on irreverent and frank discussions about oral sex, Christianity, racial intolerance, gun control and any other topic his angry, abrasive tongue could wag about. KOA's powerful signal, capable of reaching thirty-eight states in the evening hours, meant Berg's blitzkrieg was pissing off a lot of people. "The Order," a virulent White Power/Aryan Resistance movement . . . assembled a "hate list" of those who were deemed to be threatening the existence of the white race and thus worthy targets of assassination. Among them were Henry Kissinger, David Rockefeller, Fred Silverman, and Alan Berg. Berg's assassination was a carefully planned paramilitary operation fueled with bank robbery money.[3]

Berg's story became an Oliver Stone movie, which was based on Eric Bogosian's play, *Talk Radio.* During the final two decades of the twentieth century, overnight radio became a hot zone of contentious rhetoric and combative discourse, something listeners seemed to like as audience figures expanded.

TECH TALK

Technology played an increasing role in late-night radio in the 1980s, as satellite-delivered talk programming made significant inroads in markets throughout the country. Meanwhile, FM—the radio band with the superior sound—was sapping AM of its music programming. This forced the older, static-plagued broadcast

The Best of RADIO forever young℠ Yesterday

The Golden Decade

What a time it was. The whirlwind that was American popular music was blowing up a storm. The home grown phenomenon of rock n roll, the invasion of the Brits, and the gentler incursion of the Brazilians had America dancing and singing as never before. The last days of the big bands were producing some glorious moments. Broadway turned out hit after hit musical. And new composers and artists were sprouting like mushrooms everywhere.

Trying to Recapture a Magic Time.

There was no musical decade like the early sixties through the early seventies. After that, music on radio settled into a now familiar groove – almost entirely vocal, with the three mainstreams of country, rock and adult contemporary flowing steadily, sometimes boringly onward, in their wake a host of "alternatives" and niche music. Some of the so-called "adult standard" formats of recent years have tried to recapture that magic time. None have even come close.

The Birth of Easy Listening.

For, you see, to reprise the Golden Decade of American music, you almost had to live it. And Charlie Whitaker and Lynn Christian did. When the two young Texans stormed the radio citadel of New York in the mid-sixties, they brought with them an already successful format they had created on top-rated KODA FM in Houston. And within weeks after the all-new WPIX FM debuted in October of 1964, New York had fallen head over heels in love with The Sound of the Good Life. That sound – a carefully orchestrated blend of pop vocals and instrumentals – went on to become a major market success story across the country. So unusual and distinctive was its sound that Claude Hall, radio editor of Billboard Magazine, dubbed it Easy Listening.

But as the 70s went by, Easy Listening lost its way and eventually became the all-vocal format known today, in its various mutations, as Adult Contemporary. Somehow, the best of the non-rock favorites of that era – a vast body of great music -- was ignored, all but disappearing from the radio dial.

The Great Sound is Back.

Now that great sound back in a brand new radio programming service called Forever Young. All the elements are there: the bright, swinging hit instrumentals; the great artists that turned out hit after hit, the best of everything of that turbulent, creative, exciting era. The ballads, the broadway hits, the bossa nova, the movie music, just as it was when this very same format swept the country from coast to coast. Forever Young. The great songs of the past that could become your radio station's bright future.

Delivered to your station on a reliable, versatile, Scott Studio System.
Christian/Whitaker Productions 214.340.6690 310-476-6170

Figure 9.1. Syndicator services were used to fill all-night dayparts. Courtesy Lynn Christian.

service to all but abandon melodies in favor of around-the-clock chatter.

> **Rollye James:** The dawning of the '80s saw another crisis for radio, AM in particular. Just as television threatened radio's existence in the '50s, FM radio, with its cleaner signals and fuller fidelity, threatened to bury AM. AM stations found themselves in the "nothing left to lose" category. So if music was no longer an option for AM, what about talk?

The use of telephones in late-night talk shows was enhanced with the employment of 800 numbers and the growth of the cell-phone industry. It was easier and, with toll-free numbers, more economical to contact a station. Subsequently, the increase in the volume of calls rose dramatically, requiring stations to install more phone lines, hire producers and assistants, and ultimately embrace computer technology. As might be expected, it was the larger-income stations that found this level of upgrading less of a burden. At small stations, the all-night host typically served as his own producer and assistant.

> **Dick Fatherley:** It was amazing how all this improved telecommunication technology resulted in greater audience participation. That was a solid and positive development. Local access and network 800 numbers, not to mention the cell-phone phenomenon in the '90s, really gave radio talk programming a boost. It was a boon to both day and night shows. More and more listeners went from being "passives" to "actives."

> **Art Bell:** Technology makes being out here on the Nevada desert the same as being the next-door neighbor anywhere in the country. The phones never stop ringing, even after the show is over, and these are people calling from thousands of miles away.

> **Larry Miller:** Over the past 20 years, talk on AM stations rose because of the political environment and the enhanced accessibility of stations. Something else is also a factor in this as well. Boomers have gotten discouraged with the narrowness and playlist strictures prevalent at music stations and have turned to talk. Maybe it's the age thing that makes

listeners more inclined to grapple with issues and pick up the phone and call a station in the middle of the night.

Ultimately, callers were attracted to all-night shows because they were where the action seemed to be. Many postmidnight programs featured prominent government officials and celebrities, as well as controversial figures. Recall, if you will, this statement in an earlier chapter reported by the *New York Times* in 1982:

> If some top members of the Reagan Administration have been a little red-eyed lately, it may be because they have been staying up late to appear on the all night radio talk show hosted by Larry King on the Mutual Broadcasting System. They show up at the studio at midnight and sit through three hours of questions from Mr. King and his listeners. The Administration apparently sees the show as an opportunity to deliver its message to a late-night audience of 3.5 million people without dilution or editorial intererence.[4]

ON THE LIGHTER SIDE OF DARKNESS

While the themes of most all-night talk programs were commonly of a serious and "issues"-oriented nature, there was a lighter side to be found on the radio dial. Not all overnighters engaged in the solemn and weighty. Just as many were committed to providing their sleepless audiences with a good laugh as were intent on generating provocative ruminations.

For example, Steve and Johnnie, a husband and wife team, have kept listeners tuned to WGN in Chicago since the 1980s with their engaging and topical conversations with one another and their listeners. This has made them the Windy City's favorite all-night hosts. Meanwhile, on the east coast, Joey Reynolds's audience continued to grow in the 1980s as he attracted listeners with what WOR's PR department characterized as his entertaining and charismatic personality:

> Joey's radio shows sparkle with a rare and wonderfully sharp, spontaneous wit that made him, then and now, one of the greatest personalities on radio. He has also developed a warm sort of humor that jokes with the person to whom he's talking, rather than against them [*sic*]. An approach on the air that builds friends. He's a great companion for the day's early

hours when heavy issues are simply too heavy. His stream of consciousness style offers the kind of entertainment seldom heard on radio.[5]

The overnight antics of California's Dick Whittington kept listeners tuned to KIEV-AM in the 1980s.

Gary Owens: This guy was a real original. You never knew where he would head next because of his surreal sense of humor and sometimes bizarre creativity.

Recalls writer Elizabeth Hayes:

He once dropped a giant Alka-Seltzer in the Atlantic Ocean to protest government disposal of noxious gas. He declared war on Catalina Island, staged a wedding between the Queen Mary and the harbor cruise boat Prince of Long Beach, and air-dropped human hair (sent in by listeners) onto Mt. Baldy. . . . Whittington plays a good-natured host to a hodge-podge of somewhat marginal types. His guest roster [has] included a mysterious psychologist, a man who would only speak in tongues and a psychic who claimed he has counseled Barbara Bush.[6]

In an interview with Hayes, Whittington described the nature of his audience:

At 3 in the morning, we have people on whom nobody else would. . . . Sometimes you think you're in "The Twilight Zone." I think that because I don't take it all that seriously—and most importantly, I don't take myself seriously—people, issues, causes don't frighten me. . . . In some talk shows I've listened to during the daytime, the audience becomes an addendum. They don't participate. To me, on all night radio, they have to be part and parcel. Six hours is such an amorphous time that the audience dictates the content, you don't. . . . Most people listen in the dark, I've ascertained. . . . They're all age groups. . . . You're dealing, I think, with lonely people. Understanding that and being compassionate and not trying to be better is important.[7]

What contributed to the late-night antics at some stations was the altered state of their on-air hosts. Not unlike the pot-smoking overnighters of the late 1960s and early 1970s, certain deejays and talkers of later years were not always in full control of their mental faculties. This would sometimes inspire peculiar performances and programs that veered into idiosyncratic regions, to put it euphemistically.

> **Doug Steckler:** A lot of these guys were boozing before and during their airshifts, so as you might imagine things were not always as coherent as they might have been. Who knows whether it affected their performances in a positive or negative way.

MORE STARS IN THE SKY

The prominent all-nighters of the 1970s continued to rule the airwaves in the 1980s, and some grew to light the night as supernovas. Aside from Larry King, popular personalities like Tom Snyder, Bruce Williams, Larry Glick, Ray Briem, Eddie Schwartz, and dozens of others from all parts of the country attracted greater and greater attention. During this period, New York's Music Radio 77's overnight lineup featured nightmen Howard Hoffman, Mike McKay, and Mark Sommers before it dropped its legendary music format in favor of 24-hour talk.

> **Sheena Metal:** In the 1980s, I think radio was all about the disc jockey with the larger-than-life personality throwing on some hot tunes and acting as ringmaster in an unending flow of crazy call-in requests and huge contests. Sure, there was always talk on at night, but I think many people dismissed this as radio for pseudointellectuals and college graduates over 65.

> **Eric Rhoads:** In my book, *Blast from the Past,* I wrote about some of the stars of late-night radio. Here's an example: "Lighting up every evening across America, ABC's Tom Snyder became one of the most beloved radio personalities." As I already mentioned, Yvonne Daniels in Chicago was another giant personality during that time. These people really meant something to listeners.

> **Robert Feder:** While talking about all-nighters in Chicago, no one personified the power and intimacy of overnight radio with greater success than Eddie Schwartz, a one-of-a-kind character whose passion for the city and concern for others

Figure 9.2. Chicagoans loved listening to overnight radio host Ed Schwartz. Courtesy Robert Feder.

were matched only by his oversized girth. Throughout the 1980s, and even before, he was the undisputed, king-sized king of the wee hours in the nation's third-largest media market. To hundreds of thousands of night owls, insomniacs, and third-shift workers, "Chicago Ed,"—as he was affectionately known—was a trusted companion and a friendly voice in the dark. Whether he was chasing down overnight fires and power failures or chatting with the world's top show biz stars and politicians, Schwartz cheerfully presided over the biggest all-night show around. As the most unlikely star many Chicagoans had ever heard, Schwartz possessed a wheezing, high-pitched voice, a thick diction, and an unabashed civic boosterism that baffled the so-called professionals but endeared him to a loyal following. "With a lot of late-night radio listeners, I've become kind of like an old bathrobe or an old pair of slippers," he once said. "They know who I am and what I do, and they're comfortable with it. They're glad to find out that I'm here at night, and we get together and maybe everything's okay with

Table 9.1. Herb Jepko on the all-night airwaves in the 1980s at KBOI in Boise, Idaho.

50,000 WATTS · 24 HOURS

BOISE, IDAHO

Program Schedule

	MONDAY TUESDAY WEDNESDAY THURSDAY FRIDAY		SATURDAY SUNDAY
6 AM	THE DUNN AND SCHNEIDER SHOW LON DUNN PAUL J. SCHNEIDER NEWS SPORTS TRAFFIC UPDATES		RELIGIOUS PROGRAMMING
10 AM	MARK ALLEN MUSIC NEWS		KBOI WEEKEND NBC SPORTS UPDATES
2 PM	"THE GOOD DOCTOR" DREW HAROLD MUSIC NEWS SPORTS TRAFFIC UPDATES		
6 PM	DICK STOTT MUSIC NEWS	JEFF THOMAS	PUBLIC AFFAIRS
12 AM	THE HERB JEPKO SHOW TALK SHOW		

NEWS
Barrett Rainey
Don Wimberly
Terry Thurber
Dan Leach

SPORTS
Paul J. Schneider

FINANCIAL NEWS - Merrell Lynch
TRAFFIC UPDATES - Boise Police Department
WEATHER

the world." After 8 years of top ratings at WIND-AM (where he started out as music librarian and worked his way up to music director, community affairs director, executive producer, assistant program director, and finally all-night host), Schwartz was lured over to 50,000-watt giant WGN-AM in 1981, where his audience got even bigger. At the height of his popularity, he attracted more than 300,000 listeners a week in the Chicago metropolitan area—and many more nationwide. Frequent guests included such celebrities as Bill Cosby, Jay Leno, Steve Allen, and Robert Conrad, as

> well as senators, governors, and mayors. "His audience is larger at midnight than most others are at noon," Dan Fabian, former general manager of WGN, observed in 1991. "If there's something going on in the world and he decides, 'We're going to find out about this,' . . . he had a real sense of urgency, a fever. He believes very much that, in fact, this is full-service, full-time live radio, regardless of the hour." An outspoken advocate for the downtrodden, Schwartz launched his most successful crusade in 1981 when he learned that the then-mayor of Chicago, Jane Byrne, was spending $100,000 to light up the city's bridges and set off New year's Eve fireworks at a time when the shelves of local food pantries were bare. "That made me angry," he later recalled. "I said, 'If she won't do something about hunger in this town, I will'." For the next 12 years, he hosted his annual Good Neighbor Food Drive, an all-volunteer effort that grew into the largest one-night antihunger event in the country, credited with collecting more than two million pounds of food and more than $1 million in cash.

Bruce Williams's star ascended further in the 1980s as he assumed coast-to-coast overnight hosting duties for "Talknet." At one point in his career he even conducted his program from a hospital bed during recovery from an operation. His fans responded with bags of mail.

> **Joseph Buchman:** He's one of the maestros of late-night radio broadcasting and I've been lucky to have him as a friend. The guy's published several books. In one, if I remember correctly, he has a description of how he hounded a radio station in New Jersey or New York to get his first radio job. He did, and the rest, as they say, is history, because he's left his amazing mark on all-nights.

Meanwhile, Ray Briem's career hit its high watermark in the 1980s with his tremendously informative and revealing late-night chats with Soviet talk-show host Vladimir Pozner via telephone from his studio in Los Angeles to Pozner's in Moscow.

> **Ray Briem:** Yes, we actually hooked up several times with Pozner from Moscow and discussed our two countries' important issues. It was a pretty exclusive event in radio communications, and it was taking place in the very early

morning hours. Besides talking about current domestic events, the world was my beat. If a story was unfolding in a foreign city, I would call there and get a firsthand report. Just before the Soviet Union invaded Czechoslovakia, I was talking with the CTK news agency in Prague. They were telling me that the meeting in Bratislavia with the Kremlin leaders would never bring about an invasion of the Czech Republic. Being a ham radio operator, I would monitor shortwave stations and had many "firsts" on my show, such as the one and only news report from Radio Beijing during the Tienneman Square uprising or the broadcast of Radio Pyongyang in North Korea that broadcast the so-called confessions of the crew from the USS *Pueblo*. I also called small towns across the United States and talked to police chiefs, officers, and anyone else on duty. Where else were you going to find out about the "Chitlin Festival" in Salley, South Carolina? I was stationed in New York City with Armed Forces Radio for 2 years, and I emceed *One Night Stand*, which would broadcast name dance bands from places like the Astor Roof of the Hotel Astor or the Cafe Rouge of the Statler. Harry James, Tommy and Jimmy Dorsey, Woody Herman, and many others appeared. So in my KABC overnight show I would interview band leaders, singers, and arrangers. Among my guests were Tony Bennett, Nelson Riddle, Henry Mancini, Artie Shaw, and Ella Fitzgerald, to mention only a few.

Greg Hardison: I must say that Ray was one of the classiest, least-egotistical, and fairest people I have ever worked with in the business. Even though I rarely agreed with his conservative politics, I never lacked motivation in doing my best for the show because of Ray himself. I also took note of the time difference with the rest of the world as producer of the show. Our air hours were "their" 9-to-5 business hours. We used this to our advantage in maintaining regular contacts with, for instance, South Africa's government ministers as apartheid was dismantling in the 1980s. We also did two interviews with Philippine President Ferdinand Marcos. The first marked his first-ever appearance on any medium with audience participation. Marcos enjoyed the experience and agreed to a second show with Ray. The

> *Nightline* staff heard the show, and I soon provided them with Marcos's contact information, noting the office and home telephone numbers for Marcos's main press aide, Hermie Rivera. Marcos agreed to the *Nightline* appearance, during which he caved to pressure to hold free elections in the Philippines. That election led to his ouster, as he was replaced by Corazon Aquino. Of course, most recall Ray's programs with Vladimir Pozner from Radio Moscow. Vladimir made his first in-studio appearance on the Briem show during the Chernenko regime, and he was extremely nervous the entire 5 hours of the broadcast. His next appearance came a year or two after Gorbachev assumed power. At that time, Vladimir was considerably more at ease and open.

Throughout the 1980s, several more radio stations entered the 24-hour arena, among them KKLA-FM in Los Angeles, which offered religious programming. At the same time, due to the decline in the fortunes of AM radio because of the vast migration of listeners to the FM dial, a large number suspended all-night operating hours.

Last Days of the Century's Nights

The level of talk in overnight broadcasts took a dramatic leap in the 1990s as President Clinton became the near-obsessive topic on call-in shows. The contempt for and fascination with the commander in chief appeared to have no bounds. The themes encountered on all-night radio in the last decade of the second millennium ran the spectrum from love to hate, with the latter emotion nearly always prevalent in conversations about the Clinton administration. Observed all-night monarch Joey Reynolds, radio personalities like "Rush Limbaugh [have] to make fun of the president or [they don't] have a show."[8]

All-night radio seemed to be reaching its highest point of popularity in the 1990s as the country stayed up later and later and more and more people were available to tune in. Overnights were no longer the dead zone. Researchers noted a marked increase in the amount of postmidnight activity in almost every part of the country.

> Sociologist Murray Melbin has observed that the night hours are filling up with activity as America becomes a 24-hour

> society. He describes night as a kind of frontier—a sparsely populated but rapidly growing area where new settlers seek wealth by exploiting new opportunities. These new opportunities include 24-hour stores, overnight-delivery services, and global bond-trading offices. What are the demographics of the frontier people, and how are they changing? Surveys taken in 1965 and 1985 reveal unexpected changes and similarities in the character of late-night America.[9]

According to *Talkers Magazine*, the following were the most popular topics on talk radio as the decade came to a close:[10]

1. Politics/Legal System
2. Crime & Violence
3. Youth & Education
4. Foreign Affairs
5. Sex, Scandal, & Gossip
6. Personal Relationships
7. Sports & Entertainment
8. Economy
9. Health & Health Care
10. Science & Technology

NOCTURNAL TRANSMISSIONS

While right-wing extremists like Ernst Zundel, Alfred Strom, Pete Peters, and Mark Koernke were exploiting the late-night airwaves to promote their messages of hate and violence, programs designed to get people together were claiming a segment of the late-night audience pie. Wrote Joshua Kadison:

> Beau's All Night Radio Love Line,
> the show for hearts in despair
> If you got somethin' to say to a love that got away,
> Beau wants to put you on the air.[11]

And the Beaus of all-night radio did just that. In February of 1997, Jacor Communications began syndicating *Love Phones*, a late-night radio talk show about sex and relationships. It took over the show from Westwood One Entertainment with thirty affiliates and was hosted by Dr. Judy Kuriansky and Chris Jagger. *Love Phones* began with Kuriansky at New York's WHTZ in the early 1990s and soon went national as its focus on relationships and lifestyles struck a cord with listeners. The somewhat-less-explicit *Love Lines,* hosted by Dr. Drew Pinsky and Adam Carolla, was retained by Westwood One and aired over twenty-seven affiliates.

This unique program genre not only attracted an impressive number of listeners in this country but made its way as far as Asia with a show called *The Late Night Clinic* on Philippine station Monster Radio RX93.1. Hosted by Tom Alvarez, it consisted of love messages and love songs:

> In the first part of the program, Doctor Love, Tom Alvarez, reads out love messages on the pager and plays requested love songs. In the second half, listeners with "love problems"

Figure 9.3. Joey Reynolds is one of all-night radio's most popular performers. Courtesy Joey Reynolds.

> consult fellow listeners on solutions and approaches to their particular situations. Doctor Love does not give any advice. He relays feedback from the listeners and plays a "love cure" in the form of a song that relates to the "lovesick patient's" situation.[12]

Late-night shows featuring sex therapists, fortune-tellers, and alleged clairvoyants carved a niche as well. Listeners sought solutions to their problems and concerns by dialing up the "Psychic Friends Radio Network" and others. These programs were often thinly disguised infomercials for an array of products and services not typically available at the local Wal-Mart.

Also hitting the late-night stage in the 1990s, but with a far more conventional and conservative agenda, was a former president's son, Michael Reagan, whose show was distributed by Premiere Radio. Thinking to benefit from his name and ride the wave of anti-Clinton sentiment, Reagan managed to attract a modest following. That is, modest compared to the soothsayers and sexologists flooding the airwaves.

COMINGS AND GOINGS

The 1990s witnessed both the continued ascendancy of all-night personalities and the departure from the postmidnight shift of others. Larry King abandoned the overnight radio waves in favor of the bright lights of CNN while Chicago's popular late-night liberal Mike Malloy got the boot from WLS for what station management described as his "mean-spiritedness" with callers. Other late-night experts, such as Eddie Schwartz, left the air because they seemed to have either tired of it or outgrown it. Meanwhile, while many of all-night radio's longtime practitioners departed the airwaves, WOR's Joe Franklin celebrated the 50,000th episode of *Joe Franklin's Memory Lane,* which he began in 1949.

The decade also contained the demise of several of overnight radio's finest practitioners, among them Barry Gray, Gene Chase, John Luther, Felix Grant, Alison Steele, Franklin Hobbs, Jean Shepherd, and Norm Nathan. In the case of Shepherd, his legions of fans mourn his passing to this day by paying lavish tributes to him in dozens of chat rooms on the Internet. For many, he was the greatest radio performer ever, not just in overnights, and for an equal number of Shepherd aficionados, the medium is no longer the appealing place it once was to spend a few hours. Marking Shepherd's passing. Don Kaul wrote

> Jean Shepherd died last fall and, I realize now, not enough attention was paid. Shepherd was a genius of radio, a precursor of Garrison Keillor and better than Keillor (who is very good). He was, above all, a storyteller and he would sit in his studio at WOR in New York night after night, enchanting his listeners with tales. He never disappointed.[13]

Jim Parsons expressed similar sentiments for the loss of Franklin Hobbs.

> You couldn't forget the voice. It was as rich as gravy and as soft and soothing as a velvet cloak. . . . Hobbs was a pioneer in all night radio, playing "beautiful ballads and music from the big bands" for a national audience—thanks to WCCO's 50,000 watt signal. . . . Hobbs's on air style was California cool before California invented it. He ad-libbed many of his commercials because he knew the advertisers so well. And he talked about music and musicians in much the same way.[14]

The *Los Angeles Times* had this to say about the passing of Alison Steele:

> Known as the "Nightbird" for her pioneering all night radio show, Steele developed a loyal following as one of the first female disc jockeys in the United States and received numerous accolades, including membership in the Rock 'n' Roll Hall of Fame in Cleveland. Through nearly three decades, she entertained late night listeners with her sultry voice, accompanied by her dog, a French poodle named Genya, as she fielded calls. . . . She broke into big-time radio as one of four women among 800 contestants to secure a spot on the rock station WNEW-FM, where she worked for 14 years. . . . In 1976 she was the first woman to receive *Billboard Magazine*'s FM Personality of the Year Award.[15]

The loss of Boston radio's Norm Nathan was felt deeply by his vast army of late-night fans. In memory of Nathan, media specialist Bill Walsh downloaded his thoughts to the Internet:

> I hate calling people "personalities," but Nathan defies a more precise description. Disc jockey, announcer, newsman,

> talk show host—he quite literally did it all in his 70 years. He will be missed. I know they say that about everyone who dies, but for Nathan it's true. A sometimes silly, self-effacing, always gentle man, he was most recently WBZ radio's weekend all night talk host. In a world where talk show hosts are more apt to deal with hot political issues and call people "swine," Nathan kept his 14 hours a week light, fun, very human. He willingly traded controversy for chatting, name-calling for genuineness, and politics for silliness. His motto was "Leave the world a little sillier than you found it." . . . Our late nights will be a little lonelier without his gentle voice to keep us company. We will miss him as we can only miss one who used to keep us company all through the night.[16]

While many former overnighters exited the shift permanently, those who remained found the 1990s a time abundant with rich subject matter perfectly suited for their needs. One of these individuals was KABC's Ira Fistell, who'd been fanning the all-night flame since the 1970s.

> **Ira Fistell:** There was so much going on. I landed at KABC in 1977 and stayed there until 1992. Then I came back in 1994 for 2 more years until I was dumped in favor of Art Bell. Memories of my time at KABC include being on the air for 7 hours a night during the riots of 1992. Driving to work was surreal with the streets totally empty and buildings burning all around, nary a fireman in sight. Then there's the summer of the O. J. Simpson trial when each night that was all we focused on. Nothing has ever come close to that case in terms of dominating the public's interest so completely for such a long period of time. Saying every night that the evidence didn't add up and that I thought O. J. had been framed by crooked cops paid off by drug dealers did nothing to dampen the interest, but I wasn't saying that cynically. I believe it then and I continue to believe it. The 1990s were a heck of a time to have a microphone in front of you, and all-nights were electric.

Free All-Night Mix

The night was an increasingly picturesque radio daypart as the decade and century came to an end, and often the most heterogeneous and

Table 9.2. A listing of syndicated talk shows carried at night. Courtesy Rollye James.

Syndicated Talk Radio Programs

1. **The following shows were listed as carried at night by at least *one* facility covered by th survey. This information is current as of March 1, 1999.**

2. Programs carried by the station which originates the show are marked with an asterisk (*).

3. **The time listed is the time the show originates in the Eastern Time Zone.** If the show emanates from a different time zone, the local time in the show's home locale is noted under "local tin of program".

4. While this survey is confined to all programs carried in the evening or overnight hours (approxima 7P-6A, local time), as indicated previously **many stations "shift" programming, taping it for latei airing (delay) or repeating it at a later time (replay).** Additionally, some syndicators will refeed program once it has aired, either directly after the first airing or some time later in the same day. Therefore **several of the shows carried at night actually originate during the day.** The list belc is in order of origination time beginning with 7PM and running through 6PM.

Syndicated programs carried at night by surveyed stations

Broad based (general interet) Talk:

Time	Host	Syndicator	local time of program (if not Eastern Time)
7-9P	Joan Rivers	WOR	
7-10P	Bruce Williams	Westwood One	
9-10P	*Dr. Ronald Hoffman	WOR	
9P-Mid.	Nolan at Night	Radio America	
10P-Mid.	*Stephanie Miller	ABC	Pacific 7-9P
10P-Mid.	Loveline - Dr. Drew	Westwood One	Pacific 7-9P
10P-1A	Jim Bohannon	Westwood One	
10P-1A	*Dave Alan	ZBS	Pacific 7-10P
10P-1A	Roger Fredinburg	Talk Radio Network	Pacific 7-10P
10P-1A	Jeff Rense	Orbit 7	Pacific 7-10P
11P-2A	Rhona at Night	Rhona Raskin	Pacific 8-11P
Mid.-5A	Stan Major	Radio America	
Mid.-5A	Mike Siegal	Talk America	
1-5A	Joey Reynolds	WOR	
1-5A	USA@Night	USA Radio/Texas State Network	Central Mid.-4A
1-6A	Art Bell	Premiere	Pacific 10P-3A
4-10A	Doug Stephan	Radio America/Talk Radio News Service	
5-9A	Phil Paleologos	Talk America	
5-10A	Daybreak USA	USA Radio	
6-10A	Howard Stern	Infinity	
9A-Noon	Mike Gallagher	Dame-Gallagher	
9A-1P	Dr. Joy Browne	WOR	
10A-2P	G. Gordon Liddy	Westwood One	
10A-3P	Judy Jarvis	Jarvis	
Noon-3P	Rush Limbaugh	Radio Active Media/Premiere	
Noon-3P	Blanquita Cullum	Radio America	
1-3P	The Dolans	WOR	
2-4P	Clark Howard	Cox	
2-5P	The Money Game	Dave Ramsey	Central 1-4P
2-5P	Dr. Laura	Premiere	
3-4P	Dr. Dean Edell	Premiere	Pacific Noon-1P
3-6P	Dr. Toni Grant	Radio Shows LTD	Central 2-5P
3-6P	Ken Hamblin	Entertainment Radio Net.	Mountain 1-4P
3-6P	Michael Medved	Salem	Pacific Noon-3P
3-7P	Howie Carr	WRKO	
4-7P	Barry Farber	Talk America	
5-7P	Dr. Gabe Mirkin	Burns	
5-9P	Michael Reagan	Premiere	Pacific 2-6P
6-10P	John & Ken	Fisher	Pacific 3-7P
6-10P	Tom Leykis	Westwood One	Pacific 3-7P

curious places to tune were the noncommercial stations located between 88.1 and 91.9 on the FM dial. Reporting on late-night radio in 1998 for *Los Angeles Weekly,* writer Michael Simmons cited what he considered the best programs and places to tune when seeking refuge from commercial radio. His list of favorites included KXLU's *Blues Hotel,* KPFK's *12 O'Clock Rock, The Fringe Element, Something's Happening,* and *Rise,* KPPC's *Rhapsody in Black,* and KXLU's *Stray Pop.* Simmons awarded honorary mention to an illegal micro-station as well. "KBLT is L.A.'s most notorious pirate station," he observed.

> It should be back on the air after a recent scare from the FCC. We've promised not to tell you where it is, but if you find it you'll hear how radio can sound 22 hours a day (the station rests for two hours) without interference from corporate thugs and their federal toadies."[17]

Much to the chagrin of mainstream radio broadcasters (both commercial and noncommercial) and the government, a new category of radio stations emerged during the 1990s. Called "free" or "neighborhood" stations by their operators and disciples, these outlets—more formally referred to as micro or low-power FMs—broadcast without the imprimatur of the FCC. Broadcasting with minute power (often a few watts), micros added further dimension to overnights in the areas reached by their intrepid but frail signals.

At the close of the decade, there seemed to be something for every overnight radio listener, regardless of how eclectic his or her taste might be. Thousands of radio signals penetrated the darkness, providing a vast audio menu of savory treats and exotic delights in addition to the more common fare that existed in far greater abundance.

NOTES

1. *De Jong v State of Oregon,* 299 US 353 (1937).
2. John Eggerton, "Birth of a Notion," *Broadcasting and Cable,* 16 October 2000, p. 7.
3. Chris T., "Talk Radio Assassination," *Lives of the Great Deejays,* www.wfmu.org, 1996.
4. Phil Gailey and Warren Weaver Jr., "Briefing," *New York Times,* 24 July 1982, sec. 1, p. 7.
5. "Joey Reynolds," www.wor710.com/personalities, 30 December 2000.
6. Elizabeth Hayes, "Dick Whittington's Back, With a Somewhat Different Shtick," *Los Angeles Times,* 2 July 1988, pt. 6, p. 10.

7. Ibid.

8. Joey Reynolds, *Let a Smile Be Your Umbrella* (New York: Hatherleigh Press, 2000), p. 135.

9. P. Robinson, " 'Round Midnight," *American Demographics,* June 1993, p. 40.

10. "The Talkers Ten," *Talkers Magazine,* December 1999, p. 40.

11. Joshua Kadison, "Beau's All Night Radio Love Line," *Painted Desert Serenade,* SBK Records, 1993.

12. "The Late Night Clinic," www.rx931.com, 31 January 2001.

13. Don Kaul, "Vulgarity Has Replaced Genius on Radio," *Houston Chronicle,* 26 May 2000, p. A38.

14. Jim Parsons, "Voice of All Night Radio Legend Falls Still," *Star Tribune,* 10 October 1995, p. 1A.

15. "Alison Steele, Nighttime N.Y. Disc Jockey," *Los Angeles Times,* 7 October 1995, p. A24.

16. Bill Walsh, "One Less Voice in the Night," www.interact.uoregon.edu/medialit, 27 January 2001.

17. Michael Simmons, "Best of LA 1998," *Los Angeles Weekly,* December 1999.

(An essay written by Ed Weigle on overnight radio can be found in the appendices.)

Chapter 10

Stars of the Night

Hail, thou art highly favoured.

—**St. Luke**

Anyone who has ever tuned radio after midnight for any length of time has his or her favorite all-night host or deejay. There is something exceptionally and uniquely personal and intimate about the experience of listening to radio in the depths of night when the majority of the world is fast asleep. A special relationship is forged and a bond develops with the guy or gal out there in radioland who is working the graveyard ether to help get the listener through the night.

In the preface, it was stated that this book makes no claim to coming close to acknowledging or recognizing all of the overnight radio personalities who have plied their special skills and talents to keep the signals flowing to the millions of listeners whose conscious hours are the opposite of the so-called normal or predominant population. Reason suggests this would probably be impossible in a single volume—that is, one that could be lifted within reading distance.

In what follows, radio fans and industry figures discuss who were their favorite overnighters and why. Wrote journalist Nell Nolan on the occasion of the Greater New Orleans Broadcasters Association's tribute to the city's foremost radio personalities—among them overnight talk-show host Larry Regan—"Huzzahs all filled the air when those who command those waves were hailed."[1]

Let the huzzahs begin!

Charles Willer: Jean Shepherd was *the* all-night radio genius, and I miss him a lot. Phil Knight was a favorite of mine, but it's hard to forget the brilliance of Shepherd. Then there's Joey Reynolds. He used to do more "theater of the mind" stuff, but he has slowly evolved his all-night show into a radio party with lots of in-studio and phone guests. For example, the inventor of multitrack recording and guitar guru Les Paul often appear on the show and engage in a three-way conversation with Joey and callers. It makes for wonderful radio.

Rollye James: Perhaps the best of all was Jean Shepherd. Emanating from New York on WOR, he was able to weave a monologue about anything (or often nothing) that could leave you spellbound. He knew how to tell a story, and he told it firsthand. Listeners were not only enthralled, they connected one-on-one with him.

Alan Colmes: The other two kings of overnights have to be Barry Gray and Long John Nebel. I grew up listening to Gray, who practically invented talk radio and took calls even before there was the technology to put them on the air. To get around this, he'd repeat what callers said to create the illusion of it being a two-way conversation. Barry was also the first talk-radio personality to have a strong point of view, politically, although he also loved talking about show business and popular culture. Long John Nebel was another all-night great. He introduced topics that would be picked up several decades later on overnights. Both of these guys were originals.

Larry Miller: I never really listened to all-night radio that much, but when I did, I didn't hear anybody better the Jean Shepherd and Norm Nathan. Nathan used to do a show that

Figure 10.1. Alan Colmes pulls double duty on TV's Fox News and WEVD overnight radio. Courtesy *Talkers Magazine.*

was sort of a "Night Flight" thing, taking you here and there. It was really the place to be if you were up at that time of night. He had a genuine warmth, too, that made it all the more attractive.

Steve LeVeille: Norm Nathan was the first overnight broadcaster I ever listened to and is certainly the biggest influence on my broadcasting style. I was very young when I first heard him, but I was hooked immmediately. . . . Norm did *Sounds in the Night* from the late 1950s into the mid-1960s. It was a music show. In 1979 or 1980 he returned to WHDH to do an all-night talk show for a couple of years. I was a guest on the show once. A few years later he became the weekend overnight talk host on WBZ. The thing I remember most about that show is listening in bed with an earphone and trying to contain my laughter so I wouldn't wake up my wife. Norm's show was so funny that you really had to laugh out loud a lot.

Van Harden: My particular favorite was Herb Jepko. His *Nitecaps* show was the best overnight radio around. It was originally out of KSL and then networked for a while. He had a mature audience age-wise and that didn't excite the network brass, but he was an excellent radio guy. I used to like another guy named Mike Hoyer, who did *Country Music USA* on WHO Radio. I grew up listening to him as well.

Gary Berkowitz: Jepko brought something great to all-nights. Larry Glick at WBZ and Charlie Greer at WABC are right up there with him.

Rollye James: When you try to evaluate or create a "best" category for all-night personalities, the criteria are not necessarily what you'd imagine. They don't have to be the quickest, wittiest, or brightest. They don't even have to be the most entertaining. What they have to do is be able to relate one on one, to bond with audience members individually by becoming a friend to them on the air. They have to be able to reveal enough of themselves to be real and, of course, they have to be likable. Herb Jepko is perhaps the best example of this. His *Nitecaps* show was the butt of jokes from programming and daytime listeners, but to his graying listeners, he was a gift.

Larry King: Jepko was good, as was Ray Briem, and Art Bell is attracting a lot of people out there. To these people, he's a very important person. Of course, my real heroes were Red Barber and Arthur Godfrey, who did early mornings on WJSV in D.C. in the 1930s. I wound up working with both of them.

Elizabeth Salazar: The first person who comes to my mind when I think about top overnighters is Ray Briem, who for decades hosted an all-night talk show on KABC in L.A. He helped develop the talk-radio format starting in the 1960s. Briem was a true pioneer. Back then hardly any station in

L.A. had a talk show, much less a talk show in the middle of the night. Longevity at any radio station is rare. Consequently any person who lasts a couple of years is considered an old-timer. That said, it's interesting to note that over the years, many of those who managed to keep their jobs through one management change after another, lasting year after year, tended most often to be all-night jocks. One such person who achieved that feat, which included at least several program directors, various incarnations of the Top 40 format, a complete format change, and eventually two new owners, all over a span of 20 years while doing overnights at KFRC in San Francisco, is Don Ste. Johnn. Talent, I'm sure, played a factor, but I'm personally aware of his work ethic and dedication, too, and it played a big part in his lasting for so long at one station. For being able to keep his job in such a volatile industry and enduring all the above at KFRC, I tip my hat to Don Ste. Johnn. He accomplished the impossible.

Eric Rhoads: There have been many great ones. It's a rich tradition, actually. I'm thinking about Barry Gray, Steve Allison, Sherm Feller, Mort Sahl, Mike Wallace and his wife Buff Cobb. Then there was Hank the Night Watchman on KFVD and Kurt Webster—"The Midnight Mayor"—on WBT in Charlotte. As I think I've commented elsewhere, Phil Knight was especially talented. He made a club out of the all-nighters. He was looser than the other personalities on the station, who had to adhere more closely to the station's format. Phil was very interactive and had developed regular callers and a special all-night vibe. What he created was very listenable and very fitting for the wee hours.

Phil Knight: I grew up in the Detroit area in the 1960s. The biggest influences on me were people like Lee Alan, J. P. McCarthy, and Dick Purtin. The stations I remember best are WXYZ, WJBK, CKLW, and WKMH. Later I "advanced" to FM. WABX, a wonderful station, comes to mind. Oh, and when I did stay up for the late show, I really got into Jim Rockwell. *Rockwell and Records* was a jazz program that even a nonjazz person could appreciate. Rockwell was just that good.

Steve Warren: When I was a kid in high school in the early 1960s, there were two rival Top 40 AM radio stations in Louisville, Kentucky—WKLO and WAKY. The latter had one of the first automation systems playing all-night music with a robot-like synthesized voice named Sam Seeburg (i.e., Seeburg jukeboxes). This was not my favorite, but it was unique. At the same time, across town at WKLO, the all-night personality was a very, very funny guy named Pat Murphy, who really liked being on all night. He was very off-the-wall and tongue-in-cheek, and had a style that—for want of a better comparison—was where Dick Clark meets Art Bell. Pat is the brother of legendary Kansas City radio personality Mike Murphy. I eventually went to work at WKLO and met Pat, who had a disability of one arm, so he did his show mostly single-handedly . . . literally. Later, back at WAKY, they went live with personality Gene Snyder, who was also very funny and involved his listeners by forming the all-night "Snydering" club. Both all-night shows were fun and far more interesting than the rest of the lineup of deejay sound Top 40 jocks.

Bruce Morrow: For my money, the best all-night personalities include Charlie Greer and Alison Steele—"The Nightbird." They were exceptional. Today, I think Joey Reynolds is darn good.

Marlin Taylor: When I think back on all the overnight personalities, a guy named Eddie Newman comes to mind. I really got a kick out of him. He was very good, but he started in New York and worked his way down.

Bill Conway: All-night radio was such a beacon to me as a kid growing up in Dallas, so it isn't surprising that a couple of people stand out in my mind as first-rate entertainers. Ron Chapman (AKA Irving Harrigan) was doing *Milkman's Matinee* on KLIF in the early 1950s before he went on to Charlie & Harrington fame on the same station and then on to TV as Ron Chapman. After that he went to KVIL. One of my all-time favorites was Don Norman, "Big Don from Big D," on WFAA radio. He had a beautiful voice and a very dry, straight delivery, always playing it seriously. He also did some character work for WFAA-TV. His nightly "Roman

Figure 10.2. Jim Bohannon entertains overnight listeners around the country via Westwood One. Courtesy Jim Bohannon.

Bingo" bit still plays in my head. It went something like this, "Greetings, oh vast unseen radio audience. It's time for 'Roman Bingo' here on the 'Big Don Radio Show.' Get your 'Roman Bingo' cards out. To win you must have a straight line vertically, horizontally, diagonally, or all four corners. And remember, the center space is absolutely free! Okay, here's tonight's 'Roman Bingo' number. Under the B, it is 'Vee-Eye-Eye.' Repeating that now, under the B, it is 'Vee-Eye-Eye.' Now, I will cup my hand ever so close to my ear, and if you have a 'Roman Bingo,' go to an open window and yell at the top of your lungs, 'Roman Bingo!!' I don't hear anything yet, but we'll give it a few more seconds. Okay, I guess we had no winner tonight, but keep your 'Roman Bingo' cards handy, and tune in tomorrow for another chance to do this all over again." Unfortunately, one of my big breaks came when I was a part-timer at WFAA while a full-time student. Big Don's son was killed in a motorcycle accident, and I was called in to do the shift. Don never went back to humor and transferred to the news department. I got the slot, but I was no "Big Don from Big D."

Art Bell: It's hard for me to point to someone who was a specific influence. There are some good people around today. I think Phil Henry is on the cutting edge. I'd say Kim Commando is there, too. She does a web radio show, and she's absolutely brilliant. These are a couple of people doing something completely different and creative. Of course, Larry King is a significant chapter in the history of all-night radio. After he left, a malaise set in, and there was not very much happening until I came along.

Don Barrett: When Larry King was doing overnights, there was no one better. His show was fresh, alive, and eclectic.

Jim Taszarek: Larry sure drew the listeners. I was general manager at KTAR in Phoenix in the late 1980s, and we ran him starting at 11 P.M. throughout the night. Big, big ratings and great overnight radio.

Sheldon Swartz: I'd have to say that for my generation, Larry King had no equal. He was heads above the rest.

Steve LeVeille: Larry King's show was another favorite of mine. He had great guests and would take the time to interview them before going to the calls. He also would tell stories from time to time, and this is a perfect use of the medium, one that most people have forgotten. King is an excellent storyteller.

Ray Briem: I don't listen to all-night radio anymore. However, when Larry King was on Mutual, I would listen when I was able. He was my direct competition, so I seldom tuned in, but he did a good show. I have to give him that.

Rollye James: Many folks saw Larry King as tremendously successful, and in terms of station clearance, that was so. However, few realize that his primary value to Mutual was that of a lure. In order to get the program, a station had to carry daytime inventory. That was mandatory. Strangely, while his station roster was impressive, I don't put him in the "greats" category. He did not create that important bond with the audience that others did. For a number of stations carrying him in the 1980s, it was not for his excellent programming as much as it was for the fact that he was free.

Ira Fistell: I think my first impression of night talk came from listening to Jack Eigen's *Chez Show.* I was a kid and had to get up for school, so I never stayed up too late, but his was the last voice I heard every night for years. He broadcast from the Chez Paree nightclub in Chicago and interviewed both the show business personalities who worked at the club and the guests who came to see them. Later, as a graduate student at the University of Wisconsin in Madison, I discovered Larry Glick, the overnight host on WBZ in Boston, which I could get easily every night. Glick was a personality. What he said and who he talked to were less important than how he said it. His own delightfully offbeat character was the attraction more than his callers or anything else. His listeners were called Glickniks, and the phrase was particularly apt. You listened to Larry because you wanted to hear Glick be Glick. He rarely, if ever, disappointed.

Steve LeVeille: Larry Glick was one of the first overnight talk-show hosts I heard. I picked him up during the first week or two that he was on WBZ. He was filling in for Bill Garcia, a disc jockey who was on vacation, but Larry was doing a call-in show. I had actually tuned in to hear Garcia, who I had never heard before. Years later, Larry informed me that Garcia had been fired and that he'd actually already been hired to replace him. I still consider Larry Glick the best talk-show host of all time. Glick's show had the key element that makes a radio show great—you never knew what was going to happen next. So you had to tune in every night, and you couldn't turn it off.

Sheldon Swartz: Joey Reynolds is the Larry Glick of today.

Doug Steckler: Yes, and Ira Fistell is *the* Ira Fistell of overnight radio. He's been doing great nights for decades, and he's smarter than his listeners and his board ops. He's right up there with the all-time best.

Greg Hardison: Art Bell certainly has a sort of magic for this daypart. Most overnight programming, though, is simply daytime regurgitated. I know my own efforts to do overnight talk at KFI have been consistently met with budget constraints. That lack of current viable overnight hosts is an ugly reflection of the general sense of crisis-management holding radio down—boot on the neck—these days. Ironically, one of the most effective hosts was Ira Fistell during his ABC Talkradio days. The show was formed as a New York-oriented forum to simply blow off steam and a venue for people to be heard nationwide, and it worked. The majority of our callers were WABC listeners—articulate and opinionated. The fact that the callers bounced their reactions off each other, one-at-a-time as Fistell moderated, made up for his general lack of on-air talent. Ira could carry a conversation, even though he was most certainly the first national host to regularly expectorate on the air.

Marlin Taylor: I'm not sure anyone out there is more interesting than Art Bell. I get up very early just to catch the last part of the show until he signs off. Of course, listening to his shows, you get the sense that the ultimate "sign-off" is coming.

Rollye James: Art Bell's success was not his interest in the paranormal, which developed rather late in his overnight career on KDWN in Las Vegas. Like Herb Jepko, it was his ability to bond with the audience. Any doubt as to that could have been witnessed with the dwindling success of the guy (Mike Siegel) who replaced Bell during his last leave. Art is another example of how overnight radio is poorly sold. When he first went national, it was on a small network that understood what it took to market direct-response late nighttime. By the time it was on a few hundred stations and attractive to a major network (Premiere), Art was concerned that he might lose programming control. What he should have focused on was sales control. When the show was given to Premiere by their parent company (Jacor), Premiere execs figured stations would be willing to give up a minute or two during the day to get the show (the "lure" concept again). That backfired. Most stations by then were not willing to part with daytime inventory in return for a night show. This was problematic as Premiere's entire sales effort relied on CPM (cost per thousand) agency buys. Not only was direct response at night exponentially less profitable, but it required a different sales staff to market since the advertiser-based was completely separate. Suddenly what was very attractive to a small-time operator became an albatross to a major player.

Kirk Harvey: There have been many great late-night practitioners, and I have my favorites, among them Bill Mack, Charlie Douglas, Ralph Emery, John Landecker, and Doctor Don Rose. These guys were real communicators and each possessed his own distinct style. All of them related to the listener and generated a special feeling and atmosphere.

Sam Sauls: Bill Mack has had a tremendous impact on overnight radio, so he gets my vote as the greatest.

Ray Charron: Bill Mack from WBAP in Dallas and Charlie Douglas on WWL in New Orleans have always been among the best in my estimation.

Lynn Christian: I always think of Dave Wiken, John Doremus, and Barry Farber when I consider the people on all-nights who did an excellent job.

Eric Rhoads: Did I forget to mention Charlie Douglas and Yvonne Daniels in my earlier statement? They were wonderful and brought something very special to all-nights.

Phylis Johnson: There was this woman on all-nights called Mona who aired classical music. She was first rate. I also like KBGA's Melissa Mason, known as "Moon Cat." KBGA is a college station, incidentally. Of course, I'd list Tom Snyder, David Brudnoy, and Wolfman Jack as among the best.

Robert Feder: Chicago's great Eddie Schwartz belongs on any list of all-night greats.

Mike Lawing: Barry Farber, Herb Jepko, Larry King. They're all there.

Larry Miller: Melvin Lindsey did this great show in the 1970s called the *Quiet Storm.* He was a real talented late-night radio person. Then there was Charles Oatson Matthews Jr., whose *Night Flight* in Detroit was a wonderful geography lesson for listeners.

Sheena Metal: No question about it. Wolfman Jack was the greatest. He had the voice, the tunes, the persona, and the auditory ambiance. He was a true creature of the night, and he made radio fun. I'm sure by the time I caught up with him, he wasn't even broadcasting live at night any more. Still his show had all the sounds of the night. He made music cool and radio even cooler. He was a presence, a personality, a character, and he seemed to be having a good time. So when you listened to him, you had a good time too.

Anne Gress: I have a great on-air talent named Frank Childs, and I liken him to Donald Fagen's song "The Nightfly." Frank is a guy who's been around the block more than once. By nature of the time of day we're talking about, you have a pretty unusual bunch of characters you're broadcasting to. I think the audience listens closer at that hour, and Frank is the person for close-up listening.

David Brudnoy: WBZ's Steve LeVeille is my favorite after-midnight radio personality. He does a fantastic job.

Paul Heyer: Back in the 1960s when I was in high school in Montreal, I used to listen to magician James Randi, who is now a famous debunker of psychics. I'd tune him on New York's WNEW. It was terrific. He had great guests and topics.

Frank Childs: I grew up listening to Southern California radio, and I was a fan of all the late-night rock jocks, like Jim Ladd, David Perry, Bob Colburn, Mary Turner. While I listened during the day, the nighttime was the most important radio for me.

Allen Ogrizovich: I used to listen to a guy on WLS by the name of Don Phillips. I really enjoyed him, and he stands out in my mind from the 1960s and 1970s.

Sheldon Swartz: There are so many outstanding examples of great all-night radio performers, but the real stars are those working at local stations, chatting with their neighbors, their voices limited by the power-reduced signals of the stations carrying them. The heroes are the ones who work for peanuts, modulating the radio waves through the night skies as they skip off the ionosphere to parts unknown and to ears still conscious.

NOTES

1. *Times-Picayune* (New Orleans), 27 April 1999, p. 47.

Chapter 11

Nights Today and Tomorrow

I couldn't have survived four hours of do-nothing boredom every other night without my old friend, Mr. Radio.

—Bob "Dex" Armstrong

They played our song on the radio, 1:30 A.M.
My feet, already frozen by the night chill, shook with anticipation
And my mind awakened to uneasy thoughts of months ago.

—Michael Van Kleeck

Today, all-night radio is alive and doing as well as might be expected. Certainly the conversion to a 24/7 society has enhanced the appeal and value of overnights, but the continued downsizing of local broadcasting due to industry consolidation resulting from the Telecommunications Act of 1996 and the growth of national syndication services has had a greater impact on this radio daypart than on others. Yet, paradoxically, there seems to be more programming variety and diversity to be found between midnight and sunrise than, perhaps, at any other time in the history of this radio genre.

Donna Halper: Society is much different in our Internet-connected world and more people are working longer hours, so finding people at a supermarket at 3 in the morning is no longer so unusual. Clearly this means a larger potential audience for all-night radio programs.

John B. Hanson: All-night radio is extremely valuable in an increasingly 24-hour society. For millions of people, overnight is what midday is to others. With as much activity taking place at night, it is important to maintain communication between the listener and the station. To fail to serve the audience would have negative consequences to the station—mainly loss of audience.

Jim Bohannon: Ours is a 24/7 society now, so people are up and about more than ever before. Retail outlets aren't open all night because they like to lose money. There's a solid market round the clock for all kinds of goods and services—radio included.

TALKING THE NIGHT AWAY

The subject matter of all-night talk radio has continued to reflect the times. Although, observes Mark Jurkowitz, "Politics and weighty issues are passé. Sex, lifestyle, and sports are in."[1] The decline in issues-oriented talk may stem from a combination of sheer exhaustion with anything political and the departure of talk-radio's favorite subject and object of scorn, President Clinton. This sentiment was reflected in a recent headline in the *New York Times:* "Radio Hosts Say Bush and Gore Pale Next to Clinton as a Talk Show Topic." Lamented KLBJ's talk-show hosts, Mark and Ed, "It won't have quite the sizzle of the Lewinsky scandal."[2]

Yet, while music programming attracts a sizable segment of the overnight audience, individual talk shows continue to command the largest listenerships.

Jim Bohannon: Night talk shows will always enjoy a public. Night people, in particular, need a chance to communicate with others, and this won't change, thus insuring the future existence of this kind of radio service.

In every part of the country, radio stations keep the talk going late into the night. Foremost among them:

In the east
WABC, WHAT, WJFK, WNEW, WOR, WPHT, WRKO, WWDB, WXXI, CJAD, KDKA, WBAL, WTOP, WCBM, WNEW*, WEVD, WLIB, WMAL, WSYR, WTOP*

In the south
KAQK, KJFK, WGST, WSB, WTAR, KTSA, KTSM, WACV, WBAP, WERC, WFLA, WGAC, WGST, WINZ, WIOD, WKHM, WLAC, WMC, WNIS, WGST*, WNWS*, WTMA, WVMI, KRMG

In the midwest
KMOX, KSTP, WIBC, WISN, WJR, WKMI, WLS, WOMP, WXYT, WHIO, WHO, WJIM, WKZO, WTAM, WTDY

In the west
KABC, KEWS, KFI, KHOW, KIRO, KLSX*, KOGO, KSFO, KVI, KGA, KGO, KIDO, KOA, KSCO, KSDO, KTAR

(Asterisks indicate FM outlets employing talk and information programming.)

Long a mainstay of AM radio stations, talk began to slowly appear on the FM dial around the country in the 1990s. This was a development that did not exactly inspire warm feelings among

Table 11.1. All Jewish, all night on WPAT in New York. Courtesy WPAT.

WPAT 930 AM Metro NY	
****** *ALL JEWISH ALL THURSDAY NIGHT* ******	
10:00 - 10:30 PM	INNER MEANING WITH KIM CHEROVSKY Interviews on Judaism and spirituality with special guest Rabbi Jacob Jungreis.
10:30 - 11:00 PM	THE TOP TEN JEWISH MUSIC COUNTDOWN FAVORITE Jewish music of the week.
11:00 - 12:00 AM	TALKLINE WITH ZEV BRENNER. *AMERICA'S LEADING JEWISH PROGRAM. LIVE CALL IN WITH NEWSMAKER GUESTS AND CELEBRITIES MAKING HEADLINES IN THE JEWISH WORLD.*
12:00 - 12:30 AM	BETWEEN THE LINES: THE TORAH CODES. With Dr. Robert Wolf and Joel Gallis.
12:30 - 2:00 AM	THE VOICE OF JERUSALEM WITH AVI. THE LATEST NEWS, SHMOOZ, AND CONTESTS LIVE FROM ISRAEL.
2:00 - 3:00 AM	THE TED SMITH SHOW. Interview show on health and social issues.
3:00 - 4:30 AM	THE TOP TEN JEWISH MUSIC COUNTDOWN.
4:30 - 5:00 AM	LIVE FROM ISRAEL. The latest up to date news from Israel with Dov Shurin.

many AM operators, who have relied on nonmusic programming to keep them viable since the takeover of the listening audience by FM in the 1980s.

Among the handful of syndicated chat programmers of all-night radio, Talk America Radio Networks is a mainstay. It provides two schedules to client stations. Its Talk 1 schedule features *Rhona at Night, DreamWeaver, Joe Mazza Show,* and *Good Day USA.* Stations opting for Talk America's second schedule receive *Ring Talk, The Rollye James Show, Uri Geller, The Next Dimension, For the People Replay,* and *Edge of Reality.*

Postmidnight talk may have shifted its emphasis from hard-core political discourse, but it has retained its homespun relevance through the efforts of hosts such as WGN's Steve & Johnnie and WBZ's Jordan Rich. On one recent show, WGN's husband and wife team devoted part of a program to a discussion of their hobby—Beanie Babies.

> The broadcasting duo's Beanie Baby collection began two years ago, when King's brother, Lee, gave them Legs the Frog and Pinky the Flamingo, Steve and Johnnie decided to have a Beanie Baby collector as a guest on their show and the listeners' interest grew from there.[3]

At WBZ in Boston, Jordan Rich discovered his audience's passion for furry, four-legged creatures dubbed "man's best friend."

> After Rich read aloud the story of a man who tossed a bichon frise into oncoming West Coast traffic, the night owls began creeping into the airwaves. . . . "The Jordan Rich Show" is not for the emphatic talk radio listener. If you're looking for long-winded debates on campaign spending, weapons research, or preserving the right of a fetus, you won't find it here. This program is not about right or wrong. It's about listening, not judging, and having a little fun. . . . For the rest of the night, Rich discussed the art of office golf with a writer from The New Yorker, and his lack of interest in the critically acclaimed movie, "American Beauty." He would promote a radio weather gadget and briefly talk about flamenco dancing. It was like Seinfeld on the radio. A little bit of something and nothing wrapped into one. Yet the call box continued to flutter. At least until 5 A.M.[4]

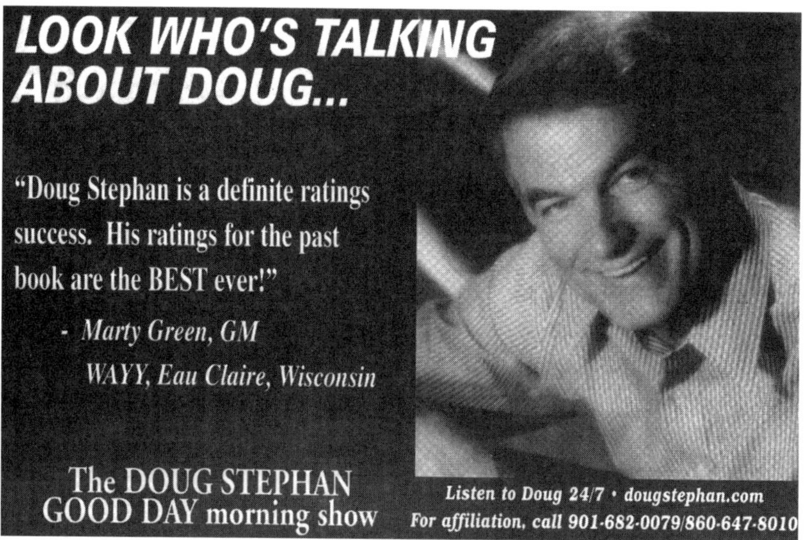

Figure 11.1. Doug Stephan is one of the country's most popular early morning talkers. Courtesy *Talkers Magazine.*

To keep his early morning talk show fresh, Doug Stephan takes it on the road, broadcasting from a broad range of locales around the world, including local diners in industrial centers.

Jason Insalaco: Doug goes the extra mile, literally, and it makes for really entertaining and interesting listening. After Art Bell, Doug's show is tuned by more overnight/early morning listeners than any other. He's on over 300 stations and does a 6-hour live show six times a week. Even if you don't care for his show, you have to give him credit for his enormous effort to bring something fresh and rewarding to his audience.

Meanwhile, the commercial viability of overnight talk, both on the local and national level, continues to be an issue for stations in the new millennium. This, claims Rollye James, has to do with the way the daypart has always been marketed.

Rollye James: In the mid-1990s, Premiere Radio Networks acquired a growing nighttime entity—*The Michael Reagan*

> *Show.* The program itself was not spectacular; however, it was offered at night and a number of stations were able to air it live (including some in major markets, such as Detroit, Seattle, and San Diego) with little, if any, commercial hassle. One of the first things Premiere did was to move the show to afternoon drive. Rapidly, Reagan lost virtually all of his live clearances. Stations that had run him live in the evening were now running him tape-delayed overnight—if they ran him at all. By all recollections, not one viable facility in a major market moved him live to afternoons. But here's the kicker—Premiere now makes more money on a cost per thousand basis than it would have by cultivating a nighttime success. This is not an isolated example. Virtually every national nighttime radio talk show has been marketed that way. Bruce Williams, with two decades on NBC's Talknet, learned firsthand how valuable daytime clearance of commercials was to his success when his night program was pulled from a Washington, D.C., station, which covered the market with 5,000 watts at night, and put on a suburban outlet in Maryland with nighttime coverage of 27 watts that barely reach the District. The 5,000-watt station refused to carry *NBC News* during the day, and the 27-watt facility (with considerably more power during the daylight hours) agreed to do so, if they could get Bruce's show. Again, it was not about who aired the newscast but all about who ran the commercials in them. Bruce had a highly rated program, but because it was on at night, the network largely ignored any sales opportunity within it and concentrated on using it as a lure. Other than Herb Jepko, when he marketed *Nightcaps* himself, only one show has ever succeeded financially as a wholly contained nighttime offering, and that was (and is) Art Bell's.

NIGHT MIX

As stated earlier, the variety of all-night offerings is impressive as the radio medium enters the second century of its existence. Many would argue that all-night radio has been and remains the most vital part of the broadcast day, and a survey of overnight programming tends to bear this out. As the new century arrived, all-night listeners in the west could enjoy KFAI's unusual blend of the features during its "Radio Theater Millennium Marathon." These included:

> *The Firesign Theater at 2* A.M.—The 4 or 5 Crazy Guys' first group recording since 1978, released October 1998.
>
> *The Insider's Lounge at 3* P.M.—Welcome to a kind of "country and western" *Twilight Zone,* a strange, yet eerily familiar parallel universe, where lonely people who don't fit in may, for the very first time, find themselves, and a home . . . if they're lucky.
>
> *Short Stories at 4 a.m.*—In this hour we bring you two short stories—"The Last Dragon to Avondale" and "Time for Bill Lizard"—of the kind that make up so much of the history of radio theater.
>
> *"Roller Madness from Outer Space" at 5* A.M.—TV characters traveling from one channel to another? Unheard of? But here we have it . . . a rare recording and bizarre story from 1974.[5]

For west coast all-night listeners with more conventional tastes, there were hundreds of other signals to tune, such as KMEL in San Francisco that aired hip-hop music and Los Angeles's KLAC that offered big band and swing standards. Meanwhile, across town, KABC's Doug McIntyre continued to engage the overnight talk-radio crowd, while sports fans could tune a station in LaQuinta, California, for *ESPN Radio All Night,*

> If you are a night person, AllNight with Todd Wright is the show for you. From 2 A.M. to 6 A.M., you'll get plenty of sports news, analysis, interviews, and listener calls. You name it, it's here![6]

On the east coast, *Early Morning with Mark Weaver* kept all-nighters tuned to WMAL in Baltimore, and in every major city up and down the coast stations boasted about superstars in their night-time air. This was likewise the case in the south, where Ed Tyril talked to people throughout the night at Miami's WINZ. On the western edge of Dixie, WWOZ in New Orleans provided listeners a reason to stay up late because *The Night Train* with Dave Hersh, *'Round Midnight,* with Kalamu ya Salaam, *Blues & Roots* with John

Sinclair, *Soul Power* with Soul Sister, *Blues Cruise* with Midnight Creeper, and *Overnight Jazz* with Dan Fitzgerald shared the on-air spotlight during the week.

In the midwest, Cincinnati's WLW maintained its overnight tradition of excellent programming by providing a holistic package to listeners. Notes broadcast scholar Lawrence Lichty,

> The programming at WLW is now what is generally described as "full service," being a combination of news, talk and sports with well known local personalities. This is a format usually found only on a few stations similar to WLW in the largest markets with very big revenues. Most are also 50 kW outlets. . . . Evenings are generally call-in talk, including sports.[7]

A few hundred miles west, St. Louis's KMOX drew weekend all-night audiences with *The Grayson Files,* a program hosted by Jon Grayson, featuring wit and reflection on topics ranging from politics to science.

Today country music remains extremely popular at stations with all-night programming. Premiere Radio syndicates one of the most popular all-night programs featuring this type of music. Called *After Midnite* and hosted by Blair Garner, it is one of the most widely distributed all-night shows, with affiliates numbered in the hundreds.

> **Ed Shane:** Blair started the show himself and created a network for it, calling it "After Midnite Entertainment." It began in 1993 and was picked up by Premiere before they went on a buying spree that snared Rush Limbaugh, Dr. Laura, and Art Bell. Blair works from L.A. and interviews country artists [Faith Hill, Dwight Yoakam, Clint Black, Dixie Chicks] who are in town for concerts. The show has become so influential that artists go there just for the interview. The music mix on the show tends toward new releases, so new artists try to get as much time on the show as they can. The show filled a real niche as consolidation began to trim budgets. Stations would pick up *After Midnite* to save an overnight salary. Now the show claims 275 affiliates.

Although many stations rebroadcast programs from other dayparts, such as Bruce Williams, during their overnight hours, the period has mostly been filled with material designed for it. This has kept postmidnight radio viable in light of the growing competition from other 24/7 media.

Public and Foreign Nights

For those who fancy radio sans commercial interruptions, the public sector of the medium offers a broad array of all-night listening options. National Public Radio's *World Radio Network* is intended to serve as a lead-in to the extremely popular *Morning Edition* and *Weekend Edition* shows. *World Radio Network* airs from midnight to 5 A.M. weekdays and remains on slightly later weekends.

> Each night of the week, public radio listeners from Juneau to Abilene to Annapolis are guided through the overnight hours with English language news of the day from two dozen of the world's finest public broadcasters, including live top-of-the-hour newscasts and breaking news coverage from the NPR newsroom. For the first time, NPR listeners have a place to turn for a comprehensive and decidedly non-US perspective on the news, with reports from dozens of newsrooms—Tokyo, Johannesburg, St. Petersburg, Sydney, Jerusalem—WRN is often the first source for stories that eventually make headlines in the States.[8]

Public Radio International gives listeners an option to the round-the-clock news of NPR with a program called *Jazz After Hours,* hosted by Jim Wilke, whose "easy-going presentation has won the praise of such jazz stars as Dizzy Gillespie, Ray Brown, Max Roach, Joe Henderson, Milt Jackson, Joshua Redman, Billy Taylor, Larry Coryell and others who have been guests on [the show]."[9]

> "Jazz After Hours" ranges from classics to the latest releases for late night listeners across the U.S. The program is broadcast Friday and Saturday nights for seven hours each night starting at 12 midnight Eastern Time. It can be heard on more than 70 public radio stations in the U.S. and Canada.[10]

For listeners looking for something a bit more exotic on the noncommercial end of the FM band, college, community, and microstations around the country are prepared to serve. For example, there's *Boogie Chillun* hosted by the Iceman on KVXR in Austin, Texas. The program features the best in blues music, replete with crisp and insightful commentary on the artists. Other listeners in Texas, as well as throughout the country, can get their fix of religion by tuning *Praise in the Night* ("Come and visit us often as we begin to tell what God is doing through his [radio] ministry."[11]) heard over KVTT in Dallas and distributed countrywide by the International Broadcasting Network.

In the northwest, blues listeners can tune in *Night Shift FM,* with hosts David Samson and Jonathan Richards, on KBCS in Seattle. Then there's the *Madness Network* broadcast over WNUR that promises listeners something completely different. Claims the show's website, "Listeners won't find a better mix of comedy/dementia/novelty music."[12] Similar eclecticism can be found on the east coast, where Albany-area listeners can tune *The All Night Crew* on WRPI at midnight on Saturdays, and in Ann Arbor, Michigan, where *Radio Ping-Pong* airs a diverse blend of melodies for the more discriminating listener.

Outside of the United States, all-night listeners have plenty of choices as well. For instance, insomniacs and third-shift workers in Ireland can tune FM3 for all kinds of music ranging from jazz to show tunes, and the availability of overnight-radio programming has been on the rise in England and elsewhere overseas since the late 1990s. Writing in the *Observer,* Tom Hibbert noted:

> The recent proliferation of all night radio stations has been a boon to persons suffering from the unable-to-slumber scenario. Good book? Mug of cocoa? Pah. Here is my recipe for your sleepless night. Start off on the World Service. John Tidmarsh is talking about fireflies in Angola. This is the stuff! Except that then "Tidmarsh's Outlook" ends and some ghastly jazz programme comes on so you turn yer knob to Radio Five Live, upon which there's a raging debate about the future of rugby league, and so you turn your dial a bit more to Talk Radio, upon which Mike Dicker is trying to be "controversial" by saying that women drivers are useless. So it's down the dial again to LBC (heard only in the London region, unfortunately) for Clive Bull. This man is a genius. There you are trying to fall asleep, having tuned in to "obviously boring," when Bull comes on saying, "And tonight's topics are 'What happens when you are cremated?' and 'Which members of Crossroads are dead?' " Bull has a certain dry wit that keeps one from going mad in the wee hours.[13]

In Canada, late-night radio has been scheduled by CBC for years. The corporation has "been beguiled by late-night or all-night radio for about 30 years,"[14] inspiring it to experiment with many different formats and programs variously called *Nightlines, RealTime,* and *Wired for Sound.* The latter was launched in 1997 with host Dave Bidini, who brought his own unique musical tastes to the program. Meanwhile CBC's Radio Two has offered a late-night classical-music program called *That Time of the Night,* which it claims is endorsed by "Insomniacs, night owls, shift workers, nursing mothers, long distance truck drivers, the sophisticated music lover, cabbies, the aesthete, bakers, artists and artisans, the casual listener, and the late night solitary jogger."[15]

From the Philippines to Russia, all-night radio programs are enjoying expanded audiences as they provide everything from local to global music programs and news and talk shows. The 24/7 society has spread far beyond the boundaries of the Western Hemisphere. China is a good example. Over the past decade, all-night radio has taken root in the most densely populated nation on earth.

> Late night shows with names such as "With You Till Dawn," "Night Date," and "The Night Is Not Lonely" have sprung up across China, giving people a chance to tell it like it is. After decades of not daring to voice an opinion lest it be held against them—even resisting sleep for fear of blurting something incriminating while dreaming—people are now staying up late for a chance to talk about subjects that were once taboo.[16]

In the Midnight Dreary

Not everyone is enamored of what all-night radio has to offer. In fact, some of its practitioners, both present and past, complain that much of overnight radio, including music and talk programming, has become rather insipid. In a recent article in *Talker's Magazine,* KLSX talk-show host Tracey Miller lamented,

> I've survived in this radio business for years by working hard and keeping my head low, but I'm becoming increasingly agitated with the state of talk radio today. . . . I used to think that talk radio was about the exchange of ideas and stimulating conversation. Apparently those days are over.

Flip around the dial and you'll hear nothing but banal banter.[17]

Larry King: I'm not one to say that the good old days were better, but when it comes to all-night radio I think that is true. Of course, I grew up listening to the radio greats, like Arthur Godfrey and Edward R. Murrow. People who made radio classy. Radio is not classy today. It's a hodgepodge of people on soapboxes, people with agendas from either the political right or the political left. Even a lot of sports talk shows have become ranting and raving festivals, because the host feels he or she has to make a point. The angry host is what you find out there. That loses a lot because it becomes knee jerk. I don't hear any surprises. I know what's coming, because it's so predictable. Today, the really good ones stick out, but years ago there was more class. There are lots of things on all-night radio, and radio in general, that are just tripe.

Frank Childs: It's interesting and rather sad how radio has changed over the years. In the beginning of my career, radio seemed to possess more passion. The music meant more to us. The jocks meant more to us. We would polish our cars and cruise the strip with our radios tuned to the same great nighttime personality. When I started out in the business, I wanted to express myself with the songs I played on my show. In those days you could bring your own records in and basically program your own show. I would smoke a fat joint before I'd go on the air. I would have my music picked out beforehand to match whatever mood I felt or mindset I was in. It could be a political or social statement I was going for that night. I'd have my coffee and my cigarettes ready, and I'd do the crossover with the jock leaving. The light would go down low and it began. I always felt like I was conducting a symphony. Jackson Browne for the "no-nukes" rallies, the Doors for war and acts of terrorism, and the Eagles for making love. You worked at creating an atmosphere of intimacy and connection. It's hard to find that anymore.

Dick Summer: As a listener, which is what I am now, radio has things backwards. It thinks it's servicing my needs, but it has no idea of who I am, what I want, or when I want it, and it obviously doesn't really care. There was a blackout here

> recently, and I tuned in the local talk station to hear some stories about what was going on in the city . . . not "news" stories, people stories. But the on-air guys were just reading wire copy or tossing around the same old trash that the daytime guys had left at the curb. I remember one hurricane night at WBZ when a listener called from his home near the beach. He graphically described the waves as they eventually pounded on his front door. And I remember a Christmas Eve in the broadcast trailer on Boston Common when I casually invited people to come down and sing some carols with me. By midnight I knew I was in big trouble. The traffic was stopped for blocks around. There were thousands of people on the Common, including Tom Rush, Jose Feliciano, and Arlo Guthrie with their guitars. Have you ever heard a couple of thousand people sing "Silent Night"? Fortunately, the cops were understanding. Some of them even joined the singing, and then it began to snow. Something is gone out of all-night radio that made it special.

While one of radio's true masters, Garrison Keillor, admits to not tuning all-night radio, his wife has long been a fan but has become disenchanted with what is available today.

> **Garrison Keillor:** Jenny was a regular listener for some time to Art Bell but has tapered off listening to Minnesota late-night radio because she has found it to be too pleasant and not cranky enough.

So Long and Good Nights?

Art Bell's return to the airwaves in February 2001 was generally received with enthusiasm and a renewed sense of optimism for the future of all-night radio, but even Bell expressed concern that certain trends in the industry, in particular the consolidation movement of the past several years, may have taken a toll on overnight, if not on all radio dayparts, that will be difficult to overcome. Reported Robert Worth in the *New York Times,*

> These are dark days for local radio. The number of independent stations falls every year . . . big business is killing radio's democratic promise, severely limiting the number of voices that can be heard.[18]

Art Bell: I fear that all-night radio will not continue to evolve as things now stand. The consolidation that's been going on in radio has been unhealthy, and I have been a part of it. There's probably going to be a shift in the pendulum back to the local all-night show, and that will be a mostly positive thing because it will encourage individual creativity, something radio needs. Consolidation does the opposite. When stations simply air syndicator feeds, there is no venue for young and local talent to evolve. If I'm on 500 radio stations, I'm taking away 500 jobs from prospective radio talent. To be honest, I've felt guilt over that. It's not good for radio. Large organizations tend not to nurture local or young talent. They play it conservative and safe. Of course, this situation often inspires rebellion and some local maverick may take off and help change this. That's the way it seems to go.

Larry King: Well, I'm accused of being a catalyst of the decline in local overnight programming. Put a lot of people out of work. When I left overnights, we were on about 500 stations. All the big stations, too. I've run into a lot of people who said they operated the board while I was on. It started a sad trend, because I think the more talent the better. I'm very worried about companies being able to own as many stations as they can afford. I don't think that's good for the market. They say it's good for competition, but I say it's terrible. I think the inmates are running the asylum. Much of what is on radio today is a lowering of the standards, and you're never going to see young talent come along if they don't get a chance. If you're a kid today and you want to break into radio, say you want to be a talk-show host, how do you get on a station if it's carrying 18 hours of national programs each day? It's an economic reality. There are no training grounds left.

Layoffs, as the consequence of station consolidations, were having their effect on the industry during the first year of the new millennium. Job duplication is inevitable when companies merge and staff downsizing is typically the result. This "Top of the Week" story in *Broadcasting and Cable* makes the point,

Clear Channel Communications, the world's largest radio company, last week acknowledged that it is laying off 400

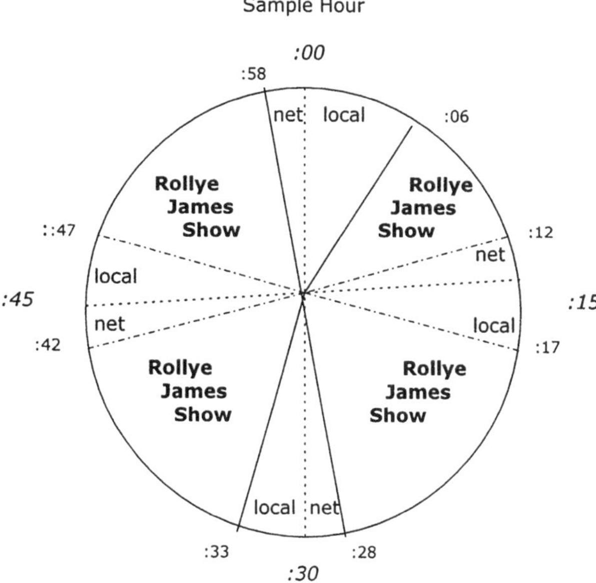

Figure 11.2. A programming clock for *The Rollye James Show.* Courtesy Rollye James.

> employees. The dismissals come on the heels of Clear Channel's $23.8 billion merger with AM/FM.[19]

One of late-night radio's true free-form innovators, New York's Vin Scelsa, found his program, *Idiot's Delight,* on the skids at WNEW-FM as the new millennium began. The station cited business reasons for the show's shutdown.

> The last installment of "Idiot's Delight," Vin Scelsa's long-running radio show, ended at 3:25 A.M. on New Year's Day. . . . His station did not renew his contract . . . into the new year, so he is without a station. Mr. Scelsa, 53, was one of the last practitioners of "free-form radio" on a commercial station, playing whatever music he liked, indulging himself in monologues and conversations with guests and breaking rules of brevity and programming consistency.[20]

> **Fred Jacobs:** Given continued consolidation, a tougher economy, and general belt-tightening, I would be surprised if this condition would be reversed any time soon. At most

> stations, positions are being cut and stations are opting for mechanical means to keep their signals out there at night.

Another impact of the rabid station buying prompted by the Telecommunications Act of 1996 is the buyout of small independent stations. The huge offers are hard to resist and the resulting loss of programming diversity obvious. One such example was the $165 million purchase of Chicago's WNIB-FM, which had aired a quirky classical-music format for over 45 years.

> For nearly half a century, lovers of classical music in the Chicago area have been tuning WNIB-FM (97.1) for eclectic and sometimes obscure programming. They hear live broadcasts of the Cleveland and the San Francisco Orchestras, interviews with contemporary composers and even, on April Fool's Day, broadcasts of a work by John Cage that consists of 4 minutes and 33 seconds of silence. . . . The mix of the fine music and down-home warmth has been the station's trademark since it began broadcasting in 1955.[21]

The new owner, Bonneville International Corporation, quickly announced a probable change in format to a more lucrative contemporary music sound. This alarmed longtime WNIB listeners, who have witnessed a sharp decline in fine-arts programming, but they were without recourse, as the FCC does not dictate a station's programming content.

> The demise of classical music on WNIB would reflect a nationwide trend. By one count, the number of commercial stations in the United States that offer mainly classical music has dropped to 37 today from 52 a decade ago. . . . In another reflection of this trend, the only commercial radio station broadcasting mainly classical music in Denver, KVOD, was recently sold. Its classical broadcasts ceased on Dec. 31.[22]

> **Nick Anthony:** Well, you know, consolidation hasn't exactly changed the landscape of all-night radio, but it has accelerated the changes that have been evolving over the last several years. With stations making very little money overnight and with the growth of digital automation systems, many outlets no longer have a "live" voice on after midnight. If they do, it is usually one of the syndicated satellite-delivered voices.

Don Barrett: The challenges facing all-night radio are monetary in nature as the mega-companies look to keep expenses in line with a rebroadcast of their daytime material or by picking up a network. All-night staffs are cut.

Kirk Harvey: In this age of consolidations, where you have the big companies gobbling up the smaller ones all across the country, assembly line production is the result. It's made to sound live to fool the audience, but it is not what nighttime radio is about.

Paul Ward: Radio is now a nongrowth industry. Clear Channel, a group that controls hundreds of radio stations, does not use programming from any supplier that is not company-owned. Thanks to the Telecom Act of 1996, this deregulation has ruined American radio. As the Clear Channels of the world acquire more outlets in more markets, this downturn will only continue.

Night Losses

Of course, there are other factors contributing to the perceived slide in the fortunes of all-night radio—and radio in general—besides widespread station consolidations, although these may be considered part and parcel of this trend. For instance, a recent story in *Broadcasting and Cable* concerning the decline in the number of entries in the annual Peabody Award competition suggests that the giant station mergers have had a negative impact on the amount of news and public-affairs programming broadcast. "Judges received only 145 radio entries this year, down from 200 in 1999 and 185 last year."[23]

Melissa: I'm afraid late-night radio is going the way of the 8-track. Radio stations are looking to cut corners and unfortunately one of the first places they seem to snip away at seems to be the hours between midnight and 6 A.M. Instead they choose to use automation, board-ops, and syndication rather than use live in-house air talent. While this may seem to make sense economically initially, I think, it's a mistake in the long run. While it's true that these hours are for the most part nonrated and nonrevenue generating, the audience member who tunes during this time slot generally spends

Figure 11.3. Melissa, popular Boston late-night radio host. Courtesy Melissa.

more time listening to the radio than their drive time listening counterpart. Not only do they listen longer, they generally listen more attentively. There are a number of reasons for this, the biggest reason being that there are not as many outside distractions during the late night/early morning as there are during the day. Good feelings about a radio station generated by a listener in their quietest moments, I believe, carry over into their daytime radio-listening habits.

Elizabeth Salazar: I think the prospect for broadcast radio, including all-nights, is a bleak one. Erosion of AFTRA, the national performers' union, has permitted the handful of station group owners to cut costs. Those stations that have no union protection are usually the first to see cutbacks. These big radio companies have exploited this situation and have made their all-night music shows nothing but computer-run jukeboxes, interspersed with prerecorded voice tracks. Sans any air personality to pay, management saves a lot of money, but in my opinion, they cheat their listeners into thinking that someone is actually in the studio hosting the local program.

Jim Tinker: Many stations in L.A. are dropping local content and going with network or satellite programming. This is displacing well-paid union "air personalities" with lower-paid board operators. The cost of consolidation. Eliminate personnel costs to pay the mortgage.

Dick Summer: All-night radio is now a throwaway, due to many factors, among them station downsizings and national program feeds. That's a real shame. There is no time when people pay as much attention to radio, so it's a real opportunity for the medium to secure a hold on its constituency.

Rollye James: All of this just deepens the perception of all-nights as fringe time. Something to be thrown away by all the majors. That can't be good for its future.

Syndies and Nets at Night

Steve LeVeille: Network and syndication programming long ago killed most of the overnight radio on AM stations, even before the current multiple ownership was allowed. It is now only the biggest of the big-market stations that have a live show on all night on the AM dial. But network and syndicated programming has killed much of the local programming on AM stations in every daypart.

Rollye James: Many stations rerun their own local daytime show or rerun syndicated shows overnight. This, of course, means that listeners are not able to participate and have no role in the on-air activity. Management hopes listeners will enjoy professional-sounding programs more than a lesser-quality live show.

Eric Rhoads: The syndies and nets constitute the majority of all-night's radio programming. The downside to this, and not the only one, is that this eliminates a training ground for newbees. All-nights were once a place for experimentation, a place where people could develop their on-air sound. We have no farm team and we need one if we're going to exist in the future.

Don Hallett: Syndicators ask their affiliates to rerun the show from the day before in the next overnight daypart. Clear Channel is running satellite programming after midnight on many of its one thousand plus stations. They beam in the programming and this way they do not have to invest in local talent. In my travels around the country, I am astounded by the number of stations that have no "local presence" overnight. I'm even more astounded when I hear nothing but music and commercials and no attempt to voice track. Too often the only local element is a prerecorded weather forecast or a promo directing listeners to the station's morning show. Although I don't have the statistics, there are a surprising number of stations in smaller markets that simply sign off. One of our client stations in a top 100 market is on that list. Their reasoning is to save on electricity.

Gary Berkowitz: Today all-night radio is mostly syndicated programming. There are still a few great places to catch live radio at night but the numbers are shrinking. For better or worse, syndication is the major trend in all-night radio.

Peter Van De Graaff: I think the state of overnight radio is both wonderful and tragic. Wonderful for those of us in the syndicated satellite-transmitted world because we provide stations with the opportunity to be on all night for a fraction of the cost of hiring their own overnight host. Since the "graveyard shift" has traditionally been the place where the least experienced announcer is placed, there's also the added benefit of providing a host of high quality with the syndicated service for that time slot. At the same time, the tragedy of it all is that there's a good deal of local flavor lost when media giants send their product out to hundreds of stations with very little localization. We try hard to address that at the Beethoven Satellite Network with local inserts every hour that we voice in advance, but there's really no substitute for the real thing. I guess it's just a case of economics, and it's certainly an understandable phenomenon, with the audience for classical music shrinking and stations being bought up by media conglomerates. The bottom line is that things are great in the overnight radio world as far as production values, but something is missing with regards to the local connection.

Ray Briem: Most overnight radio has become network or syndicator-oriented in its coverage and content. This is due mainly to economics. A station would much rather take a network feed than pay a local emcee. That's a way to stay out of the red. Thanks to a well-organized retail sales department, my show was almost always sold out, and it brought in $1 million a year. No other station can claim that. In fact, most will operate in the red. KABC tried local talent when I retired, but it was nonproductive and took the network feed of Art Bell to turn a profit.

Dick Fatherley: Network and satellite program suppliers continue to grow in number. They barter their payments, and that's attractive to stations. You can see why they're succeeding.

Charles Willer: As the entertainment pie gets sliced thinner and thinner (narrowcasting to tiny demographics), the economics for supporting live overnight deejays on a local station become poorer. As live local talent gets laid off, networks move in. I love Joey Reynolds, but he's not here. He's in New York City. I can relate with him on many levels, but I cannot ever expect to meet him at a remote broadcast in Fort Wayne, nor will he ever do anything tangible for our community.

Robo Radio

Technology has always been as much a part of the development of radio as its programming. However, the advances in technology during the past decade have had an impact on the medium in ways that are perceived by many in the industry as detrimental to live local programming, particularly overnights. A number of innovations—among them Internet-streamed audio and direct-broadcast satellite—threaten traditional over-the-air radio broadcasting. For several years, the National Association of Broadcasters has argued against the rollout of digital satellite radio, contending that it poses a threat to local broadcasting. Meanwhile, the NAB has supported the consolidation movement, which has resulted in reduced levels of local all-night programming in every part of the country.

Despite the formidable resistance of the nation's largest broadcaster's association, the new millennium was being hailed as the age of satellite radio. Wrote Tim Jones in the *Chicago Tribune:*

> The biggest development in radio since the popularization of the FM band will launch next month, putting to test a multibillion-dollar bet that millions of consumers will gladly spend $9.95 a month to hear what they want, when they want it and to escape the barrage of commercials they hear every day going to and from work. After years of anticipation and long technical delays, satellite radio will make its debut. Its proponents hope to build an in-the-car radio business on the same sort of consumer demands and frustrations that have made cable television a potent competitor to broadcast TV.[24]

Among the technological innovations that have played a key role in the reduction of local programming are computer automation and satellite feeds. These are considered the principal roadblocks to the future of local all-night radio. "Some fear that all night radio soon will become an automated wasteland of no discernible worth to station owners."[25]

> **E. Alvin Davis:** Many stations are using this technology to eliminate local evening and weekend air talent. Digital "virtual" programming (imported programming via hard drive) has reduced the number of live and local all-night shows. The obvious concern is what impact will all of this have on the future development of on-air talent. At some point, the current crop of air talent will move into management, retire, or die. Where will the next generation of talent come from now that radio has eliminated many of those shifts where talent have typically learned and polished their craft?

> **Rich De Leo:** There were plenty of all-night music shows around on the local level just a few years ago, but then management decided to begin cost cutting and make the overnight an automated thing.

Bill Conway: The rules have now changed because of a combination of technology and economics. The technology allows us to use the digital audio systems to "voice track" overnight, which is what we do at KOIT. Satellite-delivered formats, both music and talk, make it simple for others to do the same. Technological advances permit us to automate transmitter controls and readings, too. If something fails, the computer calls an engineer or programmer to fix the problem. It is a rare station that has a live announcer or even a live body in the station from midnight to sunrise. A few months ago, a 5.2 earthquake hit Napa at 1 A.M. My wife and I were up and felt the trembler. We tuned the local major news and talk station, KGO, but it had no newscaster on duty, and it was forced to go to a network feed to provide its listeners with information.

Anne Gress: I'm extremely concerned by all this. With the invention of voice tracking and satellite, local overnight stations are turnkey operations. It's like the saying, "The light is on, but no one's home."

Randy Lane: There are a lot fewer people on the air live because of computerized automation voice tracking systems, which allow broadcasters to record a show by a quality talent that sounds very "live."

Bill Cahill: Stations opt for automation to save money, but that is a big mistake in my estimation. This drives night owls to some other communication medium, like the Internet, where they can find live companionship.

Nick Anthony: Well, with stations making very little money overnight and with the growth and availability of digital automation systems, many stations no longer have a "live" voice after midnight. If they do, it is usually one of the syndicated satellite-delivered voices. Most of the major consolidators own digital automation software companies. Clear Channel, for example, owns the "Prophet" digital system, allowing them to voice track many shifts, especially overnights. Cumulus owns the "Wave Station" system, giving them the same money-saving advantages. Cutting costs through voice tracking, digital automation, and satellite-delivered shows is the way these radio groups are going. Doing live, local, and compelling all-night programming is fast becoming a distant memory.

Fred Jacobs: This is true. All-night positions are being cut at most stations for bottom-line reasons. They are now either voice tracking (prerecording) this daypart with in-house talent, or they're simply programming songs and production via an automation system like Prophet (AKA "Profit"). Unfortunately, the days when the "overnight guy" could be developed into a strong bench player have given way to economics. They're a dying breed, and early evenings (7 to midnight) may be next.

Frank Childs: Today the music is on a hard drive of an automated system. Everything is researched down until the life is removed from it. All-night stations are run by HAL (re: *2001: A Space Odyssey*).

Joel Raab: As listenership levels and revenue potential for overnight radio are minuscule compared with other times of the broadcast day, operators are eliminating air talent in favor of prerecorded overnight shows, syndication, or automation systems. The money saved by doing this is either put to the bottom line or redirected to another, more lucrative daypart.

Elizabeth Salazar: This doesn't bode well for overnights, and with the advent of the Internet and live streamed audio available from worldwide sources and with the recent approval by the FCC of mobile satellite digital radio (nonbroadcast radio), the picture for local terrestrial radio, not only local all-night radio, is becoming bleaker and bleaker.

THE BRIGHTER SIDE OF NIGHTS

Not all the news and views about all-night radio are gloomy. In fact, there is much to feel optimistic about as the size of the overnight radio audience holds steady in the face of so many new and evolving listening alternatives.

Alan Colmes: As we become even more diverse, as we get further away from the traditional home-office commute, and as more people work out of their homes, there will be a greater audience for these off-the-beaten-track dayparts. As Long John Nebel showed years ago, and as Art Bell has proven recently, there are dollars to be made in the all-night hours.

Sam Sauls: I believe there will always be a need for programming provided to the "traveling" listener. Until direct-broadcast satellite broadcasting becomes a true reality, and who knows when that will be, radio will continue to fulfill this need, particularly to the overnight audience. Additionally, the all-night listener will continue to look for a companion—one found in the overnight radio domain.

Steve LeVeille: You know, I don't see any major changes ahead. I don't expect much of an increase in the amount of local programming nor much of a decrease. I'm sure there will be changes at individual stations, but I don't see big changes industry-wide. I am curious about how the Internet will affect radio in the future. It's possible that the future of radio will be closely tied to the future of the Internet.

Sheena Metal: I think that as we move into the first decade of the new millennium there will be new and exciting forms of overnight programming. For example, we're going to find that a hybrid of talk and music will become stronger and attract audiences.

Steve Warren: As I now work for one of the new satellite radio companies, I believe that a new chapter in all-night listening may be underway with a vast selection of formats coast to coast. As for local radio, our cities and populations continue to grow and, therefore, more people will be thrust into jobs and responsibilities in the overnight hours. This will keep live, local all-night radio a going enterprise.

Gary Owens: The future of all-night radio will definitely be high-tech and cutting edge, but that is not necessarily a bad thing. Topics heard on all-night talk will continue to be as diverse as they are today. Look, it's not going away, despite what the prophets of doom and gloom have to say.

Walter Sabo: Historically, all-night radio has been undervalued by both owners and advertisers. As a former head of a major market radio chain—the NBC FM owned stations—I can assure you that all-night radio is a gold mine. It is by far the best advertising medium in the world. That's because the audience is giving it almost 100 percent attention, particularly the overnight talk shows.

Wayne Cornils: All-night radio will never go out of style as a companion, new technologies or not. The one-on-one value of all-nights far exceeds that of other dayparts. The future is terrific for all-night radio if it turns off the jukebox and remains intimate.

Marlin Taylor: As long as people are awake in these hours, and more and more are, there's room for good programming. That alone will keep overnight radio relevant.

Dick Summer: We know that society is adapting more and more to a 24/7 schedule. As it does, overnights will become more financially viable. It doesn't take a genius to figure that out.

John Butler: There's still plenty of live, local all-night programming out there. It's important here in Baltimore at WMAL and around the country. Our overnight guy, Mark Weaver, is a real value to the station and its audience.

Elroy Smith: Despite all the changes in the radio industry, we continue to do a live show on both WGCI and WVAZ. They work for us, so why change?

Craig Stevens: Let's not forget that syndicated shows have brought many new listeners to the radio medium. They offer listeners high-quality entertainment and information with top-quality personalities. Air talent with major market experience is brought to small-town America, and that isn't such a bad thing.

Charles Willer: Well, in the future, I wish for some sort of a local radio revival, something so magnetic that sponsors flock to it and support it. Everything is cyclical, so this may happen.

Larry Miller: I think the challenge for overnight radio is to find the next Jean Shepherd. It has to make room for originality and creativity. If a station sounds the same at midnight as it does at noon, then something has been lost. All-night radio needs another generation of broadcasters who possess the ability to be real entertainers on the air. In the end, this is what has kept radio viable through the years, and it seems to always return to this.

Joel Raab: The good news about all the new technology is that overnight radio's sound has improved significantly.

Steve LeVeille: Another piece of technology has had a very positive impact on overnight talk radio. The proliferation of cell phones has really helped. The people working the night shift or out and about in their cars were unable to call the shows until the cell phone came along. Because we now live in a 24/7 world, there are more people working the overnight shift, or evening into late night, or getting up early to beat the morning rush or get to the gym before the morning rush. And they all have cell phones. Another example is truckers who have always worked overnights, a huge audience, but until the advent of the cell phone, they couldn't call in. My show on WBZ airs from midnight to 5 A.M., and 50 percent or more of the calls I receive are from cell-phone users. This brings me to another change in overnights. The 4 A.M. hour is becoming a "morning drive" period in many ways. It used to be that morning drive started at 6 A.M. As radio stations and advertisers got hip to the fact that people were going into work earlier and thus getting up earlier, that start time got pushed up. Now I have mostly people in cars calling me at 4 A.M. Some of these people are headed home from work, but most of them are headed to work, and they start tuning in between 3:45 and 4:30 A.M. Because of this, I reintroduce the topics I started the show with at midnight. Also in the 4 o'clock hour, I do more time checks than in the other hours. I've added an additional weather check, too, and we've added a traffic report at 4:30. Sure, I'll admit, there isn't much traffic at that hour, but on those mornings when there is a big

> tie-up or an unscheduled detour, people are glad to get this information. Let's face it, over the coming years there will be more and more traffic at 4:30 in the morning, and the sponsors are catching on and buying spots at this hour. So overnight radio is going to change for the positive.

For those who doubt that listeners are tuned in during the late-night hours, a recent incident in Miami may make believers of them. At Spanish-language station WQBA, a brawl between guests occurred forcing host Martha Flores to appeal for help over the air. Reported the *Miami Herald,* "So many listeners called 911 that the emergency system collapsed."[26]

AND THE SUN WILL RISE

Tens of millions of Americans tune the estimated nine and a half thousand radio stations that keep their signals radiating throughout the night. These loyal listeners do so for companionship as well as to be entertained and informed about the world in which they reside, for they consider themselves no less a part of it because they are night people. The overnight audience is not confined to one type of listener, but rather its listenership is diverse and multifaceted. It is a listening constituency that is rich and varied.

Since the 1920s, when the medium was born, late-night and early-morning programs have been an integral part of the American radio scene, as well as the culture. These broadcasts grew in popularity and importance during the war years of the 1940s, and in the decades to follow, by providing listeners with the kind of music and talk they desired and needed.

For people in the radio business, overnight was (and still is—although at fewer and fewer stations) a part of the schedule when they could experiment and develop their skills and talents and enjoy freedoms uncommon to any other shift. This engendered many extraordinary radio talents and brought new listeners to the medium.

All-night radio has been and still is a very unique and special form of mass communication. Michael Harrison, the publisher of *Talkers Magazine,* summarizes why:

> It has provided companionship for the lonely—namely insomniacs and all night workers who are thus reminded during the wee hours that there is a world out there to which

they are connected. This quality served to keep radio strong in the face of the competition provided by early television (which shut down shortly after midnight) and provided media legitimacy to the idea that the "real world" is a 24/7/365 enterprise.

It has contributed to the expansion of what is considered "morning" in American life by providing commuters and workers information before the traditional 6 A.M. start of the waking day leading to the fall of the idea of a standard "9 to 5" workday.

It has served as one of the first Internet-like media in so much as people could hear local stations from far away regions due to the impact of late-night atmospheric conditions on long-range AM reception. Contributed to the concept of the global village becoming a reality.

It has provided certain advertisers with a less expensive way to be heard on big time stations, enabling them to carve out a unique image and contributing to the development of direct response marketing.

And it has provided listeners with the opportunity to hear personalities and programming that are not as restricted by commercial and ratings considerations as daytime radio, increasing the diversity and creativity of the medium.[27]

Indeed, all-night radio has provided its listening public with a compelling reason to remain awake.

Frank Childs: I still get a charge out of playing the music, cranking up the monitor speakers as loud as I want without someone telling me to turn them down. I still enjoy turning the lights down low and making that perfect segue. And I still love to look out my window on the city at night and watch the lights, knowing out there somewhere is some night clerk, hospital worker, cop, fireman, factory worker, or any number of people working or playing and enjoying the music of the night.

One wonders if nineteenth-century poet Edward Fitzgerald could have been anticipating the creation of all-night radio when he wrote:

For in and out, above, about, below,
'Tis but a Magic Shadow-show,
Played in a Box whose Candle is the Sun,
Round which we Phantom Figures come and go.[28]

For millions of people, all-night radio stations are the "blessed candles" that light the way to the dawn.

NOTES

1. Mark Jurkowitz, "Talk Radio's Blue Streak," www.markjurkowitz.com, 11 October 2000.
2. Francis X. Clines, "Radio Hosts Say Bush and Gore Pale Next to Clinton as a Talk Show Topic," *New York Times,* 30 October 2000, p. 38.
3. Mary Beth Sobolewski, "Radio Duo Passionate about Beanie Babies," *Chicago Sun-Times,* 29 March 1999, p. LI-54.
4. Ron Azevedo, "He Keeps the Night Owls Awake," *Boston Globe,* 26 March 2000, p. 10.
5. www.KFAI.org.
6. "ESPN Radio All Night," espn.com, 29 January 2001.
7. Lawrence Lichty, "WLW," *MBC Encyclopedia of Radio,* ed. Christopher Sterling (Chicago: Fitzroy Dearborn, forthcoming 2002).
8. "World Radio Network from NPR," www.wrn.org/overnight, 21 February 2001.
9. "Jazz After Hours," www.kuow.org, 29 January 2001.
10. Ibid.
11. "Praise in the Night," www.ptn.org, 29 February 2001.
12. "Madness Network," www.kiwi.pyro.net, 16 February 2001.
13. Tom Hibbert, "Sleep Talk," *Observer, 9* March 1997, p. 77.
14. Peter Goddard, "Breath of Fresh FM Air at the Corp.," *Toronto Star,* 9 August 1997, p. Arts J-5.
15. "That Time of the Night on CBC Radio," www.radio.cbc.ca/programs, 29 January 2001.
16. Maggie Farley, "Radio Programs Tell It Like It Is," *Los Angeles Times,* 8 November 1994, p. 4.
17. Tracey Miller, "Has Talk Radio Become Nothing but Banal Chatter?" *Talkers Magazine,* February 2001, p. 33.
18. Robert Worth, "Is Democracy Still on the Dial?" *New York Times,* 3 March 2001, pp. A-15 & 17.
19. *Broadcasting and Cable,* 20 November 2000, p. 16.
20. "Free Form D.J. Loses Weekly Radio Show," *New York Times,* 4 January 2001, P. B-10.

21. "Quirky Classical Beacon May Shake, Rattle, and Roll," *New York Times,* 31 January 2001, p. 41.

22. Ibid.

23. "We Can't Hear You," *Broadcasting and Cable,* 19 February 2001, p. 4.

24. Jim Jones, "Satellite Radio Industry Sends Signal," *Chicago Tribune,* 2 January 2000, p. 37.

25. Gregg Quill, "Free Spirits of the Airwaves Who Only Come Out at Night," *Toronto Star,* 10 January 1989, p. E-3.

26. "People," *Broadcasting and Cable,* 11 September 2000, p. 86.

27. Personal correspondence, 17 February 2001.

28. From the poem *The Rubaiyat of Omar Khayyam* (1859).

FURTHER READING

Bain, Donald. *Long John Nebel.* New York: MacMillan, 1974.

Barfield, Ray. *Listening to Radio.* Westport, Conn.: Praeger, 1996.

Barlow, William. *Voice Over: The Making of Black Radio.* Philadelphia, Pa.: Temple University Press, 1999.

Bell, Art. *The Art of Talk.* New Orleans: Paper Chase Press, 1998.

DeLong, Thomas, A. *The Mighty Music Box.* Los Angeles: Amber Crest Books, 1980.

Ditingo, Vincent M. *The Remaking of Radio.* Boston: Focal Press, 1995.

Doll, Bob. *Sparks Out of the Plowed Ground.* W. Palm Beach, Fla.: Streamline Press, 1996.

Douglas, Susan. *Listening In: Radio and the American Imagination.* New York: Times Books, 1999.

Dunning, John. *On the Air: The Encyclopedia of Old-Time Radio.* New York: Oxford University Press, 1998.

Fong-Torres, Ben. *The Hits Just Keep on Coming.* San Francisco: Miller Freeman, 1998.

Fornatale, Peter, and Joshua E. Mills. *Radio in the Television Age.* New York: Overlook Press, 1980.

Foust, James C. *Big Voices of the Air: The Battle Over Clear Channel Radio.* Ames: Iowa State University Press, 2000.

Gray, Barry. *My Night People.* New York: Simon & Schuster, 1975.

Halper, Donna. *Invisible Stars: A Social History of Women in American Broadcasting.* Armonk, N.Y.: M. E. Sharpe, 2001.

Hilmes, Michele. *Radio Voices: American Broadcasting, 1922-1952.* Minneapolis: University of Minnesota Press, 1997.

Jack, Wolfman. *Have Mercy! Confessions of the Original Rock 'n' Roll Animal.* New York: Warner Books, 1995.

Keillor, Garrison. *WLT: A Radio Romance.* New York: Penguin, 1992.

Keith, Don. *Wizard of the Wind.* New York: St. Martin's Press, 1996.

Keith, Michael C. *Talking Radio: An Oral History of Radio in the Television Age.* Armonk, N.Y.: M. E. Sharpe Publishers, 2000.

———. *Voices in the Purple Haze: Underground Radio and the Sixties.* Westport, Conn.: Praeger, 1997.

King, Larry. *On the Line.* New York: Harcourt Brace, 1993.

Looker, Thomas. *The Sound and the Story.* Boston: Houghton Mifflin, 1995.

Maltin, Leonard. *Great American Broadcast.* New York: Dutton, 1997.

Morrow, Bruce. *Cousin Brucie: My Life in Rock 'n' Roll Radio.* New York: Beech Tree Books, 1987.

Munson, Wayne. *All Talk: The Talk Show in Media Culture.* Philadelphia, Pa,: Temple University Press, 1993.

Nachman, Gerald. *Raised on Radio.* New York: Pantheon Books, 1998.

Passman, Arnold. *The Deejays.* New York: Macmillan, 1971.

Reynolds, Joey. *Let a Smile Be Your Umbrella.* New York: Hatherleigh Press, 2000.

Rhoads, Eric. *Blast from the Past: Radio's First 75 Years.* West Palm Beach, Fla.: Streamline Press, 1996.

Shepherd, Jean. *In God We Trust, All Others Pay Cash.* New York: Doubleday, 1991.

Singer, Arthur J. *Arthur Godfrey: The Adventures of an American Broadcaster.* Jefferson, N.C.: McFarland & Co., 2000.

Sklar, Rick. *Rocking America: How the All-Hit Radio Stations Took Over.* New York: St. Martin's Press, 1984.

Spaar, Lisa Russ, ed. *Acquainted with the Night.* New York: Columbia University Press, 1999.

Sterling, Christopher H., ed. *MBC Encyclopedia of Radio.* Chicago: Fitzroy Dearborn, 2002.

Vowel, Sarah. *Radio On: A Listener's Diary.* New York: St. Martin's Press, 1997.

Williams, Gilbert A. *Legendary Pioneers of Black Radio.* Westport, Conn.: Praeger, 1998.

Appendix 1

The Nitecap Radio Movement, by Joseph Buchman

I am a Nitecap. I believe in the Nitecap Movement as a great vehicle to make the sentiments of the brotherhood of man among all nations, creeds, and races a fact, not merely a saying.

—The Nitecap Creed

"Herb?"
"Yes."
"This is Shirley Stephens calling from Salt Lake."
"Yes, Shirley."
"I just wanted to say happy birthday to the Nitecap Show. You know, Herb, it was my mom's whole life. She came here in 1964. She was Harriett Congers, a charter member Nitecap."
"Oh yes! I remember her."
"She just adored your show. We just think it's the most wonderful service. It's fun and a network of friends for everyone. Oh, she loved the conventions, and I heard you're going to have one in 1984."
"We hope so. I think it's time that we all got together again."
"Fantastic! And we're looking forward to the newsletter and the magazine. There's no need for anybody to be lonely as long as you're around, Herb."
"Thank you, Shirley."
"I would like to say hello to my mom's many Nitecap friends out there, the ones that she wrote to and the ones that she loved. This was her whole life in the last decade before she left at ninety-four. Herb, we just adore you and your whole concept there. In night-time radio, there's just nothing like what you do."

"Thank you, dear."
"Love you."
"Bye. Shirley Stephens here in Salt Lake this morning. That opens our Utah line . . ."

—*The Herb Jepko Show,* **February 1984**

It's hard to imagine a time before television, but for some—for those awake in the wee hours of the morning—the last television-free sanctuary stretched into the late 1970s. Nighttime then was filled not by the ceaseless roar of cable television, 24-hour independent stations, VCRs and Blockbuster movies rentals, but by radio. Even without overnight competition from television, many radio stations still signed off the air after midnight. Even some clear-channel, 50,000-watt AM stations found no reason to remain on the air overnight.

Advertisers were loath to reach the small, disenfranchised, and older audience that was assumed to inhabit late-night radio. Media buyers were utterly unwilling to purchase time in a period not even measured by ratings services. With neither ratings nor revenues, why stay on the air? Overnights were perceived as a dark, empty desert, pockmarked by a handful of radio stations offering the lowest-cost programming possible. Not particularly attractive.

In the high mountain desert city of Salt Lake, the management of radio station KSL, a 50-kW clear-channel owned by the Mormon Church, reached a similar conclusion. Why use a church-owned facility to broadcast to an audience that—one can imagine church leaders concluding—had no business being awake in the middle of the night? Why use a church-run business to employ someone who should be home with his family at those hours?

Yet, on February 11, 1964, Herb Jepko opened a mike into that void and began what would become almost 30 years of connecting with the disenfranchised, widowed, lonely, fearful, elderly, or just plain up-all-night oddballs. Within little over a year, dozens of local

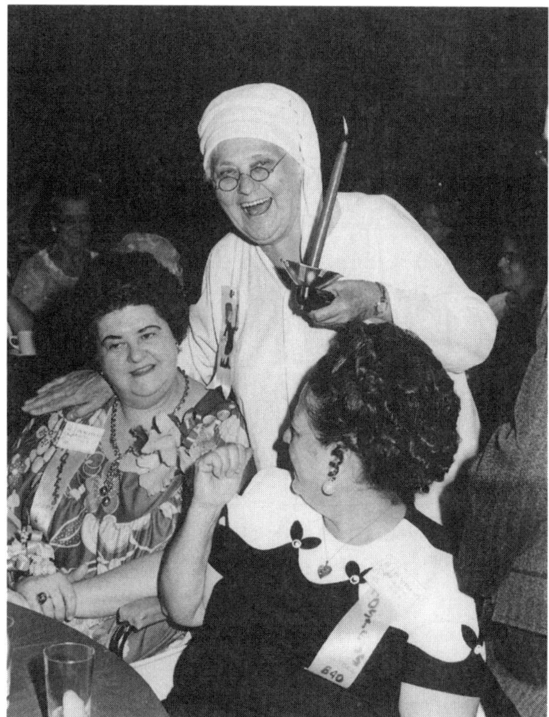

Figure A.1. Nitecap conventioneers take it literally. Courtesy Joe Buchman.

Nitecap clubs had organized, a monthly magazine was launched, and tens of thousands of membership cards were issued to listeners across the United States and Canada.

The first annual Jepko convention was held in Salt Lake in July 1965, with listeners arriving—much to KSL management's surprise—from over thirty states. Over three hundred couples met and married as a direct result of the program. Hundreds of thousands of others developed friendships, exchanged photographs, ran up long-distance phone bills, and traveled miles to meet a fellow listener.

The success of the show was unprecedented and remains unequaled in the history of broadcasting. Before the world wide web, before the cyber community, before Internet dating and virtual relationships, there were the Nitecaps connected by the old web created by radio signals.

I will do all in my power to help build the Nitecap organization and to carry out all of its projects designed to lend friendship, comfort, and pleasure to all persons, particularly the ill, the aging, and the unfortunate.

—The Nitecap Creed

Following his stint in the army in 1954, Herb pursued a series of radio jobs in sales and sales management, eventually becoming promotion director for KFI in Los Angeles. During this time, he met Ben Hunter, who was doing a late-night talk show called *Night Owls.* In 1961, Herb was hired by KCPX to play late-night jazz but quickly found himself bored by only playing music. Between jazz cuts, Herb began talking to his listeners about the mountains, the weather, and the news of the day. There were no means for airing calls over the air, so Herb talked to his listeners during the music.

Mail began arriving from all over the Rocky Mountain west, and it was not long before the management of KSL knew of the talented air personality across town. While KSL had a history of hiring only Latter-day Saints (Mormons), exceptions were sometimes made for on-air talent. Herb's nominal Catholicism and occasional drinking would later create significant tensions.

In 1962 Herb began hosting KSL's midday program, *Crossroads,* and things began to look up, but he realized that this was a different audience than the one he had been connecting with in his late-night shift at KCPX. It was his late-night audience for whom he felt the greatest affinity.

Herb had so much confidence in his ability to make the overnight period work that he pitched his doing it to the station's board of directors. After a few months of continued pressure from him, the board relented and offered him a make-it-or-break-it deal. He could have the midnight to six time slot only if he would agree to a 50 percent pay cut and a 6-week trial period to show it could work. If not, he was out the door. While it was a tremendous financial risk for him and his family, he agreed.

We love to hear each other chat, to hear each glad hello. But most of all we love to hear the voice of our own Herb Jepko. We're the Nitecaps, nightly Nitecaps, and our hearts are light and gay as we rally round our Nitecap show on the brand new side of the day.

—"The Nitecap Song" by Dame Edmunds

Just after midnight on February 11, 1964, Herb began what would become the most successful program in KSL history. For the first few weeks station engineers had managed to rig only one phone line that could be put on the air. Yet even on that first night, Herb was not at a loss for callers. One of the first advertisers was the publisher of a venison cookbook and Herb's wife, Patsy, soon found herself listening to the show while filling orders all night at the kitchen table. The volume of letters from loyal listeners was literally overwhelming, and Patsy struggled to keep up. Each morning, after a night on the air, Herb would return home to shower, change clothes, and begin making sales calls, while Patsy took care of their kids. For the first year of the show, they subsisted on 2 or 3 hours of sleep, catching up on the weekends.

The show, initially called *The Other Side of Damn,* was an immediate success. Within a year, listeners, or Nitecaps, as they became known following an on-air contest to choose a name, were meeting in five states in organized service clubs, called "Nitestands." Patsy was literally buried under a mountain of paper as every day brought well over 1,000 letters.

KSL managers and Mormon Church officials belatedly realized that they had unknowingly relinquished a perfect platform from which to reach those in need of proselytizing messages from the church. Rather than risk the backlash of replacing Herb, they sought to place LDS Church advertising on the show and encouraged Herb and those of his LDS listeners to move the talk toward the value of the church.

Herb adamantly refused to allow any discussion of "denominational religion" on the Nitecap program. Some church members pressured KSL station management to make a change, raising understandable concerns that such a successful program was being run on church-owned facilities by a nonmember. As tensions reached the boiling point, Arch Madsen, president of KSL, reached a novel compromise with Herb by allowing him to buy time from KSL and operate as an independent contractor. The Nitecap operation moved out of KSL into its own broadcast studios and offices. But tensions between KSL personnel and Herb's staff continued to simmer and intensify.

> I think that programs like this, that don't get involved in denominational religion, can make fences fall down. Regardless of where a

> person votes, or worships, and regardless of the color of a person's skin, we are all human beings.
>
> **—Herb Jepko, 1978 Louisville Convention address**

Prior to the success demonstrated by Herb and the Nitecap show, most programmers in the industry felt that "all talk is local." In other words, programmers felt there weren't enough national issues of importance to generate sufficient interest among enough local listeners to achieve ratings success, while local issues, where listeners felt their opinion might make a different in the outcome, were thought to be the key to talk-radio programming.

In disagreement with this view, network talk radio was born in January 1968 when KXIV in Phoenix signed on as the first Nitecap Radio Network affiliate. The following month, WRFM in New York announced a Nitecap format would originate locally, hosted by Gordon Owen. An article in the *Wick* announced that the Nitecap Radio Network would be built in the west via affiliates carrying the Herb Jepko program from the flagship station KSL, while affiliates east of the Mississippi would join flagship station WRFM with Gordon Owen in New York City.

In April 1968, KBIG became the third Nitecap affiliate, joining KSL and KXIV in the west. Unfortunately, WRFM dropped the Nitecap format in June 1968. The first talk-radio network ended operations in August of 1968 when both KBIG and KXIV dropped the show. While some listeners were disappointed, most could still hear the program over KSL. In an era before overnight radio ratings, an article in the August 1969 edition of the *Wick* blamed a lack of listener letters to the stations as the cause of the loss of affiliates.

Network talk radio was reborn a little over a year later in October 1969 when 50,000-watt clear-channel KVOO, Tulsa, affiliated with the Nitecap Radio Network. This incarnation of network talk radio lasted almost 2 years but ended when KVOO dropped the show in September 1971.

For Herb and Nitecaps everywhere, the third time proved to be a charm. In January 1973, WHAS in Louisville, another big clear-channel signal, affiliated with NCRN. KSL and WHAS were situated perfectly, geographically, and gave Herb the first-ever coast-to-coast coverage for an independent broadcaster. By mid-1974, over eighty Nitestands were active, with members meeting and organizing service for others in their areas. When KIRO in Seattle and KRLA in Los Angeles also signed on as affiliates, the program began to generate interest among the radio networks.

Arbitron was now measuring radio listening between midnight and 1 A.M., the first hour of Herb's show. Estimates showed a surprising number of 18-24 year olds tuned in during the first hour of the program. Based on calls to the show, many appeared to be lonely college students studying late at night. However, the show retained a reputation for attracting a mostly older, rural audience.

Outside of the cities where NCRN affiliates were based, the sky wave AM signals were too easily distorted by the normal electrical noise of a city to be heard. Thus most of the audience was found in less-populated rural areas, where distant AM signals could still be easily heard. Understandably this largely rural, older audience was not exactly attractive to advertisers or to the national networks.

> We screen the products we advertise. Our following is so dependent upon us that we want to back up everything we advertise. We don't advertise anything that we don't believe in ourselves.
>
> **—Herb Jepko, March 1975**

Almost all revenue for the show was derived from direct-response advertising, and Herb insisted, with very few exceptions, that all order fulfillment be handled personally by the Nitecap staff. Too often he had seen listeners of other programs robbed by direct-response advertisers who went bankrupt without filling paid orders. So Herb required almost all Nitecap Radio Network sponsors to ship sufficient inventory to his Salt Lake offices to cover anticipated orders. Only after inventory arrived would he allow the commercials to air.

In November 1974, WBAL in Baltimore affiliated with the Nitecap Radio Network, providing a clear-channel signal into Washington, D.C., Philadelphia, and New York. This created the first exposure to the program for many media executives living on the east coast and would result in the tragic demise of the program.

> From Salt Lake City, high in the Mountain West, the Mutual Broadcasting System presents the Herb Jepko Nitecap Show.
>
> **—Mutual's introduction to show**

On November 4, 1975, the Mutual Broadcasting System began carrying the Nitecap program nationally. Thanks to the dozens of new affiliates, the number of requests for membership cards in the Nitecaps International Association soared to over 300,000. Within a year Arbitron estimated that ten million listeners were tuned into the program. Following the affiliation with Mutual, the Nitecap organization moved into larger and more expensive studios and offices in Salt Lake City.

As part of the agreement with Mutual, Herb relinquished control of order fulfillment and sales strategy to the network. MBS sales executives attempted to sell the show on a cost-per-thousand basis to national advertisers. However the reputation of the show as appealing primarily to an older, less-affluent audience made this a nearly impossible sell. MBS sales personnel quickly abandoned their efforts to sell the program. Ironically, although Herb was enjoying the largest audience in the history of the program, he began to suffer huge financial losses. The combination of the increased expenses of operating his own studios and the decrease in revenue resulting from the shift away from the direct-response approach would quickly prove disastrous.

> *I believe it is my obligation as a Nitecap not to carp and criticize, but to support and encourage my fellow Nitecaps. To this end, I hereby pledge myself to the building and supporting of the Nitecaps International Association, its founder Herb Jepko, this Nitestand, and every sincere Nitecap.*
>
> **—The Nitecap Creed**

By the fall of 1976, Herb was under intense pressure from MBS to change the program content in an attempt to attract a younger audience. Mutual felt more controversy and conflict would serve to attract the younger demos, which would be easier to sell on a cost-per-thousand basis to national advertisers. Herb in turn pressured MBS to continue to serve the audience with whom he had developed such strong friendships and for whom he felt such a strong public service commitment. With Mutual account executives unwilling, or unable, to work deals for sufficient direct-response advertising, and with Herb unwilling to compromise, the show began to collapse.

On May 18, 1977, Mutual replaced the Nitecap program with Long John Nebel and Candy Jones. When Long John died less than a year later, Mutual gave Larry King his first shot at a national audience. Larry King and others later mistakenly cite King's program as the first network late-night talk show.

Immediately following the Mutual cancellation, the Nitecap Radio Network was reborn with ten affiliates, including KSL, but without WHAS. By late 1977, fourteen affiliates had joined the network, but most were low power at night and the vast majority of the core audience felt betrayed by the inability to receive their program. Network radio, in an era before satellite distribution, required expensive AT&T land lines, which were only feasible with the economics of scale offered by scores of stations sharing the cost.

Larry King's Mutual program, along with other all-night radio programs, FM stations, 24-hour broadcast television, and cable TV had fractionalized the late-night radio audience. Where Herb had found a pockmarked desert in 1964, he now found himself attempting to stand out in a cacophony of late-night media entertainment options. Eventually old tensions between KSL management and Herb resurfaced, and in August of 1978, without advance notice to listeners or to Herb, KSL dropped the Nitecap program.

> *I will seek and exalt the good I find in all persons and seek to overlook their errors and weaknesses just as I trust others will accept me with both my strengths and weaknesses.*
>
> **—The Nitecap Creed**

The NRCN continued on for another year before going off the air in August 1979. Two significant attempts were made to resurrect the program, but the show lasted only a few months. However, the legacy of Herb Jepko lives on. No one has yet duplicated what he created through the intense love and passion he possessed for his audience. His was radio based in humanity.

> We need to stop looking at people suspiciously but accept them more generously as human beings with kindness in their hearts. With this as our motive, I think we can achieve a wonderful kind of communications.
>
> **—Herb Jepko, 1978 Louisville Convention**

Appendix 2

An Overnight Radio Reminiscence, by Ed Weigle

Pittsburgh radio will always be closest to my heart. Although I never really did anything of much importance in radio in the Steel City, it was home until I married and moved away. The warm feeling I get when I think of the legacies of KDKA, WAMO, WTAE, and KQV assures my everlasting allegiance. Dear friends like WAMO's Porky Chedwick and WTAE's Hank Baughman were my mentors when I began my radio career in voiceovers at the ripe old age of 13.

Still, some of my fondest memories as a youngster, and an early part of my learning, originated far from my hometown, carried to me aboard the ionospheric roller-coaster of nighttime radio. There was something almost mystical about eavesdropping on a secret society of night owls hundreds of miles away, while my parents and most of eastern America were sound asleep. There was always the hope that one day, just maybe, the voice on the other end of that sky wave would be mine. The 50,000-watt monsters that were hidden by daylight gave up their secrets between dusk and sunrise.

As an aspiring broadcaster, it was a great opportunity to listen and learn from the big boys. Call letters like WNBC, WLW, CKLW, WLS, KMOX, WBZ, WOWO, and others bounced down into my receiver with varying degrees of clarity. For those magical hours, New York, Cincinnati, Windsor, Chicago, St. Louis, Boston, and Ft. Wayne were only as far away as my pillow or nightstand. This was a surreal novelty that I'm afraid is lost today on my kids, who can conjure up crystal-clear Internet audio from stations around the world, at any time of the day or night, by the mere click of a mouse. Imagine, no tuner to fiddle with.

Overnight radio was just downright cool! Satellite programming had not yet become the easy alternative it is to local programming today. Back then, network programming came to us via terrestrial phone lines, vinyl discs, or reels of tape. There was music on AM back then, not just talk. The "boss jocks" hadn't yet been run off the air as they would be by 1980, the year I entered the business, by stifling FM formats that promise "less talk, more music, and NO personality." The talent that ruled the pre-1980s nighttime airwaves were of the same creative, energetic, and exciting caliber as the jock who manned the drive time on-air chair. Today, sadly, at most stations, the late hours serve as little more than a proving ground for neophyte broadcasters, baby-sitting the omnipotent satellite feed, if automation has completely taken away the need for human staffing.

For me, overnight radio was my classroom. I was able to hear many broadcasters, from many cities, all in a single night, without the daytime distractions. Since a broadcaster is, after all, the sum of everyone he ever listens to, many of those "stentors-of-the-night" live on in my mind's ear and have benefited me almost as much as Hank and Porky. Sadly, the voice that bounces into my nightstand radio from afar today is usually the same one I can pick up on the station across town.

While I never did find myself on one of those 50-gallon giants (outside of doing station IDs, promos, and commercials for some of them), I was lucky enough to have enjoyed several overnight shifts in the course of my career. In the 1980s, the graveyard shift was perhaps the only daypart, except morning drive, that hadn't been completely sapped dry of all personality or creativity. Program directors during this bleak period in radio history were sold on the lifeless "liner-card" mentality that pervaded the industry at the time. Talking them into deviating from it was about as difficult as giving a wolverine an enema and just as dangerous, since the industry was so rabidly "anti-jock" then. For that reason, I gained an instant appreciation for the night shift and the wonderful listeners who made it so special. A continuous cavalcade of lonely hearts, insomniacs, inebriates, college students, cranks, those on the lunatic fringe, and the just plain curious, kept the shift interesting and enjoyable.

As I soon discovered, what makes overnight radio unique is that any deejay or talk host has the ability to establish a connection with the audience. This is not necessarily a testament to an announcer's "winning personality," but the tendency of listeners to want to form an attachment with the voice emanating from their nightstand radio.

The overnight host has a listener's attention when their daily problems are not yet their immediate concern. Until dawn breaks up the party, you, the host, are their closest pal. If you take their calls and listen to what they have to say and treat them with respect, you're their guru. Think about it. What better place to establish intimacy but in a person's bedroom during the wee hours?

That "intimacy" should be respected by a broadcaster for what it is and is not. Every deejay has heard, or perhaps lived, a horror story where a long-anticipated meeting at the station with a listener ends awkwardly when the deejay discovers they've just made a date with Quasimodo or a close kin thereof. The fact is, however unkind, the dreaded possibility of such a romantic disappointment may be more of a motivation for avoiding in-studio rendezvous than the obvious security reasons for doing so.

Generally, it's best not to take a relationship with a listener beyond where the signal alone takes it. Overnighters have to use some caution regarding those they invite to the studio, since the announcer is often left alone when the cleaning crew leaves. The solitude can be both inspiring and unsettling, particularly if your station is situated in a house trailer deep in a mountain forest, like a popular Pittsburgh area oldies outlet I once worked for.

An ominous memo in the control room warned, "Be kind to listeners, otherwise they may try to kick the shit out of you!" The notice was inspired by one deejay's encounter with an inebriated listener who felt the jock didn't fully appreciate his offer to visit the station to personally say hello. The man showed up anyway and attempted to kick the trailer door in, all the while promising to do the same to the ungrateful deejay inside. Fortunately, the jock was able to alert police before there were any casualties beyond a broken doorjamb.

In other cases, listeners feel they know the host a bit too well, as I experienced while pulling overnights at a Pittsburgh classic rocker in the late 1980s. For a couple of months, a young woman would call me each morning just to tell me about her day. She was always very soft-spoken and polite, until one day when she asked whether I'd be attending a station function at Three Rivers Stadium. I told her that my girlfriend and I planned to call it a date. To that, she screeched, "Girlfriend!?," followed by a blistering stream of Elizabethan epithets. Before slamming the phone down, vowing to never call again, she sobbed, "So I guess that means I won't find a daddy for my little boy!" Although my heart went out to the poor kid, you better believe I looked over my shoulder for days afterward expecting to meet my presumptuous admirer face-to-face.

Still, some listeners can take generosity to a shocking level, like one perky, elderly man who used to call radio stations in Lexington, Kentucky, years ago. When the deejay would answer the request line, he'd be greeted with a friendly "Hi! How about a blow job?" The hell of it was, this guy was serious! As far as I know (or care to know), no one ever took the man up on his offer.

Anyway, I left the on-air aspect of radio in 1994 in order to pursue the more profitable production side. If I miss any airshift, it's certainly the one between midnight and five. While my industry has changed considerably over the past 2 decades, the people who listen to overnight radio haven't. It remains a world unto itself. One that I was fortunate enough to sample a small part of. Today, while I listen to national hosts like Art Bell or Joey Reynolds, I wonder if they truly realize how lucky they are.

INDEX